T0330117

The Digital Business Ecosystem

The Digital Business Ecosystem

Edited by

Angelo Corallo

Researcher, Scuola Superiore ISUFI, University of Lecce, Italy

Giuseppina Passiante

Professor of Management, Scuola Superiore ISUFI, University of Lecce, Italy

Andrea Prencipe

Associate Professor of Management of Enterprise, University G d'Annunzio, Pescara, Italy and Senior Fellow, SPRU, University of Sussex, UK

Edward Elgar
Cheltenham, UK • Northampton, MA, USA

Published by
Edward Elgar Publishing Limited
Glensanda House
Montpellier Parade
Cheltenham
Glos GL50 1UA
UK

Edward Elgar Publishing, Inc.
William Pratt House
9 Dewey Court
Northampton
Massachusetts 01060
USA

A catalogue record for this book
is available from the British Library

Library of Congress Cataloguing in Publication Data

The digital business ecosystem / edited by Angelo Corallo, Giuseppina
Passiante, Andrea Prencipe.
    p. cm.
  Includes bibliographical references and index.
    1. Business networks—Computer network resources. 2. Communication in
management—Computer network resources. 3. Digital communications—
Economic aspects. I. Corallo, Angelo. II. Passiante, Giuseppina. III. Prencipe,
Andrea.
HD69.S8.D54   2007
302.3′5—dc22

                               2007000149

ISBN 978 1 84720 043 3

Printed and bound in Great Britain by MPG Books Ltd, Bodmin, Cornwall

Contents

Contributors

Max Boisot
Max Boisot is Adjunct Professor at INSEAD, Fontainebleau, France and Associate Fellow at Templeton College, University of Oxford. He is also a research fellow at the Sol Snider Center of the University of Pennsylvania Wharton School, and Associate of the Centre for International Business and Management at the Judge Institute of Management Studies at the University of Cambridge. He holds an MSc in Management from MIT as well as a doctorate in technology transfer from the Imperial College of Science, Technology and Medicine, London University. From 1984 to 1989 he was Dean and Director of the China–EC Management Program, the first MBA programme to be run in the People's Republic of China in Beijing. The programme has today evolved into the China–Europe International Business School (CEIBS) in Shanghai. Since 1994 he has set up the Euro–Arab Management School in Granada, Spain for the EU Commission. Max Boisot has carried out consultancy and training assignments for a number of multinational firms – Shell, BP Exploration, GEC-Alsthom, Thomson CFS and UBS are the most recent ones – in the field of international management and technology strategy. He is currently undertaking research at the Wharton school; this involves building a simulation model of knowledge flows within and between organizations. In addition to his China experience, Max Boisot has taught in Japan, the USA, Hong Kong, South Africa, the Middle East, Russia and France. He is the author of *Information Space: A Framework for Analyzing Learning in Organizations, Institutions and Cultures* (Routledge 1995) and *Knowledge Assets: Securing Competitive Advantage in the Information Economy* (Oxford University Press 1998). He was awarded the Igor Ansoff Strategic Management Award 2000 for the latter book. He has also published numerous research articles.

Erik Brynjolfsson
Director of the Center for eBusiness at MIT (http://ebusiness.mit.edu) and the George and Sandi Schussel Professor of Management at the MIT Sloan School, Professor Brynjolfsson was among the first researchers to measure the productivity contributions of information technologies. His research has been recognized with six Best Paper Awards by fellow academics. He

lectures worldwide on business strategy, pricing models and intangible assets, including keynote addresses at the Business Week CEO Summit, the Business Week CIO Summit, the Economist eBusiness Summit and the eBusiness Expo. He is Editor of the Ecommerce Research Forum (http://ecommerce.mit.edu/forum) and several books including *Understanding the Digital Economy* (MIT Press 2000) and *Strategies for eBusiness Success* (Jossey-Bass 2001). Professor Brynjolfsson has served on the Editorial Boards of numerous academic journals as well as Time Magazine's Board of Economists. At the MIT Sloan School of Management, Professor Brynjolfsson teaches a popular MBA course on Digital Business and a PhD seminar on IT, Organizations and Markets. He is an associate member of the MIT Laboratory for Computer Science and the MIT Center for Coordination Science. Professor Brynjolfsson previously taught at Stanford Business School and at Harvard University. He holds Bachelors and Masters degrees from Harvard University in Applied Mathematics and Decision Sciences and a PhD from MIT in Managerial Economics.

John Child
Professor Child holds the Chair of Commerce in the Birmingham Business School, University of Birmingham, UK. His research interests include the internationalization of firms from emerging economies and new organizational forms. His MA and PhD are from the University of Cambridge, which also awarded him a higher doctorate (ScD) for his outstanding scholarly work. In 2002, he was elected a Fellow of the Academy of Management and in 2004 received the Distinguished Contribution Award of the International Academy for Chinese Management Research. He was Dean and Director of the China–Europe Management Institute in Beijing 1989–1990 and has also been Distinguished Visiting Professor at the University of Hong Kong. Professor Child was Editor-in-Chief of *Organization Studies* from 1992 to 1996. He is the author or co-author of 18 books and over 120 articles in learned journals. He published two new books in 2005: *Organization: Contemporary Principles and Practice* (Blackwell) and (with David Faulkner and Stephen Tallman) *Cooperative Strategy* (Oxford University Press).

Angelo Corallo
Angelo Corallo is Researcher at the Department of Innovation Engineering at the University of Lecce. He graduated in Physics at the University of Lecce and has been researcher at the Osservatorio Astronomico di Capodimonte. He teaches within the Master and PhD Programmes of Scuola Superiore ISUFI (University of Lecce) and the PhD Programme in

Complex Industrial Systems. His research interests encompass mainly the co-evolution of technological and organizational innovation, with a specific focus on business ecosystems, extended enterprise, knowledge management and collaborative working environments in project-based organizations. He is currently involved in many research projects related to technological and organizational issues both at an Italian and European level (Knowledge Hubs, Technological Systems for Tourism and Cultural Heritage, Multi-channel Adaptive Information Systems, Digital Business Ecosystems). Angelo collaborates with the Massachusetts Institute of Technology in projects related to enterprise process modelling, enabling business to e-business transition and social network analysis in the innovation community. He collaborates with the Business Enterprise Integration Domain Task Force of OMG (Object Management Group) to define an organizational metamodel supporting the architecture of business modelling frameworks.

Paolo Dini

Dr Paolo Dini is a Senior Research Associate in the Department of Media and Communications at the London School of Economics and Political Science. His research is concerned with complex systems at the boundary between social science, computer science and natural/physical science. Dr Dini received his first degree (BSc) in Mechanical Engineering and Aeronautical Engineering from the University of California, Davis in 1983. He received his MSc and PhD in Aerospace Engineering (low-speed aerodynamics modelling and design) from Pennsylvania State University in 1987 and 1990 respectively. Dr Dini taught undergraduate physics for five years at Carleton and St Olaf Colleges in Minnesota, then worked as a system integrator, digital design engineer and project manager for a wearable computer company for three years, also in Minnesota, followed by one year in the Software Engineering and Applications group of Philips Research Laboratories, UK. He then spent two years at the MIT Media Lab Europe in Dublin, where he led research projects centred around the concept of self-organization in a wide range of fields, from the self-assembly of proteins around carbon nanotubes to biological design patterns in software engineering, communities of software agents on mobile devices and resource sharing in *ad hoc* networks. He also led the Wireless Ad hoc Network for Dublin (WAND) project in collaboration with Trinity College Dublin. This involved the specification and deployment of a wireless 802.11 network infrastructure in the centre of Dublin, a qualitative and ethnographic study of different potential user groups and the development of distributed applications such as interactive narratives based on stories taken from the local community. Dr Dini is the Scientific Coordinator of the FP6 (Sixth Framework Programme) Digital Business Ecosystem integrated project, a partner in the BIONETS integrated project, and coordinator of the network of excellence OPAALS (Open Philosophies for Associative Autopoietic DigitaL EcosystemS).

Robert M. Grant

Robert Grant is Professor of Management at Georgetown University. He was born in Bristol, England and studied economics at the London School of Economics. He has held faculty positions at St Andrews University, London Business School, University of British Columbia, California Polytechnic and City University, London. He has been a visiting professor at UCLA, INSEAD, Bocconi University and University of Bologna. His current research interests include the nature and development of organizational capability and strategic planning processes within large companies. His book *Contemporary Strategy Analysis* (5th edition, Blackwell, 2005) is the leading strategy text among top-tier MBA programmes in Europe and North America. The book is supported by more than 20 case studies that he has authored.

Michael Hobday

Michael Hobday is Professor of Innovation Policy at SPRU, University of Sussex and Professor of Innovation Management at the Centre for Research in Innovation Management (CENTRIM), University of Brighton, UK. He is the co-director of the CoPS Innovation Centre (based at the University of Sussex). He has produced more than 140 publications and reports, including 6 books and 43 refereed journal articles, for instance in *Industrial and Corporate Change*, *Management Decision*, *Oxford Development Studies*, *Research Policy* and *Technology Analysis and Strategic Management*.

Chuan-Leong Lam

Chuan-Leong Lam is an Ambassador-at-Large with the Singapore Ministry of Foreign Affairs. He is also the Chairman of the Infocomm Development Authority of Singapore and Chairman, Competition Commission of Singapore. He is an Adjunct Professor at the Lee Kuan Yew School of Public Policy, National University of Singapore and Adjunct Professor at the School of Social Sciences, Nanyang Technology University, Singapore. He holds an MBA from Harvard Business School and a First Class Honours in Physics from the University of Singapore. Mr Lam has recently retired after serving 36 years with the Singapore Civil Service. During his career, he headed key ministries in charge of communications and information, trade and industry, national development and the environment. His key interests and direct experience are in the area of macroeconomics, regulation of monopolies (for example telecommunications, power and water), competition policy, pricing and market efficiency, privatization of government services (for example telecoms, power, incineration plants) transport economics, structuring of public and private financing initiatives, e-government systems, development project evaluation, discounted cash flows, option valuation, and risk management and scanning. Mr Lam has been a member of the Board of the Monetary Authority of Singapore. He has been either chairman or a board member of several companies and statutory bodies in Singapore.

Robert Laubacher

Robert Laubacher is a Research Associate at MIT's Sloan School of Management. His work there examines how information technology is transforming business strategy, organizational practices and social patterns. His current project, Activity Based Performance Measurement, is developing new tools to measure the financial pay-off from investments in information technology. Mr Laubacher has published in academic fields and in *Harvard Business Review*, the *Financial Times* and the *Boston Globe*. His work has also been featured on national public radio and in the *New York Times*, *Wall Street Journal* and *Fast Company*. He co-edited *Inventing the Organizations of the 21st Century* (MIT Press 2003), a collection of articles based on a multi-year MIT research initiative. During his time at MIT, Mr Laubacher has served as a consultant to many corporations and was also an adviser to the organization practice of McKinsey & Company, assisting with development of new service offerings and in client engagements. In addition, he has been executive producer of two independent feature films, *Home Before Dark* (1997) and *American Wake* (2005). Prior to coming to MIT, Mr Laubacher was with JSA International, a strategy consulting firm that served Global 1000 clients based in the USA, UK, France and Germany. During his time there, JSA was acquired by the consulting practice of EDS, which subsequently merged with A.T. Kearney. He holds an undergraduate degree from Northwestern University and has completed a Master's degree and doctoral coursework in modern history at Harvard.

Swapan Kumar Majumdar

Swapan Kumar Majumdar is Professor in charge of Management Information Systems and eBusiness Management at Al Akhawayn University of Ifrane, Morocco. Professor Majumdar holds a BTech degree in Chemical Technology from Jadavpur University (India), an MBA from IIM Bangalore (India), an MSc in Analysis, Design and Management of Information Systems from the London School of Economics (London), an

MPhil in Management of Software Engineering Projects from the Imperial College of Science, Technology and Medicine (London) and a PhD in eBusiness Management from the Indian Institute of Technology, Delhi (India). Professor Majumdar has over 25 years of experience in consultancy, teaching and research in the business application of ICT. His teaching, research and consulting interests are analysis and design of business information systems and management of ICT-enabled processes and systems, especially eGovernance, eLearning and eHealthcare initiatives. He has published several papers, articles and case studies in national and international journals. He is a life member of the Global Institute of Flexible Management.

Jordi Molas-Gallart
Dr Jordi Molas-Gallart is a research professor at the Spanish Council for Scientific Research (CSIC). He works at INGENIO, a joint research centre of CSIC and the Universitat Politècnica de València. He is also an Honorary Professorial Fellow at SPRU, University of Sussex. An economist with eighteen years' experience as an analyst of technological change and technology policy, he has focused an important part of his research on the study of the defence and aerospace industries. He holds a 'Licenciatura' in Economics from the Universitat Autònoma de Barcelona, an MA in International Relations from the School of Advanced International Studies of the Johns Hopkins University and a DPhil from the University of Sussex with a dissertation on the relationship between military production and technological innovation. He has led research and consultancy projects for the European Commission, the European Parliament, the UK Department of Trade and Industry, the French Ministry of Defence and the UK National Engineering Laboratory among others. He is the author of *Military Production and Innovation in Spain* (Harwood Academic Publishers, 1992) and of more than 60 articles, book chapters, monographs and reports on different aspects of defence procurement, procurement reform and science and technology policy issues.

Sourav Mukherji
Sourav Mukherji is Assistant Professor of Organization Behaviour at the Indian Institute of Management, Bangalore. An engineer from IIT Kharagpur, Professor Mukherji obtained his doctorate from the Indian Institute of Management, Bangalore. His major research interests are in the areas of corporate strategy and structure, organization learning and knowledge management. Prior to joining the faculty at IIM Bangalore, Professor Mukherji was with the Boston Consulting Group, where he worked as a strategy consultant in projects involving corporate restructur-

ing, mergers and acquisitions and market entry strategy for multinational organizations. After completing his engineering degree, Professor Mukherji had worked with information technology firms like IBM and Oracle in various product management functions. As a doctoral student at IIM Bangalore he won the 'Infosys Fellowship', awarded for research in the IT industry. During this period, he had publications in peer-reviewed journals in the area of organizational theory and knowledge management. Professor Mukherji is currently engaged with studying the managerial and organizational innovations that have contributed to the competitiveness of leading Indian organizations in software services, automotive components and pharmaceutical industries. He has presented papers at international conferences, spoken at corporate forums and published in peer-reviewed journals on topics related to knowledge management and outsourcing of knowledge-intensive services.

Francesco Nachira
Francesco Nachira is a scientific officer of the European Commission, Directorate General 'Information Society and Media', heading the Sector 'Technologies for Digital Ecosystems'. He joined the Commission as scientific officer in 1995; since then he has promoted the fields of e-Government; urban and rural areas; tourism and e-Business, with a special focus on networking and ICT technologies supporting participative knowledge-intensive local development. Francesco Nachira graduated in 'Scienze dell'Informazione' at the University of Pisa. He studied Physics at the Scuola Normale Superiore of Pisa and followed multidisciplinary summer sessions at the University of Berkeley and at the Centro de Idiomas y Computación, 'José Martí' of Avana. He was researcher at the Italian National Geophysical Institute, where he taught within the 'International Postgraduate Course in Geothermics', supported by UNESCO. He worked in the R&D Department of a large enterprise operating in software development and services in the area of artificial intelligence (AI) and software engineering. He was assistant to the Vice Director of a state-owned Italian conglomerate, fostering the deployment of ICT in an Italian region, defining strategies for public intervention and for the involvement of local actors and constituency building. He was Technical Director of a small Belgian software integration and R&D company managing EC and European Space Agency projects. He was a partner of a consultancy intelligence company (Rome and Brussels), supporting decision makers in exploiting the opportunities created by the global information infrastructure. Before joining the European Commission he founded and was the CEO of Alfea Multimedia (Pisa), a pioneering innovative non-profit organization, formed by moviemakers and computer scientists

and focused on new forms of networked interactive communications. He is an active member and supporter of several grassroots associations and communities.

Giuseppina Passiante

Giuseppina Passiante is Full Professor of Management at the Faculty of Engineering, University of Lecce. She coordinates the research activities of the e-Business Management School (eBMS), a sector of the Scuola Superiore ISUFI, where she is also on the faculty of the PhD Programme in e-Business. Giuseppina Passiante's research interests encompass some cutting-edge research fields concerning the evolution of firms and networks of firms in the current scenarios of the digital economy. She has mainly focused on the dynamics of knowledge processes in innovative networks made up of virtual firms and on the modelling of 'virtual knowledge networks' as complex adaptive systems; the setting up of virtual innovation systems as a conceptual framework in order to understand the transition process from an economy conceived as an allocative system towards an economy conceived as a cumulative and adaptive learning process; and the theoretical and empirical exploration of relationships existing between a firm's strategy, a firm's knowledge strategy and the criteria for selecting the most suitable Information and Communication Technology platform for these strategies. She has published on these subjects in national (*Sviluppo e Organizzazione*) and refereed international journals (*International Journal of Innovation Management, International Journal of Information Management, Journal of Small Business and Enterprise Development*) and with national (Scientifiche Italiane, Cacucci Editore) and international publishers (Imperial College Press, Springer-Verlag). She collaborates with the Sloan Management School of MIT (Boston) in a research field concerning Social Network Mapping. She is in charge of the Italian scientific programme aimed at realizing a 'Basic and Applied Research L@b on e-Business Solutions' in cooperation with the Al Akhawayn University, Ifrane (Morocco).

Andrea Prencipe

Andrea Prencipe is Associate Professor of Management of Enterprise at the Faculty of Economics of the University G. d'Annunzio and Senior Fellow at SPRU (University of Sussex). He holds a BA (Hons) in Economics and Commerce from University G. d'Annunzio, an MSc in Innovation Management from Scuola Superiore S. Anna, Pisa, an MSc in Technology Innovation Management and a PhD in Technology Strategy from the University of Sussex. He has been a visiting scholar at Harvard Business School and Michigan Business School. He teaches in the Master and PhD courses of Scuola Superiore S. Anna, (Pisa), ISUFI (Università di Lecce) and SPRU (University of Sussex). He has been an invited speaker at Harvard Business School, London Business School, Cass Business School of the City University, London, and the University of Linköping, Sweden. His research interests encompass strategic management of technological and organizational innovation, organizational learning in project-based organizations and the implications of modular design strategies on the division and coordination of labour. He has published on these subjects in national (*Sinergie*) and refereed international journals (*Administrative Science Quarterly*, *Research Policy* and *Industrial and Corporate Change*) and with national (Franco Angeli) and international publishers (Oxford University Press). Andrea is Book Review Editor of the *Journal for Management and Governance* and sits on the Editorial Board of *Long Range Planning* and the *International Journal of Technology and Innovation Management*. He is an *ad hoc* referee for *Administrative Science Quarterly*, *British Journal of Management*, *Industrial and Corporate Change*, *Journal of Management and Governance*, *Long Range Planning*, *Organisation Studies*, *Research Policy*, *Sloan Management Review* and *Technology Analysis and Strategic Management*.

John Quimby
John Quimby is a research scientist at the Center for Coordination Science at MIT Sloan School. For the past few years, he has led the software development of the Process Handbook and been a contributing author to an *IEEE* journal article about the handbook. John spent the previous 15 years as a software engineer at Digital Equipment Corporation. There he was the architect of the TeamRoute Workflow Control System, designer of workflow control user agents and contributing architect to Digital's workflow strategy. He is the patent inventor of the Advanced Signature Data Object used for electronic signatures in workflow products, co-designer of a Business Process Re-engineering toolkit, and architect and project leader for Vax Valu V1.0, V2.0 and beyond. In addition to working on three versions of VAX VTX, he designed Digital's initial EDI architecture and architected 10 versions of Digital's VAX Remote Terminal Emulator. Prior to Digital, John was a member of the professional and technical staff of the University of New Hampshire, Durham, NH where he received his BFA in 1975. Recently he has worked on MOC (Matrix of Change).

J. Ramachandran
J. Ramachandran is BOC Professor of Business Policy at the Indian Institute of Management, Bangalore. A qualified chartered and cost accountant, Professor Ramachandran obtained his doctorate from the Indian Institute

of Management, Ahmedabad. His major research interests are in the areas of corporate transformation and competitive strategy. Prior to joining the faculty at the Indian Institute of Management Bangalore (IIMB), Professor Ramachandran was Vice President (Management Services) at Reliance Industries Limited, one of India's largest private sector firms. A winner of a number of awards for case research and teaching, *Business World* recently cited him as a Star Teacher. Professor Ramachandran is currently engaged in studying the globalization of firms from emerging markets. He has been the Harry Reynolds Visiting International Professor at the Wharton School of the University of Pennsylvania and a Visiting Professor at INSEAD, Fontainebleau, France and the Carlson School of Management, University of Minnesota, USA. He has also been a member of the Sub Committee on Strategy in Non-US Settings, Business Policy and Strategy Division of the Academy of Management, USA. Professor Ramachandran was the Chairperson of Executive Education at the IIMB. He has also directed the Global Leadership Programme conducted by IIM Bangalore jointly with the Amos Tuck School at Dartmouth College, USA, HEC France and Templeton College, Oxford as well as the MIT Sloan-IIMB Senior Management Program on Globalization, Technology and Management of Change. A former member of the board of governors of the Indian Institute of Management, Bangalore, Professor Ramachandran serves on the boards of select companies. He has also served as a consultant to various multinational and Indian companies, including Daimler Chrysler, Hewlett Packard, Philips, ITC, Colgate Palmolive, Siemens, Olam International, Wipro, Infosys, Sasken, Wockhardt, United Breweries, Eicher, Dalmia Cements, Madras Refineries and LIC.

Puay Tang

Dr Puay Tang is a political scientist with a PhD in International Relations from the Nitze School of Advanced International Studies, Johns Hopkins University, Washington DC. As a senior fellow at SPRU, University of Sussex, her research focuses on the application and development of new information and communication technologies, e-government, e-commerce, the management of intellectual property rights in a digital environment, the impact of intellectual property regimes on innovation, and university–industry relations. Her articles on these topics are complemented by a number of substantial reports to sponsors. Dr Tang also works on the evaluation of science and technology policy and research programmes and is a frequent evaluator and reviewer of European Commission Frameworks 5 and 6 Information Society Technology proposals and projects. She is a member of the Expert Panel on Information Science for the European Commission Descartes Prize, worth 1 million Euros for the winning project. She has managed and undertaken projects for the UK Economic and Social Research Council, the Engineering and Physical Sciences Research Council, the UK Department of Trade and Industry, the European Commission, the European Parliament, the Organization for Economic and Cultural Development and the Dutch Ministry of Economic Affairs. She has advised the UK Parliamentary Office on Science and Technology on the use of electronic services. Dr Tang is also an associate of the editorial board for *Information, Communication and Society*, published by Routledge. She reviews articles for *Research Policy*, *International Journal of Innovation Management*, *Telecommunication Policy*, *Industrial and Corporate Change*, *Information, Communication and Society* and *Intellectual Property Quarterly*, among others.

Glen Urban
Glen L. Urban is a leading educator, a prize-winning researcher specializing in marketing and new product development, an entrepreneur and author. He has been a member of the MIT Sloan School of Management faculty since 1966, was Deputy Dean at the school from 1987 to 1992 and Dean from 1993 to 1998. He is now Professor and Dean Emeritus, and Chairman of the MIT Center for eBusiness. Urban's research focus is on management science models that improve the productivity of new product development and marketing. For example, in a methodology he devised called Information Acceleration, he uses multimedia computer technology to simulate future sales of products such as cars, computer systems, telecommunications and drugs. Dr Urban's recent research is to develop a trust-based marketing system on the Internet. An extension of the information acceleration research, the system uses pickup trucks for a prototype web site that integrates attribute screening, expert advice, collaborative filtering and community interaction. This is being extended to understand how the click stream from such an adviser–customer dialogue can be used to discover unmet needs. Finally, research is underway to find the determinants of trust on the Internet and design a real-time adaptive experimentation system to increase the levels of trust on a web site.

Marshall Van Alstyne
Marshall Van Alstyne is an associate professor at Boston University and a visiting scholar at the MIT Sloan School of Management. Marshall received his bachelor's degree in Computer Science from Yale and MSc and PhD degrees in Information Technology from MIT. In industry, he wrote AI programs at Martin Marietta (Lockheed Martin) and at Lincoln Laboratory. He also worked as a technology management consultant for PA Consulting Group before co-founding a software and consulting firm

to provide decision support software to universities. His research focuses on the economics of information, its value, property rights and effects on productivity, firms and social systems. In designing information goods, his work concerns how firms use information strategically to compete. In control over information, it concerns who has access to what information, when and at what price. In measuring output, one long-term empirical study is investigating how information and technology make white-collar professionals more productive. In software property rights, this balances open source licences against those that are profit-maximizing. His research has received an NSF Career Award and best paper award, and has appeared in *Science* and the popular press. It is also taught in several major US business schools.

David Verrill

Mr Verrill is Executive Director of the Center for eBusiness at MIT's Sloan School of Management. He helped form the Center in 1999 and acted as a consultant until assuming the executive directorship on 1 July 2002. His professional career began as a research scientist at the famed Center for Blood Research in Boston, focusing on the major histocompatibility complex (MHC) of genetically engineered mice. After receiving his master's degree from Sloan, he joined MIT's Office of Corporate Relations, where he helped initiate and build the Financial Services sector for the Industrial Liaison Program. In 1991 he became Associate Director of Corporate Development. In 1996 he left MIT and joined Xerox as Manager of International Sales and Business Development for the Adaptive Products Division. Since 1998 he has helped start two companies, the Winchester International Group and the Hub Angel Investment Group. His areas of expertise include industry–university collaborations, technology transfer, entrepreneurship, raising capital, and topics in e-business. He has lectured widely and published in each of these areas. David was educated at Bowdoin College (AB 1983, Biology and Environmental Studies) and the MIT Sloan School of Management (SM 1987, Management). Born and raised in Maine, David lives in Carlisle, Massachusetts with his wife and their two children. He is an adventure skier and golf enthusiast.

Peter J. Williamson

Peter Williamson is Professor of International Strategy and Asian Business at the INSEAD in Fontainebleau and Singapore. He holds a PhD in Business Economics from Harvard University. In his early career, Peter worked at Merrill Lynch and The Boston Consulting Group. He was formerly Dean of MBA Programmes at the London Business School and Visiting Professor of Global Strategy and Management at Harvard

Business School. He has acted as consultant on business strategy, international expansion, mergers and acquisitions and alliances to numerous multinationals and serves as a non-executive director of several companies. Professor Williamson's research and publications span globalization, strategy in Asian markets, acquisitions and alliances and strategic innovation. His latest book, *Winning in Asia: Strategies for Competing in the New Millennium*, was published by Harvard Business School Press in June 2004. His other books include: *From Global to Metanational: How Companies Win in the Knowledge Economy* (2001), with Yves Doz and J. Santos, *The Economics of Financial Markets* (1995), *Managing the Global Frontier* (1994) and *The Strategy Handbook* (1992). Recent articles include 'China's hidden dragons' (*Harvard Business Review*), 'Strategies for competing in a changed China' and 'Is your innovation process global?' (*Sloan Management Review*). His earlier work includes articles published in *Strategic Management Journal* and *Academy of Management Journal* such as 'Use joint ventures to ease the pain of restructuring', 'Five styles of strategy innovation and how to use them', 'Strategy as options on the future' and 'Diversification, core competences and corporate performance'.

Foreword

Aldo Romano

The underlying idea of this book is related to research work of the e-Business Management Section of Scuola Superiore ISUFI. The e-Business Management Section is actively engaged with the scientific and industry communities on such topics as the management of the internet-worked enterprise, new product development in complex production domains, and innovative technological architecture of Mediterranean extra-EU countries.

Within its activities, the e-Business Management Section organizes an International Summer School whose aim is to create a forum for a systematic updating of new theories and managerial approaches in the networked economy. Each year the Summer School represents a gathering of world-renowned speakers from Europe, the United States, Japan, Australia and Middle Eastern and North African Countries. The 7th session of the International Summer School, held in Ostuni in July 2005, was devoted to 'The Emergence of Novel Organisational Forms in the Globalising Planet: Toward the Business Ecosystem?' The results of the discussions in Ostuni have been collected in this book, which opens the debate on the Digital Business Ecosystem concept. The book explores four topics:

- **Business ecosystems:** modern organizations can be described as massively interconnected networks of groups, departments, alliances, peripheral organizations, suppliers or collaborative joint ventures. In this context organizational fitness is both a property of the single organization and of the ecosystem. This loose web constitutes a business ecosystem, that is, an interconnected 'network of networks' of co-evolving organizations, with a specific relationship with a dominant organization.
- **Individualism and communitarianism:** the dramatic expansion of the business frontier in South East Asia is giving rise to an unprecedented social and economic experiment: The Asian Tigers, followed by China and India, have mixed traditional values with Western entrepreneurialism, giving rise to new organizational forms blending Asian communitarianism with entrepreneurial individualism.

- **Organizational models:** organizations are being increasingly structured as portfolios of projects, in which modules and competencies can be reconfigured around emergent needs. At the same time we are witnessing the emergence of temporary networks that swarm and dissolve around specific projects. Transient networks and organizations as project portfolios constitute new organizational species that match connectivity, flexibility and adaptiveness.
- **Diversity and business ecosystems:** globalization of markets and industry generate powerful forces towards on the one hand increasing homogeneity and on the other hand, by opening new markets and cultures, towards increasing heterogeneity. These two trends cross through business ecosystems. We can conceptualize business ecosystems as meta-organizational structures that manage the tension between on the one hand heterogeneity of resources leading to innovation and potentially to chaos and, on the other hand, to homogeneity of actors and behaviours which leads to higher coherence and focus.

I must congratulate the editors for the scientific depth, rigorousness and multidisciplinary nature of the papers presented in this book. These features are the foundations of our International Summer School. Preparing a book like this one has been a team effort. I would like to thank the researchers who participated in the 7th International Summer School and contributed with their valuable work to this editorial effort.

Preface

Michael Hobday

How best to understand, analyse and interpret the firm? This is not a trivial question. It goes to the heart of understanding the new (and old) economy. However, until now we have not yet had an approach which deals with the firm as part of the environment in which it is born and grows and competes. Neoclassical economics treats the firm as an entity devoid of history and context, operating only to maximize profit in its competitive setting. The Penrosian resource-based view is a far superior way of looking at the business firm, showing how it evolves through the development of capabilities and the allocation of resources by management to profitable new activities. However, a weakness of the Penrosian perspective is that it focuses on the business firm and cannot explain its relationship with, and embeddedness within, the environment in which it operates and evolves. By contrast, the evolutionary perspective examines how the environment selects among firms, by rewarding some and punishing others. Yet, somehow, the evolutionary perspective does not really capture the central role of business firms in actually shaping the environment.

By bringing together elements of a radical new approach to the firm, based on the biological metaphor of the ecosystem, this book goes beyond the limits of existing theories and tries to show precisely how the modern business firm competes and cooperates within its market and technological environment – equally, it touches on how firms actually shape the environment through their deliberate actions and investments. This new approach, called digital business ecosystems (DBEs) also allows us to understand the way new digital technologies feed into the environment and shape the ways in which firms and groups of firms compete and cooperate.

This book presents a fascinating collection of papers from different perspectives all addressing the DBE. It is both highly original and groundbreaking in its achievements. From a theory point of view, the study argues that the concept of region and history fails to account for the fact that the firm is not merely a member of a single industry but a part of a business ecosystem which cuts across a variety of industries. The ecosystem is supported by enabling technologies and, more specifically, digital software which changes and shapes not only the internal structure of firms but the ways in which firms work together. While the new theory is closely linked and sympathetic to the evolutionary theory of the firm pioneered by Nelson and Winter, DBE is less concerned with firm selection and more interested in path dependency of organizational forms and the emergence of 'organizational genotypes'.

The work is also rich in empirical evidence. The chapter on regional development in Europe is particularly interesting as it attempts to conceptualize and explain the challenges posed by the huge numbers of small and medium-sized enterprises within the European DBE. Another chapter deals with how DBEs relate to other historical organizational forms, pointing to the fundamental tasks of all business organizations, namely coordination and cooperation. Within the international context the research shows that, in fact, very few major companies have developed DBE structures effective enough to harness the potential of 'global knowledge diversity', implying that a change in business leader mindset is needed before the benefits of DBEs are to be fully realized.

Evidence to interpret and examine the impact and implications of DBEs is provided from a wide range of developed and developing countries, including the European Union, China, India, Singapore and the USA. With the emergence of China and India as important global players it is fascinating to see, for example, how Indian software service organizations created a particular form of DBE with a network of external linkages which both 'scaled up' and sustained the growth of this industry. A chapter on China shows that this rapidly growing economy will soon force a fundamental strategic rethink on the way transnational firms choose to globalize through DBEs. A second chapter on China deals with precisely how the new information and communications technologies which underpin DBEs will affect China's entire development trajectory and the very nature of globalization as it is currently understood.

The book provides frameworks and methods for understanding DBEs, covering issues of intellectual property, costs and benefit assessment techniques and a series of other useful tools. Perhaps one limitation of the book is that it does not go very far in showing how leading firms actually construct the DBE within which they compete. The concepts of 'self-organization' and 'co-evolution' do not seem to capture this vital role of leading firms. However, there are some fascinating glimpses into this issue (for example the chapters on Cisco, IBM, Microsoft and Netscape). What these chapters suggest is needed is more in-depth research and conceptualization on how and why particular firms introduce the new technologies, build the infrastructures and stimulate the markets within which they then compete – and how these processes underpin the self-organization of the DBE. In fact, the strict biological notion of self-organization may be challenged by these new conceptualizations of DBEs in the book, which suggest the importance of leadership, decision making and 'conscious' human strategy and action on the evolution of the DBE. No doubt these issues will be taken up further by the authors in this exciting new research agenda.

In summary, this is a unique text rich with theory, novelty and significant new arguments and empirical data. It extends our understanding of the firm in many positive new ways and is a very welcome and important contribution to the field of innovation studies.

Introduction

**Angelo Corallo, Giuseppina Passiante and
Andrea Prencipe**

BACKGROUND

Radical changes in the geography of costs, production, and human and social capital have affected the organization of business activities, modifying both geographic and sectoral dimensions. Business organizations have reacted by decentralizing production and innovation, shifting activities to external partners and adopting distributed, modular organizational structures. This trend has led to the emergence of the business network.

The business network is ubiquitous throughout the economy. The production and commercialization of products and services rely on a network of interrelated firms which contribute directly or indirectly to its design, creation and delivery (Powell 1990, Castells 1996). Although research has made important contributions towards the understanding of business networks, further theoretical and empirical research is required to develop a better understanding of the processes underlying their structure and evolution.

As early as 1959, Stafford Beer compared business systems to biological systems and argued that an industrial organization is an organism which responds to its environment. The ecological perspective does not see the economy as a machine; on the contrary it argues that the market economy is best understood as a living, evolving ecosystem (Rothschild 1990). Departing from these contributions, this book aims to provide a better understanding of how business networks were born, under what conditions they can survive and what the main variables to be considered are in order to support the design, implementation and evolution of an effective business network structure. Moore (1993) defined the business ecosystem as a loose network of suppliers, distributors and outsourcing firms that work cooperatively and competitively to support new products, satisfy customer needs and incorporate innovations. In Moore's (1996) approach, innovation becomes the locus where business ecosystem species co-evolve. Innovation is a catalyser element for the creation and evolution of the ecosystem.

This ecosystem concept is widely used by Intel, IBM, HP and Microsoft in defining alliances and networks and promoting their products and services. According to Mayer and Kenney (2004), Cisco has successfully grown through the conscious and deliberate acquisition of high-technology firms to become the dominant global networking equipment provider with an active involvement by both the firm and its employees in its ecosystem. As suggested by Iansiti and Levien (2004a), the biological ecosystem can provide a powerful metaphor for understanding these business networks: like a biological system, a business ecosystem is a non-homogeneous community of entities, made up of a large number of interconnected participants with different interests, who depend on each other for their mutual effectiveness and survival, and so are bound together in a collective whole. The structure of a business ecosystem, its relationships among members, the types of connections existing among them and the differing roles played by the members, follow a similar path to that of biological ecosystems (Iansiti and Levien 2004b). At a meso level, business ecosystems show an evolutionary dynamic. As described by Saviotti (2001), the structure of these networks emerges when the individual components of the systems, which are initially combined in a random way, assemble in particular organizations, whose interactions are influenced by institutions. At first the new structure is loosely organized, but gradually becomes more interconnected and rigid. This structure becomes unstable due to changing environmental conditions both internally and outside existing institutions and organizations, in the sense of requiring new firms and new institutions to define the rules. Such rules will be available *ex ante*, but can also be created simultaneously with the diffusion of innovation.

The diffusion of information and communication technology (ICT) has allowed organizations within business ecosystems to use Internet-based technologies in conjunction with face-to-face interaction in order to undertake and coordinate joint tasks. Value generated in Internet-enabled business transcends traditional industrial sector firms belonging to different sectors but to the same business ecosystem (Gossain and Kandiah 1998) or business web (Tapscott *et al.* 2000) and can provide unique and customized solutions to individual customers. Each organization adds one or more distinct aspect of product/service value to the value generated by the ecosystem, by exchanging digital knowledge with other members: the business ecosystem evolves into the digital business ecosystem (DBE).

A digital ecosystem can be defined as the ICT-enabling infrastructure that supports the cooperation, the knowledge sharing and the building of a digital business ecosystem. The digital ecosystem is the pervasive soft support infrastructure populated by digital species able to evolve, adapt and mediate services and knowledge. In this metaphor the digital ecosystem is 'populated by digital species', exhibiting the structure and behaviour of natural species as much as a business ecosystem is populated by business species.

OBJECTIVE AND APPROACH

To date no published academic work has provided a theoretical, analytical or empirical grounding of digital business ecosystems. This book draws on and presents different perspectives of digital business ecosystems to fill this gap, taking an interdisciplinary approach to broaden and deepen the understanding of DBEs. The book is divided into four main parts. Part I presents the theoretical and analytical dimensions of digital business ecosystems. Contributions concentrate on the emergence of business ecosystems and their theoretical underpinnings. Part II explores the organizational dimension of digital business ecosystems. Contributors delve into the main organizing principles using different industrial examples. Part III takes industry- and firm-level approaches as well as some policy implications. Contributions focus on different sectors and highlight the specificity of digital business ecosystems in various industrial domains. Part IV is mainly oriented towards the definition of tools and frameworks supporting DBE design and implementation.

Part I Digital Business Ecosystems: Theoretical Underpinnings

Part I presents two chapters describing the emergence of business ecosystem concepts and evolution toward the digital business ecosystem.

Chapter 1 analyses the business ecosystem metaphor through the lens of biological ecosystem theory. The biological metaphor of the ecosystem is becoming attractive for scholars and managers. The first question addressed in the chapter is related to the effectiveness of the ecosystem metaphor. Although this seems strongly alluring for highlighting emerging organizational structures and behaviour, it is not clear whether it will be possible to extend the well-known properties of natural ecosystems to a business environment. This leads to the second question – the definition of an evolutionary model that supports a business ecosystem. In the business ecosystem perspective, the key question is far from being related to firm selection and is closely related to path-dependent histories of co-evolving organizational forms. Padgett (2001) defines this as the emergence of an organizational genotype (logic of identity) and the process of creating an organizational phenotype (through interaction with surrounding social networks).

Starting from the problem of sustainable regional development for European regions, Dini and Nachira in Chapter 2 trace the rationale for the creation of a new area of research in digital ecosystems in the presence of challenges of socioeconomic development specific to Europe and characterized by an overwhelming predominance of small and medium-sized enterprises (SMEs). Dini and Nachira define the digital ecosystem concept as the enabling technology for a business ecosystem as it represents the digital software environment that supports the development of distributed and adaptive technologies and evolutionary business models for organizations. Throughout the chapter they show how language and the formalization of knowledge play a key role in the dynamics of sustainable socioeconomic development, how digital ecosystems naturally take advantage of this fact, and how this has led to the emergence of a new and very effective paradigm for interdisciplinary research.

Part II The Organizational Dimension of Digital Business Ecosystems

Part II presents the emergence of new organizational models that are mainly independent of geographical and industrial sectors and are fundamental for understanding the organizational dimension of a digital business ecosystem.

Chapter 3 focuses on the histories of the main organizational forms and on the analysis of network organizations with specific reference to open source organization. Grant begins by examining the principal features of conventional corporations and the changing environmental conditions which are creating the need for different types of organizational structures. On the basis of a diagnosis of why these organizational innovations have failed to take root, he considers the fundamental tasks of organization – coordination and cooperation – and the mechanisms needed to achieve these. Grant recognizes that the networked organization is an organizational form that has long been an alternative to the integrated corporation. In this chapter, the more recent and entirely novel form of network organization that is open-source software (OSS) communities is analysed.

Chapter 4 argues that, despite this globalization, few companies have developed their strategies and structures to harness the potential value of global knowledge diversity. Indeed, most companies still see diverse, context-specific knowledge as an impediment to their globalization strategies, rather than as a fount of new competitive advantage. Williamson explores the changes in mindsets, organizational forms and processes that will be required for companies to break free of globalization strategies based on projecting home-grown advantages around the world and to harness more fully the latent value of global knowledge diversity within

DBEs. Using China as a core example, he proposes that as the planet globalizes, companies will need to rethink fundamentally the way different locations within their international networks can contribute to success.

Part III Empirical Studies on Digital Business Ecosystems

Part III is devoted to the analysis of empirical evidence of emerging business ecosystems in different industries and geographical areas, highlighting the specificity of each business ecosystem.

Chapter 5 identifies unique structural features of the Indian software service organizations that have led to the creation of DBEs with a network of relationships, which have facilitated rapid scaling and sustained growth of this industry. These inter-organizational relationships accommodate both complementarities and competitiveness among their members. Free of any grand design, they have emerged as a consequence of the survival and growth strategies of individual members and have led to the creation of interdependencies which are flexible yet resilient. In this chapter Ramachandran and Mukherji debate whether the network of relationships can be conceptualized as an emergent ecosystem.

Using the language of the Cynefin diagram, Chapter 6 argues that the DBE is placed at least in the complex space of the diagram and may possibly be moving towards the chaos space. Some suggestions are offered on how key people like managers of companies and leaders and economic planners of countries can respond to this development, particularly in the field of innovation and economic policy. In this chapter Chuan-Leong Lam draws parallels and examples from the experience of Singapore in dealing with this issue in the past and also some of the future developmental projects.

In Chapter 7 Boisot and Child examine the impact that ICTs might have on China's development trajectory and ask whether network capitalism is but a station on the way to fully-fledged market capitalism or an institutional order in its own right. They use a conceptual framework, the Information-Space or I-Space to explore the institutional options that confront the country under conditions of rapid social, economic and technical change. They argue that China's institutional responses to the transformations that it is experiencing throw new light on what the term 'globalization' can reasonably be expected to cover. This has implications for the country's own emerging business systems as well as for those who invest in China.

Part IV Tools and Frameworks for Digital Business Ecosystems

Part IV deals with frameworks and tools supporting the design and implementation of the digital business ecosystem.

Chapter 8 explores organizations involved in the joint development, production, operation and maintenance of large complex systems. These organizations are increasingly using electronic networks to plan, schedule, monitor, cost, design, procure and support them. Yet the same information technologies (IT) that facilitate such exchanges of information threaten ownership control over the results of R&D and design efforts. Tang and Molas-Gallart discuss how intellectual property (IP) issues affect the deployment of IT networks to share technical data in the context of research and manufacturing collaborations. From an in-depth study of IP management practices in UK defence firms and customer organizations involved in joint projects, they derive a set of recommended practices and policies for improving IP management in such contexts.

Chapter 9 creates a connection between the digital business ecosystem perspective and e-business models through ICT adoption. The diverse character of emerging business ecosystems, the complex nature of ICT and the innovative character of e-business have made it very difficult to comprehend and construct a viable business model without assessing the features of the digital business ecosystem in question and the unique resources and capabilities of the e-business initiating organization. In this chapter Majumdar defines the MAP-STEPS model which provides a roadmap for developing effective and sustainable business models for organizations considering the resources, capabilities, competencies and strategic competitive advantages of the organization; and he suggests guidelines for the implementation of e-business projects.

A digital business ecosystem can be defined as the e-business infrastructure enabling a business ecosystem with each of the ecosystem players as participants. The digital business ecosystem is the space in which digital organizations interact, compete, collaborate and co-evolve around innovation, using e-business technology. In Chapter 10, Brynjolfsson, Quimby, Urban, Van Alstyne and Verrill describe tools and frameworks related to the relationships a firm can develop with its customers and market and the measurement of productivity of a digital organization in its business ecosystem.

Chapter 11 discusses the impact of radio frequency identification (RFID) and smart devices using the results of a study of two US firms. Laubacher also draws implications for other organizations based on an MIT study that is examining the impact of RFID at a leading US consumer goods manufacturer and of smart devices in the sales group of a leading US technology firm. This study looks at how these technologies are reshaping internal processes and reconfiguring interactions between trading partners. In addition, it shows how activity-based performance measurement (ABPM) can be used to measure the costs and benefits of digital ecosystem technology and other management interventions.

Companies which use a business ecosystem approach to understand their environment and develop their strategies have had tremendous success. Each business ecosystem needs an infrastructure supporting interaction and knowledge exchange mechanisms.

FUTURE RESEARCH AGENDA

Although many essential questions have been answered in this book, many other questions remain and require further research. Significant effort is needed to develop social theories and technology models which underpin the design, structuring and evolution of digital business ecosystems.

From a theoretical perspective it is fundamental to explore further the genotype of an organizational structure, its space of possible evolutionary patterns and the relationships between phenotype trajectories and environmental conditions. This analysis, suggested by Fontana (2003) and Padgett and Powell (2003), calls for exploration of the evolution of organizational roots.

Another key question is related to the conceptualization of the interaction between a business ecosystem of firms and a digital ecosystem of software entities as a 'structural coupling' (Maturana and Varela 1998) across different types of interfaces. Structural coupling assigns an equal role to two interacting entities, such that neither is seen to determine the other completely.

From an empirical viewpoint, future research needs to focus on analysis of the micro-elements that underlie DBE structure and, more importantly, the social, economic, and technological processes that lead to DBE formation and evolution over time. To do so, in-depth case studies may help identify the relevant dimensions of digital business ecosystems.

REFERENCES

Beer, S. (1959), *Cybernetics and Management*, London: English Universities Press.
Castells, M. (1996), *The Rise of the Network Society*, Oxford: Blackwell.
Fontana, W. (2003), *The Topology of the Possible*, Draft, May, http://www.santafe.edu/~walter/Papers/top.pdf, 15 September 2006.
Gossain, S. and G. Kandiah (1998), 'Reinventing value: the new business ecosystem', *Strategy and Leadership*, **26** (5), 28–33.
Iansiti, M. and R. Levien (2004a), *The Keystone Advantage: What the New Dynamics of Business Ecosystems Mean for Strategy, Innovation and Sustainability*, Boston, MA: Harvard Business School Press.
Iansiti, M. and R. Levien (2004b), 'Strategy as ecology', *Harvard Business Review*, March, 68–78.

Maturana, H. and F. Varela (1998), *The Tree of Knowledge: The Biological Roots of Human Understanding*, revised edition, Boston, MA: Shambhala.

Mayer, D. and M. Kenney (2004), 'Economic action does not take place in a vacuum: understanding Cisco's acquisition and development strategy', *Industry and Innovation*, **11** (4), 299–325.

Moore, J.F. (1993), 'Predators and prey: a new ecology of competition', *Harvard Business Review*, May–June, 75–86.

Moore, J.F. (1996), *The Death of Competition: Leadership and Strategy in the Age of Business Ecosystems*, New York: HarperBusiness.

Padgett, J.F. (2001), Organizational genesis, identity and control: the transformation of banking in Renaissance Florence, in A. Casella and J. Rach (eds), *Networks and Markets*, New York: Russell Sage, pp. 211–257.

Padgett, J.F. and W.W. Powell (2003), *Market Emergence*, Draft, May.

Powell, W.W. (1990), 'Neither markets nor hierarchy: network forms of organization', *Research in Organizational Behavior*, **12**, 295–336.

Rothschild, M. (1990), *The Inevitability of Capitalism*, New York: Henry Holt.

Saviotti, P.P. (2001), 'Special issue: variety, growth and demand', *Journal of Evolutionary Economics*, **11** (1), 119–142.

Tapscott, D., D. Ticoll and A. Lowy (2000), *Digital Capital*, Boston, MA: Harvard Business School Press.

PART I

Digital business ecosystems: theoretical underpinnings

1. The business ecosystem as a multiple dynamic network

Angelo Corallo

INTRODUCTION

Recent changes (for example technological and market) in the competitive environment have profound implications on the way that organizations compete and cooperate. Whereas vertically integrated firms are reconfiguring their value chain, focusing on added value activities, small firms belonging to industrial districts are growing globally, creating loosely coupled networks of firms. Firms experiment with alternative coordination mechanisms that transcend the traditional dichotomy market and hierarchy. These mechanisms can be arranged in a continuum-like fashion, with discrete market transactions located at one end, and highly centralized firms at the other. In the middle, various intermediate or hybrid forms of organization can be found, ranging from market pole, repeated trading relationships, quasi-firms, subcontracting arrangements, franchising, joint ventures and decentralized profit centres. Powell (1990) and Castells (1996) argued that networks are a distinctive form of coordinating economic activity and it makes sense to classify any organizational structure adopting a coordination mechanism in this grey area as a business network.

From Vertical Corporation to Business Network

The resource-based view of the firm focuses on the capabilities of organizations to leverage specialized knowledge in order to create competitive advantage (Penrose 1959, Nelson and Winter 1982, Teece and Pisano 1994). The disaggregation of the vertical industrial firm requires capabilities of low-coupled market-based organization in order to reconfigure the organization and competencies to emerging needs and explore distant learning trajectories (Coase 1937, Williamson 1975, 1987). The Japanese *keiretsu* was the first horizontally integrated group of allied firms operating across many industries (Gilson and Roe 1993). Virtual corporations are not permanent and institutional organizations like *keiretsu*, but are based on the opportunistic and temporary integration of complementary competencies (Davidow and Malone 1992).

Castells (1996) proposed the concept of the networked enterprise as the organizational form that a firm would adopt to fit the conditions of uncertain and unpredictable environments. Accordingly, different kinds of emerging phenomena precede network organizations: flexible specialization (Piore and Sabel 1984), dynamic flexibility (Coriat 1990), Toyotism with its stable and complementary relationships between producer and suppliers (Friedman 1988), multiple relationship networks between small and medium-sized enterprises (SMEs) and large firms (Ybarra 1989), franchising models (for example the 'Benetton Model') (Harrison 1994) and strategic alliances developed by large firms in specific competitive industrial sectors (Gerlac 1992, Dunning 1993).

According to Powell (1990) an empirical taxonomy of network enterprises includes networks in craft work, regional economies and industrial clusters, and strategic alliances and partnerships or business networks related to vertical disaggregation of large firms. Typical examples of network organizations are the construction industry (Eccles 1981), the book industry (Coser *et al.* 1982) and the film and recording industry (Faulkner and Anderson 1987). The aerospace industry (Mowery 1987) or technology-intensive industries (Martini and Smiley 1983, Contractor and Lorange 1988) are empirical evidence of business networks arising from strategic alliances and partnerships. Examples of vertical disaggregation phenomena that bring about the emergence of business networks are the downsizing patterns in the Italian textile industry (Mariotti and Cainarca 1986) and the automotive industry (Davis *et al.* 1987).

According to Castells (1996), the strengths of the networked enterprise lie in the shift from vertical bureaucracies to horizontal enterprise enabled by the use of digital technology to connect and relate dispersed organizational nodes. In the networked enterprise, components are both independent of and dependent on the network organization and can also be part of several other networks. The network performance is affected by its connectivity and its consistency, that is, the degree of interest sharing among network and individual component objectives. Bureaucracy is still used in some specific units that need to be stable and affordable more than flexible and effective.

Some scholars and practitioners conceive network organizations as entities in which lateral ties are substituted for vertical ones, looking like horizontal and informal structures. Other scholars define the network organization stressing the replacement of command relationships with a quasi-market mechanism. Although quasi-market relationships lie at the core of network organizations, it is possible to observe that bureaucracy will not disappear and hierarchy will remain the dominant mode of organizing. A network organization combines the advantage of bureaucratic organization with a structure that supports innovation. Networks (Quinn *et al.* 1998) could be shaped by pointing out the nodes where knowledge is created and detained, the nodes where it is used to implement solutions, and the kind of relationship that links together the different nodes. Taking into account both firm and market perspectives, the new organizational problem of the firms seems to be no longer that of achieving alignment among different department objectives, but of coordinating networks of knowledge-owning firms to create added value products and services.

From District to Business Network

Industrial clusters are conceived as a form of network that occurs within a geographical location, in which independent and informally linked firms and institutions act as a robust organizational form in the continuum between markets and hierarchies. Research on industrial clusters has emphasized the linkage and interdependence among actors. Its economic organization is in turn influenced by the local demographic, political, cultural, social and technological environments (Knox and Agnew 1998). According to Porter (1990) the power of clusters lies in intra-cluster competition, which forces firms to innovate in order to create competitive advantage. Porter's approach emphasizes the role of social structure as economic activities are embedded in ongoing social relationships.

Research has emphasized the role of social networks and geographic proximity as a medium for interactions and exchanges of localized knowledge, mainly tacit in nature, that may in turn be considered one of the main sources of the industrial cluster agglomeration rate. On the other hand, the emerging global networked environment, enabled by information and communication technologies, is creating a new cognitive space that fosters the exchange of mainly explicit knowledge and the creation of new sources of clustering phenomena. In the new economic landscape, geographical industrial clusters are evolving towards new industrial agglomerations, grasping the opportunities which come from network technologies (Passiante 2003). Inside the cluster, a co-evolution process is emerging; it develops between the networks of localized knowledge and the trans-local knowledge networks (Doz *et al.* 2001), based on digital information exchange. These inter-organizational structures, defined as virtual clusters, are characterized by collaboration and complementarities and by the exchange of mainly digital knowledge. In a virtual cluster, each enterprise adds one or more distinct aspects of product or service value to the value of the network by exchanging digital knowledge with other members. Value networks are involved in creating value in each node. The strength of a value network comes from cooperation and interaction among participating firms (Passiante 2003).

A Theoretical Model for Business Networks

The study of economic agglomeration phenomena in the networked economy suggests an approach based on a more general concept of relationship space. Bottazzi and colleagues (2002) highlighted that spatial dimension includes both geographic and metaphorical spaces: the former refers to the agent's physical position in space, while the latter concerns technological and institutional distances, inclusion and exclusion in networks and nations, level of knowledge and information sharing. The concept of space is therefore crucial. Being part of a particular space influences the single agent's identity, capacity, behaviour, interactive pattern and collective and individual performance. Spatial dimension enables analysis at different geographical levels of the environment in which relations among actors are confined and where the concept of relationship is extended to the exchange of knowledge and collective learning. Following this approach, we may extend the concept of 'actor agglomeration' from industrial district to business network, as the generalization of any agglomeration structure that is represented by a set of firms, linked by some sort of spatial proximity (geographical, technological or institutional). Business networks are ubiquitous throughout the economy. More and more services or products delivered depend on a network of interrelated firms which contribute directly or indirectly to its design, creation and delivery. Firms look with increasingly keen interest to territory-based inter-organizational models that, since the Italian Renaissance, have shown the capability of orchestrating and integrating production and distribution networks of firms. Time after time, this kind of firm network has developed the ability of autonomous evolution and collective response, being able to survive many social, technological and market changes.

   Although research has made important contributions towards the understanding of business networks, further theoretical and empirical research is required to develop a better understanding of the processes underlying their structure and evolution.

BUSINESS NETWORKS AS A BUSINESS ECOSYSTEM

The biological ecosystem seems able to provide a powerful metaphor for understanding a business network. Like biological ecosystems, business networks are communities of agents with different characteristics and interests, bound together by different mutual relationships as a collective whole. Species within ecosystems are related and interact with each other as much as firms play a specific role in a business network. The fate of each living organism in the ecosystem is related to the fate of the others; cooperation and competition, as much as in a business network, are considered ecosystem-characterizing phenomena.

Biological Ecosystem Theory

A biological ecosystem is defined as a naturally occurring assembly of organisms that live together in their physical environment (Tansley 1935). This definition, fundamental for ecological science, was developed in a long debate lasting throughout the 20th century. The two key elements of the definition are: the interactions of species with the physical environment, explained by biologists through thermodynamic models; and the relationships among species, described through the food web model. The conceptualization of 'ecosystem' started with the observation that food relationships connect different species in functional units. Functional similarity among biological communities of different species shows a strong tendency to holism.

Elton (1927) first considered the food chain, or food web, as the key element capable of defining a biological community. He also observed that living organisms that make up a food web could be arranged into a pyramidal structure that he named 'pyramid of numbers'. Each level of this pyramid from top to bottom is made of smaller and less complex species (for example the top level is made up of a few big predators, many herbivore creatures occupy the lower levels and a huge number of plants the bottom) contributing with more and more biomass to the ecosystem. The first approach to communities and ecological systems as thermodynamic systems was made by Lotka (1925). According to Lotka, the biological system is able to transform sunlight into energy; ecological systems, like thermodynamic ones, are capable of converting energy from sunlight in a way that is properly related to their mass and to their transformation speed and is inversely related to their efficiency.

Tansley (1935) first defined an ecosystem as the whole system represented by both the biological organisms and a complex set of physical factors. Starting from the definition by Tansley – the first that correlated the ecosystem with a network of relationships – Lindeman (1942) developed the modern approach to the ecosystem by adopting Elton's food web model and Lotka's thermodynamic approach. He defined the 'thermodynamic trophic approach', redesigning Elton's 'pyramid of numbers' in terms of trophic levels: each level was characterized by a quantity of available energy lower than the previous one, because of the inefficiency of energy transformation. According to his trophic-level model, energy and matter flow freely in an ecosystem through the living organisms and their activities. Photosynthesis, decomposition, herbivore and predator are relationships among different species of existing beings and are the processes through which energy and matter flow and accumulate in the ecosystem. In this perspective an ecosystem is a dynamic and complex dimension, characterized by ecological interactions and by the free flow of energy and matter among its different elements. This definition emphasizes the relation between organisms and environment and the complexity of the relationships between an organism and its thermodynamic capability to transform energy and matter. Looking at organisms as machines, it is possible to observe that efficiency is the lowest for vertebrates that have complex mechanisms of maintenance. The efficiency of the food chain is made up of each trophic level efficiency and the number of sustainable trophic levels is related to the efficiency of the organisms. The maximum number of trophic levels for an ecosystem depends on the ecological efficiency of the whole system, depending on the difference in efficiency between the subsequent trophic levels. This number ranges from the three levels of a terrestrial community to the seven levels of a plankton-based marine community.

Ecological studies are often based on population analysis. For ecologists, a population is a set of individuals of the same species in a specific geographic area; it is a key concept since demographic processes, evolution by natural selection and regulation of the community structure in terms of competition and cooperation are beyond individual perspective and can only be explained through population dynamics.

Competition is one of the fundamental processes in ecology and the keystone of Darwinian natural selection theory. In biological science, it is defined as the contention between two or more consumers of a resource. The amount of the specific resource and the intra-species competition influence and regulate the size of a population in an ecosystem. Interspecies competition can reduce the size of a single species inside the population and even exclude a species from an ecosystem. An interesting result from biology is that if two species compete fiercely for a specific resource, the size of each population is influenced by the other.

Robustness is an ecosystem property related to the topology of the food web as well as to the characteristics of competition among predator populations. The topology of the food web could be quite unstable if there were a single point of connection or just specific species that connected with many others, showing some characteristics that limited their adaptability to environmental change. The specific characteristics of competition among species and the common asymmetry of the relationships (Morin and Johnson 1988) could create instability, usually balanced by other environmental conditions or by the presence of consumers whose action could favour the weaker competitor.

Symbiotic associations provide a good example of cooperation. Symbiotic relationships could range from associations which are useful for both the symbionts, defined in nature as mutualism, to associations useful for one of the symbionts that poorly affects the others, to extreme kinds of relationship similar to a sort of parasitism.

Strong competitive and cooperative interactions affect what in biological science is defined as co-evolution: the process in which interdependent species that interact in a competitive way (consumer–prey) or in a cooperative way (mutualism), evolve in an endless reciprocal cycle (Bateson 1983). Since each element of the couple is relevant for the other's environment, variations in the first select the evolutionary response in the other one. Both parties in a co-evolutionary relationship activate selective pressure on the other, and consequently affect each other's evolution. Populations settled in a specific geographic area define a community, a dimension concerning the association of different related species.

Key aspects in a community are: the adjustment of species diversity, the set of distinctive properties coming from the specific path of co-evolution, and the relationship between community organization and its stability. It is quite impossible to frame the community borders, and ecologists usually define communities according to their members' features, their relative abundance and their mutual food relations. A key concept in community analysis is the niche that in ecology describes the relational position of a species or population in a community. More generally, the niche concept expresses the relation of an individual with regards to physical and biological aspects of the environment. It refers to the organism's life history or habitat in the food chain.

Each factor represents an axis of a multidimensional space; the niche is the volume delimited by the intervals of each axis, in which the specific individual or population can survive. Relationships among species could be described by the superposition of the respective niches, as a function of niche width and overlap. The full range of environmental conditions under which an organism can exist describes its fundamental niche. As a result of pressure from other organisms and general interactions, species are usually forced to occupy a particular niche that is not the most suitable for their survival. According to the 'competitive exclusion' principle (Hardin 1960), if two species cannot coexist consuming the same limiting resources, they cannot occupy the same niche in the same environment for a long time. In other words, a niche is the position occupied by an organism (or group of organisms) within an ecosystem, or the set of conditions creating a habitat.

The niche defines the organism's role in the ecological community. Different species can hold similar niches in different locations and the same species may occupy different niches in different locations. It should be observed that a clear relationship between the niche dimension and the diffusion of the species does not exist and a lower niche dimension and consequent specialization do not imply greater efficiency.

Another key player in a community is the keystone, a species that exerts great influence on an ecosystem, although covering a limited amount of the whole biomass. This influence can take one of several forms. In many biological environments, keystone species are the predators at the top of the food web; more specifically they can be predators that prevent the overrunning of a particular prey species. Some starfish may perform this function by preying on mussels and other shellfish that have no other natural predators. It has been suggested that it is possible to identify such keystone predators by their biomass dominance within ecological functional groups, even though they may be relatively rare as regards the ecosystem as a whole. Other examples of keystone are some ecosystem engineers that are organisms creating or modifying habitats. The North American grizzly bear is a keystone species, since, eating salmon which come from the ocean, it transfers nutrients from an oceanic ecosystem to a forest ecosystem.

Business Ecosystems

The first approach to a business ecosystem was by Moore (1993). According to him, a firm is not just a member of a single industry but part of a business ecosystem that crosses a variety of industries. In a business ecosystem, firm capabilities co-evolve around new innovation: firms work cooperatively and competitively to support new products, satisfy customer needs and eventually incorporate the next round of innovations. In his definition of a business ecosystem, he clearly rejects both regionality and the concept of industry. He claims that modern communication technology and global competition reduce the importance of geography.

Moore (1996) also suggests abandoning the concept of industry, since the fast-paced development of technology makes it difficult and fruitless to define industries. In his approach 'innovation' characterizes the ecosystem as the locus around which species co-evolve; furthermore, innovation is a catalyser element for ecosystem creation and evolution. The ecosystem perspective goes over industry boundaries, showing that value generated transcends traditional industrial sectors. A business ecosystem (Gossain and Kandiah 1998) or business web (Tapscott *et al.* 2000) must provide unique solutions to individual customers. Business ecosystems base their success on both competition and cooperation, pushed up by the expansion of democracies and market economies. The co-evolution process is the way ecosystems exploit innovation by exploring an innovative evolutionary path and characterizing industrial districts and any kind of evolving and self-organizing mechanism. Iansiti and Levien (2004a) extend Moore's biological metaphor: they adopt biologically-inspired parameters which are capable of describing the characteristics and status of a business ecosystem and identify key actors affecting ecosystem evolution.

For Iansiti and Levien the business ecosystem is a loose network of suppliers, distributors, outsourcing firms, makers of related products or services, technology providers and a host of other organizations that are related to a product or a service. Like a single species in a biological ecosystem, each member of a business ecosystem finally shares the fate of the network as a whole, regardless of that member's apparent strength. Many ecosystem firms fall out of the value chain of suppliers and distributors that directly contribute to the creation and delivery of such a product or service. A business ecosystem is usually made up of a large number of firms belonging to several different business domains (business and financial service firms, technological providers, regulatory agencies, makers of complementary products and even competitors and customers). Many IT firms, such as Intel, IBM or Microsoft used the business ecosystem approach to describe inter-organizational structures related to strands of innovation, such as the PC ecosystem or the Internet technologies ecosystem. According to Moore (1996), Microsoft and Netscape competed at an ecosystem level to shape the future of the Internet and computing, while according to Iansiti and Levien (2004b), Microsoft and IBM compete to control the computing ecosystem. According to Mayer, Cisco has successfully grown through the conscious and deliberate use of acquisitions of high-technology firms to become the dominant global networking equipment provider through an active involvement by both the firm and its employees in its ecosystem (Mayer and Kenney 2004).

According to Iansiti and Levien (2004b), the parameters that measure the health of an ecosystem are productivity, robustness and niche creation. Productivity is defined as network ability to transform technologies and other raw materials of innovation consistently into lower costs and new products. As in biology it measures the ability to convert non-biological inputs into living outputs. Robustness measures how much a business ecosystem is able to survive from the disruption caused, for instance, by unforeseen technological or socioeconomic change. An ecosystem should exhibit variety and should be able to support a diversity of species. Its capacity to create niches is comparable to the capability of applying emerging technologies in a number of new business products. The main actors in business ecosystems are keystone and niche firms.

At a business level some firms, understanding the importance of their ecosystem's health, pursue strategies that not only aggressively promote their own interests but also the wealth of their overall ecosystem. These firms, according to Iansiti and Levien (2004b), are the keystone firms. Emphasizing the keystone metaphor, they identify in keystone firms the leader and the centre of the ecosystem. They can increase ecosystem productivity by simplifying the network connection among participants. The creation of services, tools or technologies can enhance the performance of the other members, so it can finally enhance ecosystem robustness; furthermore they can encourage niche creation by offering innovative technologies to a variety of third-party organizations. While the leaders may shift over time, the role remains the same, as the IBM–Microsoft case study developed in Iansiti and Levien (2004b) demonstrates. In order to evaluate the business ecosystem perspective, a deep understanding of the ecosystem metaphor relevance and its grounding is necessary to explain social and economic phenomena. In social and economic environments, system behaviour depends on environmental variables, agent characteristics, agent behaviour and relationships among agents. To the same extent, biological ecosystem behaviour depends on energy exchange with the external environment, on the characteristics and behaviour of the species, and on food web properties – that is on the characteristics of relationships between species.

Both Moore (1996) and Iansiti and Levien (2004b) believe that the use of an ecological metaphor is effective in explaining the lack of boundaries and the need for a systemic vision of the business: using the food web model, it is possible to describe systems of organizations as a network of mutual relationships, in this way overcoming territorial- or industrial-based limitations. Other key issues such as new forms of competition, need for collaboration and the process of market co-evolution are simply explained as results of adopting the biological metaphor.

Nevertheless the biological ecosystem approach cannot be used as an instrument of analysis for the business ecosystem: it uses both thermodynamic and network theories to model interaction among populations and environment; the business ecosystem perspective is not able to model environmental conditions and cannot leverage the thermodynamic theory to build a business ecosystem theory. What Iansiti and Levien (2004b) clearly state is that the concept of community, as defined in biological science, is proper for defining their own approach rather than an ecosystem one, since community takes care of population relationships and evolution and excludes environmental interaction.

There is another key point in the business ecosystem perspective: Iansiti and Levien (2004b) identify the role of leader in the keystone species, but looking more in depth at the metaphor, it seems that biological keystone species have a role that is closer to the artificial ecosystem keystone of Iansiti and Levien than to the natural ones. From Iansiti and Levien's perspective, in the business ecosystem keystones are hubs of great importance: the ecosystem they describe tends to become a centralized network in which the central node could change and evolve without changing the topology of the network. Similar examples in nature are specific to human-engineered ecosystems: vegetable and animal species in a farm ecosystem are related to each other but both the vegetal and animal life depends on human intervention and support. As a consequence, although a business ecosystem approach is useful in an organizational perspective, allowing deep reconsiderations of the evolution of integrated firms towards distributed and flexible inter-organizational models, the same approach is not effective in a perspective of the evolution of inter-organizational models in the global evolving scenario. We are able to create strong keystone-based ecosystems as well as farm- and other human-centred biological ecosystems.

The question arising from this perspective is: how could we design, or at least support the creation and growth of natural business ecosystems? Industrial districts are examples of natural ecosystems and they may or may not have a keystone within the system. Moreover, although keystone species populate a naturally developed ecosystem, in some cases, such as for grizzly bears, their role is not necessarily related to orchestration or leadership. Although a business ecosystem may evolve towards centralized structures, moving toward what Tapscott *et al.* (2000) define as an aggregator model, a business ecosystem theory needs to be quite general in order to explain it as a kind of self-constructed and auto-organized business network. In such a context, we focus on the understanding of the rules that govern natural biological ecosystems and, as a consequence, natural business ecosystems.

BUSINESS NETWORKS IN AN EVOLUTIONARY PERSPECTIVE

So far we have only considered thermodynamic properties and the food relationship between species. We are now going to focus on another key point of ecosystem theory: the evolutionary origin of its properties. This perspective is the common ground for a theory of organizational change, capable of explaining the evolution of organizational models in terms of emergence and selection of new species.

Theory of Evolution

The study of evolutionary ecology is based on the hypothesis that differences among organisms could be interpreted as different evolutionary responses to selective pressure from the environment. Population genetic models demonstrate that evolution proceeds through allele substitution and according to their related fitness. Since the development of modern genetics in the 1940s, evolution has been defined more specifically as a change in the frequency of alleles (alternative forms of the same gene) in a population from one generation to the next. In other words, the evolution process is a change in the traits of living organisms over generations, including the emergence of new species.

Natural selection is a process by which biological populations are altered over time, as a result of the propagation of heritable traits that affect the capacity of individual organisms to fit the environment. In this perspective the great intuition of Darwinian theory (1859) is to separate mutation and selection as two co-occurring phenomena. Darwin, in contrast to Lamarck, stated that environment does not directly influence mutations but, through selection, it allows the fittest to survive. Diffusion complements selection, allowing the fittest to dominate. In the Lamarckian evolution theory, individuals adapt during their own lifetimes and transmit traits they acquire to their offspring. Then offspring adapt from where the parents left off, enabling evolution to advance. As a mechanism for adaptation, Lamarck proposed that individuals increased specific capabilities by exercising them while losing others through disuse.

The general model of evolutionary change is based on two key concepts: phenotype and genotype. Phenotype refers to the morphological, organizational and behavioural expression of an organism during its lifetime. Genotype refers to a heritable repository of information that participates in the production of molecules whose interactions, in conjunction with the environment, generate and maintain the phenotype. Genotype and phenotype are not always directly correlated. Some genes only express a given phenotype in certain environmental conditions; conversely, some phenotypes could be the result of multiple genotypes. Phenotype and genotype are useful concepts for distinguishing the roles of adaptation (phenotypes) and inheritance (genotypes) in the evolutionary process.

Evolution can be summarized as the selection of phenotypes which cause the diffusion of their genotypes, and by the generation of new phenotypes through genetic mutations. This distinction emphasizes the differences between the two related research streams of selection and generation. Selection of phenotypes is responsible for studying the survival of the fittest and is influenced by the complex relations between environment and populations. Selection is a dynamic phenomenon that occurs spontaneously in constrained populations. The classical fields of inquiry concerned with selection are population genetics and ecology. The research agenda on selection aims at characterizing the conditions under which a phenotypic innovation, once generated, can invade an existing population. The environment includes selective pressures that establish differences of fitness among different genotypes.

In order to understand how organisms' adaptation reflects their environment it would be necessary to analyse selective factors of the environment and evolutionary reactivity of the phenotype. Such a study should take into account a model of the phenotype–environment relationship that explains the fitness function of the phenotype, the genetic basis of the phenotypic variations and a model connecting functions and fitness in respect to the environment (Arnold 1983). This specific model is particularly complex since many characteristics have a polygenic basis and, as explained by Gould and Lewontin (1979), functions could be a consequence of selection of other characteristics and adaptations could be the results of past environmental conditions. In any case it is possible, according to the phenotypic optimization approach, to evaluate the impact of the environment through an optimization process that works on fitness of all the possible phenotypic models. This line of research is not related to a deep understanding of how change arises and, as a consequence, evolving entities are assumed as given and their innovation is attributed to some stochastic events. On the other hand, generation of new phenotypes through genetic mutations is more oriented towards the study of constraints that influence the mutation process. Furthermore it tries to understand how these constraints restrict the dimensionality of the available configuration space that allows some phenotypic trajectories and denies others.

The generation of new phenotype problems is involved in the exploration of the origin of the internal architecture of biological entities and in the mechanisms through which this architecture influences its own capacity to vary. Many important phenomena of phenotypic evolution cannot be explained by the neo-Darwinian thought that assumes phenotypes to be completely malleable by natural selection. These phenomena include the punctuated mode that suggests the apparently discontinuous nature of evolutionary change (Gould and Eldredge 1977) or the constraints to variation (Maynard-Smith *et al.* 1985).

As explained, the emergence of a phenotype is strictly preceded by its survival in a population through selection processes. In any case the dynamic of selection does not teach us much about the process of mutation that generates such an evolutionary innovation. It is necessary to define a model of genotype–phenotype relationship, capable of explaining what genetic change modifies the phenotype. Evolutionary trajectories are influenced by phenotype creation, since environment influences the effects of genetic mutations. It is necessary to build a space of relationships explaining the accessibility from one phenotype to another as a function of their underlying genetic representation (Fontana and Schuster 1998).

Fontana (2003) introduces the concept of a neutral network, that is, a mutationally-connected set of genotypes that maps to the same phenotype. According to Fontana, populations constantly change at the genetic level, drifting on neutral networks and thereby dramatically increasing their chances for phenotypic innovation. According to this model discontinuities are caused by the genotype–phenotype map and thus remain the same regardless of the further evaluation of phenotypes in terms of fitness assignments. The concept of discontinuity is not related to sudden jumps in fitness but is consequently related to a punctuated phenotype topology. Punctuated topology, although analogous with the phenomenon of punctuated equilibrium recognized by Gould and Eldridge (1977) in the fossil records of species, presents complex differences since it is not related to external ecological timescale phenomena but reflects the property variation of the underlying developmental architecture.

Evolutionary Theory and Organizational Change

The first and most influential biological metaphor applied to socioeconomic science was Darwinian selection on the population ecology by Hannan and Freeman (1977). The population ecology approach takes from the biological perspective the suggestion of the emergence of new species of organizations that compete for resources, emphasizing the selection aspect of Darwinian theory. Hannan and Freeman define a population according to ecological definition as a homogeneous set of organizations undertaking the same kind of activities and with the same characteristics regarding use of resources and results. Each organization is defined by its technology, structure, products or services, objectives and people. These elements cause the organization's survival in the environment or make it disappear because of environmental selective pressure. Populations of organizations are constantly under change. The change process in a population is defined by:

- the mutation stage in which a large number of mutations appears;
- the selection stage in which some new organizations find a market niche and survive;
- the consolidation stage in which a small number of organizations reach large dimensions and become institutions inside their environments.

This evolutionary environment checkmates the older organizations that, limited by their rigid structures, are not able to change and adapt to the emerging conditions and slowly disappear. New populations, fitting emerging environment conditions, will substitute the previous ones, grasping resources and thriving.

As in biological science, the lack of a clear perspective on evolutionary mechanisms does not allow us to understand how these organizational alternatives emerged and which evolutionary patterns were available, starting from the previous organizational forms in the identified environmental conditions. In this perspective, economic and organizational science, more than biological science, encounters huge problems in facing the problem of phenotype generation. An attempt to adapt evolutionary theory as a metaphor for explaining business perspectives is strongly limited in the lack of a unit of analysis for the evolution process, such as the gene in biological evolution. As a consequence it is difficult to create a model which describes the emergence of organizational phenotypes in the evolution processes and their fitness with respect to environmental conditions.

Nelson and Winter (1982) suggested an evolutionary model based mainly on the parallelism between genes and routines. The Nelson and Winter evolutionary theory of the firm focuses attention on organizational routines as units of knowledge. They consider routines as behavioural patterns that workers use during their activities, which make one firm different from another.

The concept of routines includes both decision rules and production techniques and ranges from well-specified technical routines for producing things, through procedures for hiring or firing people, to ordering mechanisms or policies regarding investment or research and development strategies. Like skills for individuals, routines can be considered as the drivers of organizational behaviour: they strongly affect the final results of each worker's activities. Routines store organizational memory and allow the representation of the firms as evolving organizational entities, and identify successful firms with respect to their routine capabilities to generate competitive advantage. According to Nelson and Winter the firm evolves through the development of its own routines and, depending on its endowment of routines, fits the environment or disappears.

Looking more in depth at this metaphor, routines are subjected to variation, selection and retention in any organizational environment, and organization survival depends on the fitness of its routines. In other words, if routines represent the genotype of an organization, this implies that the fitness of the organization is a direct function of its genotype, enabling direct influence of the environment on the organizational genotype. The main consequence is that Nelson and Winter's (1982) evolutionary approach is partially Darwinian and partially Lamarckian, since routine evolution could occur through both a stochastic event and as a result of a learning process. Whereas in the population ecology perspective, stochastic events generate mutations in the population, according to the Nelson and Winter evolutionary approach, organizations can change their routines equipment through chance, as the result of an unpredictable event, or as a choice, adopting a strategy that modifies existing routines as a result of learning processes.

The routine approach can be extended, separating the perspective between behaviour and thing (Fontana 2003). According to Fontana, behaviour is not a thing but is the property of a thing. It follows that the only way to change behaviour is to change the thing that generates it. The change of a property is necessarily indirect. As an example, consider a computer program that implements a function. A function is not a thing, so you cannot directly alter it. To alter the function you must alter the program text that implements the function. The mapping from program to function is what computer scientists call the semantics of the programming language in which the program is written. This example opens the door to other social, technological, economic or organizational examples.

Following this approach, organizational routines represent the functions and dynamic principles that govern interactions between the parts of the organization and represent the semantics of the routines. In this perspective Nelson and Winter's routines became the phenotype of more complex genotypic elements that Padgett defines as the logic of identity. In his work on the Florence banking model evolution, Padgett (2001) focused attention on the systematic relationship between processes of organizational birth and the surrounding social and economic contexts out of which organizations are constructed. According to Padgett, the essential theoretical problem is causal feedback between organizational form and environment. His main objective was to understand how to analyse systemic interactions and feedbacks in such a way as to explain the emergence of new organizational forms.

In both biological and social systems, birth is rooted in a logic of recombination; the absence of a theory of recombination inhibits the social science understanding of genesis. Padgett argued that the analogue to DNA in social organization is the set of ideas, practices and social relations of the founder, which he defined as the 'logic-of-identity' of the founder. He defined the genotype as the specific genetic make-up of an individual and the phenotype as its total physical appearance and constitution, or the specific manifestation of a trait, such as size or eye colour, that varies between individuals. Thus a phenotype is any detectable characteristic of an organism (that is structural, biochemical, physiological or behavioural) determined by an interaction of its genotype with the environment. At the genotypic level of analysis, social science needs to understand the recombinatorial history of these ideas, practices and social relations, controlled through social interactions among individuals; in fact, organization genesis could be explained as the recombination of different logics of identity influenced by surrounding environmental conditions. According to Padgett, organizations – social or biological – are developmental products of these founder logics, interacting with the inherent properties of the social or biological raw materials being assembled. In economic organization, these raw materials are in large part the social networks of business interaction partners, selected through trading and personnel flows. Out of this soup of founding logics-of-identity and cross-cutting social networks, an autonomous organization emerges and sustains itself through time if an autocatalytic 'metabolic chemistry' of technology and work routines crystallizes out of this ideational/social mixture. In the context of Florentine banking, Padgett (2001) analysed 'logics-of-identity' as the historically variable rules for capital formation and pooling in Florentine society. He referred to 'social networks' as the socially structured channels (family, neighbourhood, social class, patronage) through which potential bankers with capital found each other to form and re-form firms. The possible evolutionary trajectories of a social network (such as economic partnerships) are shaped by the structure of the surrounding social networks in which that one is embedded. Because of such network interaction effects, it is impossible to explain organizational trajectories without taking into account environmental conditions. In the Florentine banking example, at an organizational genetics level, this involves career matching; at an organizational development level, this involves bankers' logics-of-identity. Finally, at an organizational speciation level, this involves the realignment of cross-domain bankers' identities, which function at a system level as dialogues or protocols through which politics and markets communicate with each other.

A key point in this perspective is to understand the topology and dynamics of the networks and the interaction and feedback among multiple networks that is the main mechanism for organizational novelty generation. According to Padgett and Powell (2003) social and political networks have the twofold roles of generation and regulation of markets. Recombination and refunctionality are the key elements through which organizational ideas and models are transposed from one domain to another. Social and political networks operate through negative feedback as a regulatory mechanism for transposition and reproduction, granting stability and equilibrium to the systems. In a horizontal and distributed market perspective it becomes clear how co-evolution among business, social and political networks, ignored by scholars in market analysis, is a key element in understanding emergence and transformation phenomena of the market.

Padgett and Powell (2003) model a multiple network identifying three separate layers: the economic domain, the kinship domain and the political domain. A key mechanism for the generation of novelty is re-functionality or transposition of organizing models from one domain to another. These three domains are characterized by constitutive ties, relational social exchange and transactional flows. Constitutive ties are the building blocks of formal organizations: firms, families and factions. Relational social exchange represents what is necessary for building relationships and, as a consequence, organizational units; in other words these exchanges are the 'gifts' people and organizations give each other to make each other productive. Finally, transactional flows represent the objects or 'things' being transformed and exchanged by participant activity.

All these three network layers are strongly connected through the nodes that represent the same people with different roles in different networks. This connection explains how it is possible to exchange and transact the goods or services of one network layer with others of different layers (for example political favour exchanged with trade opportunities). Once the multiple network topology is established, it is necessary to define a development feedback mechanism that links both multiple domains and multiple levels of networks.

In their studies on Florentine banking and life science, Padgett and Powell (2003) identify brokerage as the feedback mechanism through which information and recommendations about potential economic partners are passed through multiple trusted social relations, creating connections in different network layers. In the Florentine example, the brokerage activity which is mainly concerned with supporting the business partners' research, moves from a passive search mechanism principally of family and trusted relationships to a proactive match-making mechanism in which the broker receives gifts for his recommendations. At the relationship level, relations generate trading business through the brokers and the brokers gain transactional wherewithal for further investments.

The multiple network brokerage process works in the same way at the level of constitutive ties but with the complication of appropriate matching rules, since economic partnerships, marriages and political alliances were too important in the life course of a Florentine for a trial and error learning model. This multiple network brokerage process is an autocatalytic system in which brokers catalyse other network relations, but these catalysts are themselves produced by the reproductive system. The reproduction of culture in the form of appropriate matching rules and the reproduction of elite control in the form of sets of interconnected brokers are intimately related.

CONCLUSION

How far is it possible to extend the business ecosystem metaphor? As previously stated, the ecosystem model is particularly effective in biological science since it includes both a thermodynamic and a network perspective in a single framework. The ecosystem metaphor is suggestive and rich but is not a theoretical model which deepens our understanding of business networks. If we attempt to emerge from the level of the metaphor and apply biological rules to business domains, we are strongly limited by the specificity of the ecological perspective. The food web, mainly based on autotrophic (grass and plants) and heterotrophic species (herbivores and carnivores), is delineated by key relationships such as predator–prey, parasitism and others that are too far removed from producer–consumer or partnership relationships. Nor is it feasible to extend the perspective of thermodynamic analysis to a business ecosystem. In fact, at a business level it is impossible to reduce the analysis to flows of energy, material or amount of biomass, since other variables flow among the different populations of a business ecosystem.

Fontana's analysis (1998) of the relationships existing between phenotype, genotype and populations provides an opportunity for deeper reflection on organizational genotypes, the relationship between organizational genotype and phenotype, and environmental influences on the emergence of organizational populations. A promising perspective emerges from the studies of Padgett and Powell (2003) related to organizational emergence in respect of the surrounding social, economic and political environment. Padgett's logic of identity and multiple dynamic networks represent two key issues that enable a deep reflection on the theoretical foundation of business ecosystems and provides a fundamental contribution to the development of an evolutionary model of the business network. A general finding of this approach is the importance of (re)concatenation across multiple networks to the dynamics of speciation, viewed as the emergence of new organizational morphologies (Padgett and Powell 2003).

It would be interesting to 'reuse' this finding in other more general cases. Although with differences in terms of relationships, it is possible to identify other situations in which the birth of an organization is rooted in a logic of recombination and based on a certain 'logic-of-identity'. Furthermore, the multiple networks model provides an effective perspective for analysing the entire business network through the different roles each node assumes in the different layers.

REFERENCES

Arnold, S.J. (1983), 'Morphology, performance and fitness', *American Zoology*, **23**, 347–361.
Bateson, P. (1983), *Mate Choice*, Cambridge: Cambridge University Press.
Bottazzi, G., G. Dosi and G. Fagiolo (2002), 'Sulla omnipresenza delle economie di agglomerazione e le loro diverse determinanti: alcune note', in A. Quadrio Curzio and M. Forts (eds), *Complessità e Distretti Industriali: Dinamiche, Modelli e Casi Reali*, Bologna: Il Mulino, pp. 265–298.
Castells, M. (1996), *The Rise of the Network Society*, Oxford: Blackwell.
Coase, R. (1937), 'The nature of the firm', *Economica*, **4**, 386–405.
Contractor, F.J. and P. Lorange (1988), *Cooperative Strategies in International Business*, Lexington, MA: Lexington Publishing.
Coriat, B. (1990), *L'Atelier et le Robot*, Paris: Bourgois.
Coser, L., C. Kadushin and W.W. Powell (1982), *The Culture and Commerce of Publishing*, New York: Basic Books Inc.
Darwin, C. (1859), *On the Origin of Species by Natural Selection*, Murray.
Davidow, W. and M. Malone (1992), *The Virtual Corporation*, New York: Harper.
Davis, D., M.S. Salter and A.M. Webber (1987), *Changing Alliances: The Harvard Business School Project on the Auto Industry and the American Economy*, Boston, MA: Harvard Business School.
Doz, Y., J. Santos and P. Williamson (2001), *From Global to Metanational: How Firms Win in the Knowledge Economy*, Boston, MA: Harvard Business School Press.
Dunning, J. (1993), *Multinational Enterprise and Global Economy*, Reading, PA: Addison Wesley.
Eccles, R. (1981), 'The quasi-firm in the construction industry', *Journal of Economic Behaviour and Organization*, **2**, 335–357.
Elton, C. (1927), *Animal Ecology*, New York: Macmillan.
Faulkner, R.R. and A. Anderson (1987), 'Short term projects and emergent careers: evidence from Hollywood', *American Journal of Sociology*, **92** (4), 879–909.
Fontana, W. (1998), *Mammals, Florence and Chemistry: Chance and Necessity of Change*, Commentary on the paper of J. Padgett, 'Organizational genesis, identity and control: the transformation of banking in Renaissance Florence'. Prepared for the seminar series on Philanthropy and Social Change at the Robert Wood Johnson Foundation, Princeton, NJ.
Fontana, W. (2003), *The Topology of the Possible*, Draft, May, http://www.santafe.edu/~walter/Papers/top.pdf, 15 September 2006.
Fontana, W. and P. Schuster (1998), 'Continuity in evolution: on the nature of transitions', *Science*, **280**, 1451–1455.
Friedman, M. (1988), *The Misunderstood Miracle*, Ithaca, NY: Cornell University Press.
Gerlac, M.L. (1992), *Alliance Capitalism: The Social Organization of Japanese Business*, Berkeley, CA: University of California Press.

Gilson, R. and M. Roe (1993), 'Understanding the Japanese keiretsu: overlaps between corporate governance and industrial organization', *Yale Law Journal*, **102**, 871–884.

Gossain, S. and G. Kandiah (1998), 'Reinventing value: the new business ecosystem', *Strategy and Leadership*, **26** (5), 28–33.

Gould, S.J. and N. Eldredge (1977), 'Punctuated equilibria: the tempo and mode of evolution reconsidered', *Paleobiology*, **3**, 115–151.

Gould, S.J. and R.T. Lewontin (1979), 'The spandrels of San Marco and the Panglossian paradigm: a critique of the adaptationist programme', *Proceedings of the Royal Society of London*, **B205**, 581–598.

Hannan, M.T. and J. Freeman (1977), 'The population ecology of organizations', *American Journal of Sociology*, **82**, 929–964.

Hardin, G. (1960), 'The competitive exclusion principle', *Science*, **131**, 1292–1297.

Harrison, B. (1994), *Lean and Mean: The Changing Landscape of Corporate Power in the Age of Flexibility*, New York: Basic Books.

Iansiti, M. and R. Levien (2004a), 'Strategy as ecology', *Harvard Business Review*, March, 68–78.

Iansiti, M. and R. Levien (2004b), *The Keystone Advantage: What The New Dynamics of Business Ecosystems Mean for Strategy, Innovation and Sustainability*, Boston, MA: Harvard Business School Press.

Knox, P. and J. Agnew (1998), *The Geography of the World Economy*, New York: Arnold.

Lindeman, R. (1942), 'The trophic-dynamic aspect of ecology', *Ecology*, **23**, 399–418.

Lotka, A.J. (1925), *Elements of Physical Biology*, Baltimore, MD: Williamson and Wilkins.

Mariotti, S. and G.C. Cainarca (1986), 'The evolution of transaction governance in the textile-clothing industry', *Journal of Economic Behaviour and Organization*, **7** (4), 351–374.

Martini, P. and R.H. Smiley (1983), 'Co-operative agreements and the organizational industry', *Journal of Industry Economics*, **31** (4), 437–451.

Mayer, D. and M. Kenney (2004), 'Economic action does not take place in a vacuum: understanding Cisco's acquisition and development strategy', *Industry and Innovation*, **11** (4), 299–325.

Maynard-Smith, J., R. Burian, S.A. Kauffman, P. Alberch, J. Campbell, B. Goodwin, R. Lande, D. Raup and L. Wolpert (1985), 'Developmental constraints and evolution', *Quarterly Review of Biology*, **60**, 265–287.

Moore, J.F. (1993), 'Predators and prey: a new ecology of competition', *Harvard Business Review*, May–June, 75–86.

Moore, J.F. (1996), *The Death of Competition: Leadership and Strategy in the Age of Business Ecosystems*, New York: Harper Business.

Morin, P.J. and E.A. Johnson (1988), 'Experimental studies of asymmetric competition among anurans', *Oikos*, **53**, 398–407.

Mowery, D.C. (1987), *Alliance, Politics and Economics*, Cambridge, MA: Ballinger.

Nelson, R.R. and S.G. Winter (1982), *An Evolutionary Theory of Economic Change*, Cambridge, MA: The Belknap Press of Harvard University Press.

Padgett, J.F. (2001), 'Organizational genesis, identity and control: the transformation of banking in Renaissance Florence, in A. Casella and J. Rach (eds), *Networks and Markets*, New York: Russell Sage, pp. 211–257.

Padgett, J.F. and W.W. Powell (2003), *Market Emergence*, Draft, May.

Passiante, G. (2003), 'Industrial clusters in the net economy: empirical evidence and some theoretical approaches', in G. Passiante, V. Elia and M. Massari, *Digital Innovation*, London: Imperial College Press, pp. 1–39.

Penrose, E. (1959), *The Theory of the Growth of the Firm*, Oxford: Oxford University Press.

Piore, M.J. and C.F. Sabel (1984), *The Second Industrial Divide: Possibilities for Prosperity*, New York: Basic Book.

Porter, M.E. (1990), *The Competitive Advantage of Nations*, New York: Free Press.

Powell, W.W. (1990), 'Neither market nor hierarchy: network forms of organization', *Research in Organizational Behavior*, **12**, 295–336.

Quinn, J.B., P. Anderson and S. Finkelstein (1998), 'New form of organization', in H. Mintzberg and J.B. Quinn (eds), *Reading in the Strategy Process*, Upper Saddle River, NJ: Prentice Hall, pp. 162–173.

Tansley, A.G. (1935), 'The use and abuse of vegetational concepts and terms', *Ecology*, **16**, 204–307.

Tapscott, D., D. Ticoll and A. Lowy (2000), *Digital Capital*, Boston, MA: Harvard Business School Press.

Teece, D.J. and G.P. Pisano (1994), 'The dynamic capabilities of firms: an introduction', *Industrial and Corporate Change*, **3**, 537–556.

Williamson, O. (1975), *Markets and Hierarchies: Analysis and Antitrust Implications*, New York: The Free Press.

Williamson, O. (1987), *The Economics of Institutions of Capitalism*, New York: The Free Press.

Ybarra, J.A. (1989), 'Informationalization in the Valencian economy: a method for underdevelopment', in A. Porter, M. Castells and L. Benton (eds), *The Informal Economy*, Baltimore, MD: Johns Hopkins University Press, p. 224.

2. The paradigm of structural coupling in digital ecosystems

Paolo Dini and Francesco Nachira[1]

INTRODUCTION

European governments at the national and regional level have a mandate by their citizens to promote policies of economic development and of increasing prosperity, innovation and competitiveness. In the last 20 years these objectives that used to depend on a strong industrial infrastructure have been described increasingly in terms of a dependence on information and communication technologies (ICTs). The greater role of ICTs in every aspect of our lives combined with the rise of the importance of the service sector has led us to describe the time we are living in as a historic transition from the 'material economy' to the 'knowledge economy'.

The European institutions have a lesser role in setting policies of growth and development through the power of initiatives of the European Commission, including the area of actions and programmes for research and innovation. The Lisbon Strategy defined in 2000[2] is a good example of such a development plan as well as of how the European Commission sees itself as facilitator in this historic transition: the Presidency Conclusions of the Lisbon European Council (23–24 March 2000) are generally summarized by the commitment to become 'the most competitive and dynamic knowledge-based economy in the world, capable of sustainable economic growth with more and better jobs and greater social inclusion' by 2010. The level of achievement of the Lisbon objectives will determine the success of the Commission and of national governments, as well as the quality of life of future generations of Europeans. To what extent the objectives will be reached and what kinds of reform are deemed necessary will determine the future of our 'distinctive economic and social model that has combined productivity [and] social cohesion',[3] a model that has been prevalent in Europe in the last half-century.

However, unfortunately the 'Lisbon goals are still far away'[4] and the gap between the EU growth rate and those of North America and Asia has constantly widened since 1995. Reversing this progressive decline in productivity (in relative terms) requires unforeseen active effort, engagement and contributions from all the Commission services. Therefore, 'the EU needs a comprehensive and holistic strategy to spur on the growth of the ICT sector and the diffusion of ICTs in all parts of the economy'.[5]

IMPORTANCE OF ICTs FOR STIMULATING GROWTH OF THE SME SECTOR

ICT is a key component of the Lisbon strategy. Its adoption is considered to be one of the major contributions to economic growth and increase in economic efficiency. 'The decline in EU labour productivity growth rates in the mid-1990s can be attributed equally to a lower investment per employee and to a slowdown in the rate of technological progress'[6] and 'ICTs are central to boosting productivity and improving competitiveness. Forty per cent of the productivity growth in the EU between 1995 and 2000 was due to ICT'.[7] The 'European productivity growth could be significantly accelerated if organisations made more and better use of ICT in their organisations and production processes'.[8]

Relevant for the economic development is not only the usage of ICT, but also the capacity to master ICT technologies, since ICT is an economic sector in itself. Indeed in 2000 the Software and Service sector on its own represented more than 8 per cent of EU GDP and 6 per cent of employment. ICT increasingly forms an integral part of all industrial and service markets through the integration of ICT in goods or service offers.

Although there is general agreement on these statements and figures, statistical evidence points to two main digital divides on ICT adoption issues within European Member States:

- The regional digital divide arising from the different rates of progress in e-business development within the EU, generally perceived as between the Nordic/Western and the Southern European Member States. While Nordic and some Western European countries are fast and sophisticated adopters of e-business – in some cases perceived as the worldwide benchmark – the situation is entirely different in regions with less developed economies, particularly in Southern Europe.
- The digital divide by company size arising from significant gaps between small and medium-sized enterprises (SMEs) and larger enterprises in the more advanced forms of ICT adoption and particularly in terms of e-business integration and associated skills. This is set out clearly in the Eurostat e-Commerce and ICT Usage by the European Enterprises survey of 2001.[9]

The effect of the two digital divides is cumulative and gaps therefore tend to widen. In fact, due to their limited resources, SMEs worldwide struggle when facing the following obstacles to ICT adoption:

• Shortage of knowledge and entrepreneurship
• Increase of complexity in all aspects (legal issues, technology, business interactions, intellectual property rights and so on)
• Un-affordability or un-availability of specialized resources and skills
• Lack of affordable technological solutions and interoperability.

Despite the achievements in EU integration when operating in the EU common market, European SMEs have to deal with additional disadvantages:

• Different regulations and legal issues
• A multiplicity of languages
• A variety of cultures, resulting in a heterogeneity of approaches, practices, business models, ways of doing business and mechanisms of trust
• A shortage of venture capital.

Thus SMEs in the less advanced regions have become the focus of specific actions devoted to promoting ICT and e-business adoption at an EU level.[10] The Commission increased the measures aimed at stimulating broader take-up by SMEs, especially within the Research and Technological Development (RTD) programme. But take-up measures based on the scattered support of individual SMEs resulted in limited impact which did not extend beyond the beneficiary SMEs.

In 2003 a new evaluative study[11] of the contributions of all Information Society programmes and policies to the goals of the 'Lisbon Strategy' identified the necessity of a more systemic approach to information society development.[12] The Commission in its proposal on new Financial Perspectives[13] responded with a more effective integration policy for RTD. A stronger link between DG-INFSO activities and the Lisbon Strategy was created by the refocusing of the Lisbon Strategy and by the Commission's recent policy initiatives (Competitiveness and Innovation Programme; Seventh Framework Programme; i2010 – A European Information Society for growth and employment).

KEYSTONES AND SMEs

If we adopt a boundary of 250 employees and/or 5m Euro turnover between 'medium' and 'large', then more than 99 per cent of European companies are SMEs and they account for roughly 50 per cent of European GDP. These figures are not significantly changed by the ten new member states. If we look at companies with 10 employees or less they account for roughly 90 per cent of all companies. Thus the European economic fabric is characterized overwhelmingly by small and micro enterprises. This can be contrasted with the much less sharp US distribution, where the number of medium-sized companies is relatively much greater. The different dimensions of the enterprises coupled with a much greater level of ICT adoption in the US and the stronger weight of diverse cultural traditions in how European SMEs are run make the two environments extremely different.

In many US regions, the large enterprises required their network of supplier, logistics and reseller SMEs to adopt electronic business technologies. Thus the presence of 'keystone' players fostered the adoption of electronic business in the value chains or in the territories where they operate.[14] It has however become apparent that the peculiar European distribution of company size, characterized by an overwhelming majority of small and very small companies, with the presence of a few giant enterprises in some regions (Fiat, BMW, Tesco and so on), hinders the wide application in Europe of such mechanisms of ICT adoption. Such economic structure is a permanent distinctive characteristic of the EU, despite attempts to create large European enterprises.

All these facts reinforce the perception that a European solution to the problem of economic development and ICT adoption should follow a different approach to development, based on ecosystems of SMEs. Europe should adjust to the necessary acceptance of such a structure. An approach alternative to the keystone therefore needs to be found in order to continue to achieve economic development, turning what the prevailing wisdom considers limitations into competitive advantages. The rest of this chapter will therefore develop the ideas that have led to one such alternative approach, spearheaded by the European Commission. We will discuss the new scientific paradigms and ICT technologies that should be developed for enabling this approach and the contribution and role of catalyst and facilitator of the RTD programmes implemented through their projects and specifically the new instruments of the Sixth Framework Programme: Integrated Projects and Networks of Excellence.

THE LIMITS OF A STATISTICAL/MACROECONOMIC PERSPECTIVE

The distribution of company size in Europe correlates well with the level of ICT adoption, leading as stated above to a self-reinforcing digital divide.

This situation tends to favour incumbents relative to upstarts, which in most socio-economic contexts leads to stagnation or at least slows down innovation. The problem then becomes how to energize the huge potential embedded in European SMEs and amplify their productive capacity through facilitating their adoption of ICTs.

The answer has been conceptualized for a few decades as a progressive and incremental process of adoption that is well characterized by the 'Cisco ladder', as shown in Figure 2.1. This view however, is problematic because the progressive enablement of each step of the ladder by the previous step, although very appealing, is an oversimplification of the markedly different contexts and situations affecting the adoption paths actually taken by SMEs. Furthermore, many SMEs are stuck at the static website or e-mail stage without any interest or ability to move up the ladder, even as far as e-commerce.

And yet, on average the Cisco ladder does seem reasonable. 'On average' is precisely the problem. Whereas the number of European SMEs (in the neighbourhood of 20 million) certainly seems to justify a statistical

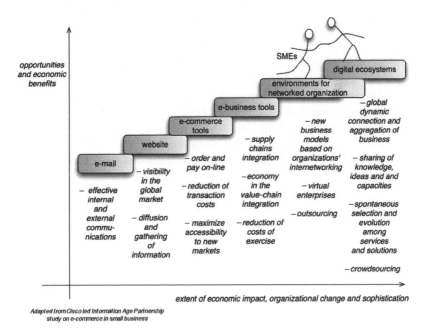

Source: Nachira *et al.* (2002).

Figure 2.1   The Cisco ladder of ICT adoption, modified to include digital ecosystems

approach, statistical models are most effective in the analysis of equilibrium systems for which the central limit theorem guarantees a sharply
spiked Gaussian around the average of any random sample. It is helpful to
use statistical averages when quantifying the size of the SME sector relative to other macroeconomic indicators. However, the SME sector is so
fragmented by different business domains and cultural and geographical
differences that it becomes very difficult to generalize about SME characteristics if one attempts a more in-depth analysis.

One such classification that seems more useful than the traditional
view (see Table 2.1) is based on a rethinking of the traditional categories
to fit better the structural characteristics of SMEs.[15] Rathbone developed a coding system for these categories. The Rathbone Codes are a
good example of how far one can push the statistical mindset in the
analysis of SMEs. These codes are useful because they not only characterize company structure but also provide an insight into company
behaviour by incorporating human and social aspects where there are
patterns that can be commonly observed to influence typical business
behaviour. Although they do better than the traditional categories, the
Rathbone Codes could be seen as a first approximation, because the convergence of average behaviour around recognizable trends is hampered
by a scale effect: the smaller the company, the less meaningful it is to
'average' its decisions or the behaviour of its employees. Social and individual dimensions become more important and social networks and
communities of practice (Wenger and Lave 1991) become more reliable
frameworks for analysis of economic behaviour than statistical averages.
The greater importance of the social dimension, in turn, implies a
greater role played by language and communications in the formation of
SME communities. This has important implications for the research, as
we shall see below.

Table 2.1   Comparison of two possible SME classifications

Traditional categories	Rathbone categories
Product code	Value code (how does the company add value?)
Size (number of employees, turnover)	Growth stage (at what stage of its life is the company?)
—	Personality (what ownership/management structure?)

THE FIRST PARADIGM SHIFT: FROM LARGE INDUSTRY TO SMEs AND THE ROLE OF LANGUAGE

When a statistical ensemble of atomized components is magnified to the point that each component is recognized as a complex network of individuals and technology, the social dimension of the technical and economic environment we inhabit and work in becomes impossible to overlook. This is when a model becomes a paradigm in the (original) Kuhnian sense, that is a body of theory combined with a community of practice and a set of research methodologies (Kuhn 1996). Over the last two decades a shift in the paradigm of the economics of large industry was forced by the problem of European development into a paradigm of socio-economic relations between small players mediated by information and communication technologies. This new perspective brought to the fore the problem presented by the 'embedded character of knowledge':

> . . . the idea that practices of different communities are highly localized and that knowledge is inextricably connected to the social processes that create and maintain it. . . . This view underlies the challenges involved in knowledge exchange across these communities and the difficulties created by the loss of context that the process of translation of knowledge entails when we try, for example, to apply the lessons learned at the level of communities to the level of businesses, public organizations, and policy. (Berdou and Dini 2005)

Embedded knowledge is also called tacit knowledge. The challenges involved in codifying or formalizing such knowledge are well recognized (Steinmueller 2000), which is why it is such an interesting area of current research in sociology.

If we apply the Kuhnian paradigm to socio-economic interactions, the body of theory becomes the knowledge – tacit or explicit – of the community of practice and the research methodologies become more simply the processes by which tacit knowledge is codified and formalized into explicit knowledge. In the regional context, the knowledge formalization process is thus recognized as the heart of a dynamic of growth, innovation and empowerment because, insofar as it can be considered a language, it reinforces the embeddedness of economic relations in social networks. This requires us to spend a few words explaining how the concept of embeddedness can be integrated with the socio-constructivist view of language.

The importance of language in the making (or breaking) of social systems has been recognized for a long time (Reinach 1913, Austin 1962, Searle 1979). If the knowledge economy is seen to depend on processes of formalization of knowledge (in spite of the challenges that this implies) and if, at the same time, the European business ecosystem landscape is strongly dependent on social relations, then clearly there is an opportunity to apply what we understand about language to catalyse economic growth through processes of socio-economic development through ICTs.[16]

The emphasis of new institutional economics on economic efficiency as the principal driver of organizational change explains the formation of corporate hierarchies in terms of lower transaction costs relative to what would be required by trading across a market interface (Coase 1937, Williamson 1975). By the mid-1980s, a different account, associated with the new field of economic sociology and with Granovetter's work in particular, was taking shape (Granovetter 1985). Granovetter argued that Williamson's reliance on a Darwinian argument to explain the evolution of the firm oversimplifies the process of organizational change. This position is particularly interesting from the point of view of research into digital ecosystems because it clarifies that biological metaphors do not necessarily apply to the business ecosystem, where other dynamics may be more important. To Granovetter, the anonymous market of neoclassical economics is virtually non-existent in economic life, and transactions of all kinds are rife with social connections, both inside the firm and in a market setting. He describes economic life as 'embedded' in a network of social relations. Thus, Granovetter sees Williamson's notion of the market to explain economic action as 'under-socialized' (very little embeddedness, or 'atomized' agents), whereas his notion of governance in the hierarchical firm appears 'over-socialized' (too much embeddedness, actors constrained by social norms and roles).

Granovetter points out that the importance of the embeddedness approach in explaining proximate causes of patterns of macro-level interest is demonstrated by the example of small firms. The persistence of small firms is usually explained by the need of large corporations to shift the risks of cyclical fluctuations in demand or of uncertain R&D activities. Granovetter instead holds that SMEs persist in a market setting because a dense network of social relations is overlaid on the business relations connecting such firms and reduces pressures for integration into hierarchical structures. This view is further supported by the observation that SMEs often do not behave rationally. Their decisions often reflect what their owners want to do rather than what is economically most advantageous for the firm. Thus, efficiency arguments are not necessarily applicable in a straightforward manner.

This however implies a double requirement: on the one hand, formalization relies on a shared language which depends on practices of collaboration for its development; on the other hand, the connection between formalization and economic behaviour needs to be made more immediate and transparent. The former requirement finds its natural fulfilment in the adoption of the open-source community process for the production of a common open-source infrastructure and basic services, shared business vocabularies, ontologies and reusable generic business models, whereas the latter requirement implies a degree of spontaneous adaptation and automation in the mediating information and communication technologies that has hitherto been unimaginable.

THE BUSINESS ECOSYSTEM

At this point an independently-developed stream of thought that fits well in the above framework was identified. Instead of seeing the 'economy as a machine' this view argues that 'the market economy' is best understood as a living, evolving ecosystem (Rothschild 1990). The metaphor was further developed and deepened by J.F. Moore (1996: 6–7), who described a business ecosystem as:

> An economic community supported by a foundation of interacting organizations and individuals – the organisms of the business world. This economic community produces goods and services of value to customers, who are themselves members of the ecosystem . . . Over time, they co-evolve their capabilities and roles, and tend to align themselves with the future directions set by one or more central companies.

Thus Moore's concept of ecosystem is based toward the keystone model.

Phenomena observed in a natural ecosystem, like competition, specialization, cooperation, exploitation, learning, growth and extinction, could also be defined in a 'business ecosystem'.

Moore, whose principal passions are 'bridging the global digital divide and increasing access to information technologies in developing countries',[17] in his analogies between natural and business ecosystems also recognizes the key role of the infrastructure:

> Like individual plants or animals, individual businesses cannot thrive alone – they must develop in clusters or economic ecosystems. Agriculture requires not only farms, but an infrastructure of roads and ports on which transport companies can move the goods, supporting a network of storage facilities, distributor, and finally consumer markets. (Moore 2003: 1)

THE DIGITAL BUSINESS ECOSYSTEM AND THE SECOND PARADIGM SHIFT

The combination of these disparate elements and requirements, together with the effort to create the conditions for achieving the Lisbon objectives, motivated the application of the ecosystem metaphor to the digital world and gave birth to the concept of the digital ecosystem. In 2002 the area of the 'e-Business' unit of the European Commission related to SMEs produced a discussion paper that introduced the concept of Digital Business Ecosystem (DBE) (Nachira *et al.* 2002). This paper and the DBE concept have been revisited more recently in a position paper on digital ecosystems (Dini *et al.* 2005), so we will only highlight a few aspects that are relevant to this discussion.

The digital ecosystem was defined as the ICT-enabling infrastructure for economies, based on fluid, amorphous and often transitory structures, alliances, partnership and collaborations among SMEs that supports cooperation, knowledge sharing and the building of a community that shares business, knowledge and infrastructure.

The aims of the digital business ecosystems strategy as originally formulated were two-fold:

1. Preserve ICT capacity building. Europe, except for a few notable exceptions, does not have large software firms. In a world dominated by large-scale ICT industries, Europe risks losing competencies and autonomy in this strategic sector. Digital ecosystems enable small and micro enterprises to produce and distribute knowledge-based components which will dynamically become part of larger complex systems. They enable ICT-based SMEs to be competitive in the global software production market.
2. Provide ICT solutions and services that support multiple and new models of business and specifically of cooperative business networking among SMEs. These solutions must also be able to 'mutate', adapting to the specific needs of the users and thereby fostering ICT adoption in local economies.

The digital ecosystem is the pervasive 'soft' support infrastructure populated by components or 'digital species' able to evolve and to adapt to local conditions and to mediate services and knowledge. In this analogy the digital ecosystem is populated by digital species, exhibiting the structure and behaviour of natural species.[18] The 'digital species' could be any useful idea, expressed in a language (formal or natural) which could be digitized and launched on the Net, and which can be processed (by computers and/or humans).[19] Thus the digital ecosystem concept also puts a great emphasis on language, but does so in a manner more aligned with Winograd and Flores (1986). Figure 2.2 shows how we might begin to conceptualize the evolution of the thought process in economic development toward a strengthening of social dimension, language and ICTs.

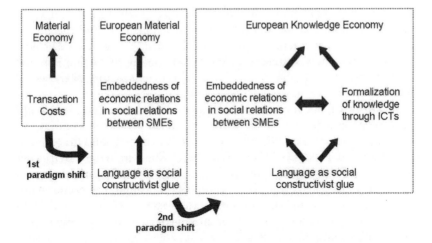

Figure 2.2   In search of the ingredients of sustainable development

Given the complexity of ecosystems, it is clear that very significant effort is needed for the development of the basic theories and technologies underpinning the structuring and the spontaneous evolution of digital ecosystems. This concept was included in the FP6 information science technology (IST) work programme, and the first FP6 call for project proposals included in its objectives 'IST as driver for small business and government reorganisation through local development processes including small business ecosystems', and 'multidisciplinary researches into complex adaptive and self-organising systems'. In response to Call 1 of FP6 the DBE Integrated Project was funded and brought together a large and radically interdisciplinary group of research/academic, industrial and business partners to address these challenges.[20]

The idea of the digital business ecosystem represents a radical departure from previous conceptualization of technology development and adoption. In this sense it can be regarded as a paradigm shift of sorts, as the term is often used in the computer science and software engineering community. More importantly, however, it introduced the possibility of conceptualizing the interaction between a business ecosystem of companies and a digital ecosystem[21] of software entities and formalized knowledge as a structural coupling across different types of user interfaces (different model development tools and run-time web interfaces for service consumption). The concept of structural coupling was introduced by the two neuroscientists Maturana and Varela (1998) as part of their theory of autopoiesis as an alternative to genetic determinism in processes of gene expression and biological evolution. Rather than assigning to DNA the role of 'independent variable' and to cell metabolism the role of dependent process entirely determined by DNA,[22] structural coupling assigns an equal role to two interacting entities, such that neither is seen to determine the other completely. Rather, each entity can only trigger changes in the other, changes that depend on the state and previous history of the entity being triggered.

The appeal of this model in this discussion is that it refutes both technocentric approaches where the users have to adapt to the technology as well as approaches where the users are entirely in control and the technology is entirely dependent on them (early discussions within the DBE project leaned toward this view). In the DBE there are mechanisms of adaptation over long time scales, triggered by run-time business transactions but clearly dependent on the current state of the system. The business users, in turn, respond to the opportunities granted by the technology, discovering new partners and new markets through synergies based on their current needs and offerings. Interestingly, this kind of interdependence between users and infrastructure is also discussed in a completely different language by sociologists Ciborra and Hanseth (1998); users are encouraged to acknowledge the inertia effects in the development and use of large information infrastructures, which are therefore more amenable to being 'cultivated' than 'managed'.

The 2002 digital business ecosystem discussion paper went further and suggested applying the ecosystem metaphor to the software entities themselves. The DBE project responded to the challenge of creating an adaptive software infrastructure through the dynamic interactions of the software species that inhabit it by bringing the ecosystem metaphor several steps closer to an isomorphic model. The result, as shown in Figure 2.3, is a well-integrated set of technological and business sub-systems.

As shown in Table 2.2, the DBE is most easily understood on two different scales: the local and the distributed. The local development environment is called DBE Studio and houses, among other things, the editors for the Business Modelling Language (BML) and the Service Description Language (SDL). The distributed version is called Service Factory and also comprises a distributed Model Repository of BML and SDL models. The local run-time environment is housed by the ServENT, while the distributed environment is called ExE and is the union of all the ServENTs, plus a distributed Semantic Registry that holds the models of implemented services. The whole architecture runs over a P2P network and every service is lease-based to guarantee maximum reliability in the search and consumption of services.

The DBE Studio is a suite of editors that is used to create business models of the services and of the SMEs, thereby enabling the business

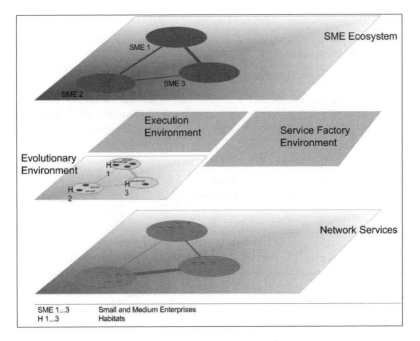

Note: Created in collaboration with Thomas Kurz, Fachhochschule Salzburg, Science Partner in DBE.

Figure 2.3   OSI stack view of the DBE

users to formalize the knowledge they create. The EvE (Evolutionary Environment) houses most of the self-organization capability of the DBE in the form of two market-driven optimization approaches. A distributed optimization enables DBE services to migrate to the SMEs that are most likely to need them based on the usage history of similar services. This optimization works over long time scales and leads to the formation of clusters of SMEs that share similar services. Having prepared these local environments, a local optimization is performed in the habitats over short time scales on the local service pools of individual SMEs by means of genetic algorithms (GAs). This provides fast customized solutions to individual SMEs' service requests. More details on the architecture and various basic services such as accounting can be found on the project website. The EvE is in fact part of the ExE and both have interfaces to the Service Factory. All three environments are distributed and rely on a P2P and dynamic network architecture.

Table 2.2   System and component views of DBE

Local view	Distributed view			
SME	Business Ecosystem			
DBE Studio[1]	Service Factory (SF)		**Digital Business Ecosystem** (All infrastructure, models and services)	**Digital Business Ecosystem**
Servent[2]	Execution Environment (ExE)	**Digital Ecosystem**		
Habitat	Evolutionary Environment[3] (EvE)	(Run-time 'Artificial Life' system)		

Notes:
1.   http://dbestudio.sourceforge.net
2.   Servent = SERV[er] + [cli]ENT; http://swallow.sourceforge.net
3.   http://evenet.sourceforge.net

STRUCTURAL COUPLING BETWEEN DISCIPLINES: THE THIRD PARADIGM SHIFT

Looking back in 2006 at the work done in what is now the Technologies for Digital Ecosystems cluster in Unit D[23] over the past four years, what started as an idea and a set of recommendations stimulated by recognized needs could be reinterpreted as an interesting case study in research policy development. Figure 2.4 summarizes the main points made so far: the realization that to optimize the interdependence between the business ecosystem and ICTs, the latter needed to be expanded to incorporate self-organizing biological models and evolutionary algorithms; the role of local government in setting policies to foster the growth of the ecosystems; and the structural coupling between technology and business mediated by the formalization of knowledge. The figure also shows how, in order to understand how to bring about this complex and multi-faceted system of technology, companies, policy makers and people, the EC had to develop an ambitious policy of interdisciplinary research. Surrounding the DBE there are now several more projects that will continue the research after the DBE ends; they look at various aspects, from theory (OPAALS) to contract and negotiation frameworks (CONTRACT, ONE), to sectoral business models

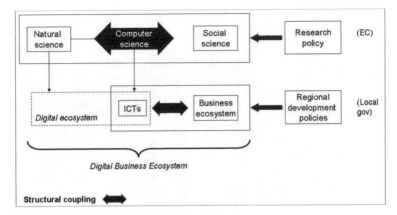

Figure 2.4   Structural coupling in digital ecosystems

and service development (SEAMLESS), to governance (EFFORT), and regional adoption (PEARDROP).

The projects of the Digital Ecosystems cluster show on the one hand a coming together of very different disciplines around a space of pragmatic problems and applications and on the other hand they have amplified a long-standing dichotomy between different epistemological and methodological traditions of research that seem to point towards a third and final paradigm shift.

The ecosystem approach has brought to the fore the deep ontological and epistemological differences between technological research borne out of the philosophical tradition aimed at designing and building 'machines' operating in a well-defined, if reductive, objective reality, on the one hand; and social science research which is more analytical and interpretative (hermeneutic) in character and aims to account for the interaction between human action and socio-economic and technical structures and processes in the context of policy development, on the other hand. But the situation is even more complex since within social science itself, sharply different philosophical positions have developed over the past several hundred years around most of the fundamental questions, that are then translated into difficult policy and political discussions.

Figure 2.5 tries to capture some of the main conceptual domains and philosophical traditions in social science. A few indicative and by no means exhaustive names are added to make the figure easier to interpret. The left-hand column is generally associated with the rationalist, deterministic tradition – it is the older of the two and grew out of naturalist philosophy. The right-hand column is more recent – it reflects a greater emphasis on the social world for defining our reality (ontology) and the construction of

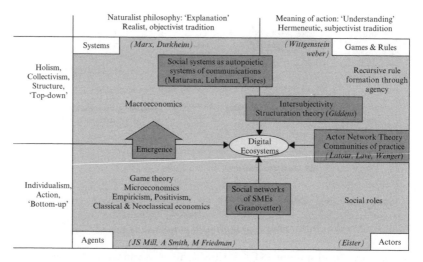

Source: Adapted from Hollis (1994).

Figure 2.5   *Digital ecosystems 'claiming the centre' in Hollis's map of social science*

knowledge (epistemology). Although interpreting the two columns in terms of an objective–subjective dichotomy can only be a gross oversimplification, the thinkers in the left-hand column could be loosely grouped as sharing a belief in some form of 'objective' reality, whereas a more 'subjective' perspective permeates the ideas found in the right column. The different widths of the columns are meant to reflect the much greater constituency, within social science, that a critical tradition inspired by naturalist philosophy still commands.

Thus, biological metaphors are certainly not new in social science. In fact, since Maturana and Varela's first publications on autopoiesis ([1973]1980), this theory has stimulated significant interest in a number of fields such as biology, sociology, law and family therapy. Although this theory has been criticized at least as often as it has been acclaimed, its most appealing characteristic in the context of this discussion is its strongly relativist position, which makes it stand out among most of the other objectivist theories of natural and physical systems. This is well summarized by Mingers (1995: 110):

> . . . I think that in a particular respect Maturana's work represents a distinct advance on classical phenomenology, a major criticism of which is that it is essentially individualist and has great difficulty in generating the intersubjective nature of social reality. Here Maturana begins from an intersubjective position. We are (as self-conscious beings) constituted through our language, and

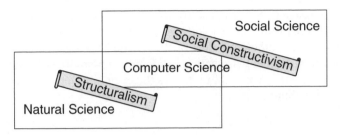

Figure 2.6   Computer science as a useful 'commons' between incommensurable disciplines

language is inevitably an intersubjective phenomenon. As Wittgenstein also argued, there can be no such thing as a private language. Thus language is essentially a consensual domain of agreements, of structural coupling that permits the operations of observers.

In spite of this very relativist outlook, autopoiesis is regarded as largely belonging to the naturalist side of Figure 2.5. Thus proposing structural coupling as a framework that can support productive interactions between philosophically incommensurable disciplines, in other words the fourth paradigm of this paper, is not likely to elicit consensus. It is the best we can do at this time, however, so we will work with it and reach some hopefully useful conclusions.

For example, the DBE research conducted so far suggests that computer science can play a double role that can be rationalized in a useful practical way from all these points of view, even if they may remain incommensurable at the philosophical level. Specifically, if computer science provides a bridge between natural and social science then it can be viewed from both sides. When we view computer science from the perspective of social science we see computers as the media of communications. When we view computer science from the point of view of natural science, on the other hand, we see logic and structure, we see machines and numbers. This is summarized schematically in Figure 2.6.

CONCLUSION

One of the most important insights of DBE research has been precisely to realize that this framework allows both naturalist and hermeneutic disciplinary domains to coexist side-by-side, without needing to compromise in any way on their respective ontological, epistemological and methodological principles whilst interacting productively through the many facets of computer science. Neither 'camp' need make any compromises on the depth and breadth of its scholarship. This framework enables a dialogue not only between different bodies of theory and between different methodologies of research, but also between different communities of practice. We can therefore safely claim that it marks the beginnings of a new paradigm for interdisciplinary research.

NOTES

1. The opinions and views expressed in this article are those of the authors and do not necessarily reflect the official European Commission's view on the subject and under no circumstances should they be taken as the EC's official view.
2. Communication from the Commission, COM (2004), 480 – 13 July 2004.
3. *Facing the Challenge: The Lisbon Strategy for Growth and Employment* ('Kok Report'), Luxembourg: Office for Official Publications of the European Communities, November 2004.
4. *Rethinking the European ICT Agenda: Ten ICT Breakthroughs for Reaching Lisbon*, PricewaterhouseCoopers, July 2004.
5. Kok Report, ibid.
6. Ibid.
7. Communication from the Commission, *The EU Economy: 2003 Review*, COM (2003), 729.
8. *Rethinking the European ICT Agenda: Ten ICT Breakthroughs for Reaching Lisbon*, PricewaterhouseCoopers, July 2004.
9. This major survey covered SMEs with 10–249 employees, in 13 EU Member States plus Norway (the gross sample was 100 000 enterprises) and reflects the situation in the period between November 2000 and June 2001. It was conducted by Eurostat together with the National Statistics Institutes and sponsored by DG Enterprise. It covered the adoption of ICT and e-commerce in all sectors of the economy. This study was followed by the launch of the e-Business Watch action in late 2001 to monitor and analyse ICT uptake and e-business practices by companies in different sectors of the European economy, www.ebusiness-watch.org.
10. *Benchmarking National and Regional e-Business Policies for SMEs*, Final Report of the 'E-business Policy Group, 28 June 2002, http://europa.eu.int/information_society/topics/ebusiness/godigital/20703report_final.pdf, 15 September 2006.
11. *Preliminary Analysis of the Contribution of EU Information Society Policies and Programmes to the Lisbon and Sustainable Development Strategies*, ECOTEC Research & Consulting Ltd, December 2003, www.ecotec.com/expertise/dginfo, 15 September 2006.
12. It also identified the key role of human capital and of the education and training systems in a knowledge society.
13. Communication from the Commission, *Building our Common Future*; COM (2004), 101, February 2004.
14. See other contributions to this same volume.
15. www.daventryhouse.com/SME.htm. Also see DBE Deliverable D7.1 at: www.digital-ecosystem.org / members / aenglishx / linkstofiles / deliverables / coreservices, 15 September 2006.
16. See Berdou and Dini (2005) for a more in-depth discussion.
17. Moore, J.F., Homepage at Berkman Center, www.cyber.law.harvard.edu/people/biomoore.html, 15 September 2006.
18. No central control, no plans defined in advance; fault-tolerant; no central point of failure; viability concept; diversity and autonomy; adaptation to local conditions; selection and evolution.

19. This includes different aspects of knowledge: software components, applications, services, knowledge, business processes and models, training modules, contractual frameworks, laws and so on.
20. www.digital-ecosystem.org, 15 September 2006.
21. Some caution is necessary: the term 'digital ecosystem' is often used in a generic and loose sense that encompasses everything, including the business ecosystem. Such a generic term is useful when speaking of different 'instantiations', such as might be possible in the multimedia sector, or the gaming sector, tourism, manufacturing and so on. However, this term is also used to signify the narrow definition of 'digital business ecosystem' which pertains only to the technology. The latter is the case in the above sentence. Digital ecosystems in the former sense are being referred to as 'innovation ecosystems' by the European Commission in FP7. It is usually clear from the context which of these two meanings applies.
22. See for instance the concept of DNA as an instruction register of the cell in Kauffman (2003).
23. European Commission, DG Information Society, **Unit D** Network and Communication Technologies, Unit D5: ICT for Business – Sector 'Technologies for Digital Ecosystems'.

REFERENCES

Austin, J.L. (1962), *How to do Things with Words*, Oxford: Clarendon Press.
Berdou, E. and P. Dini (2005), *Report on the Socio-economics of Free/Open Source*, DBE Deliverable D18.3. www.digital-ecosystem.org/Members/aenglishx/learn/Members/aenglishx/linkstofiles/deliverables/servfact, 15 September 2006.
Ciborra, C. and O. Hanseth (1998), 'From tool to *Gestell*: agendas for managing the information infrastructure', *Information Technology and People*, **3** (4), 305–327.
Coase, R. (1937), 'The nature of the firm', *Economica*, **4**, 386.
Dini, P., M. Darking, N. Rathbone, M. Vidal, P. Hernandez, P. Ferronato, G. Briscoe and S. Hendryx (2005), *The Digital Ecosystems Research Vision: 2010 and Beyond*, http://www.digital-ecosystems.org/events/2005.05/de_position_paper_vf.pdf, 15 September 2006.
Granovetter, M. (1985), 'Economic action and social structure: the problem of embeddedness', *American Journal of Sociology*, **91** (3), 481–510.
Hollis, M. (1994), *The Philosophy of Social Science: An Introduction*, Cambridge: Cambridge University Press.
Kauffman, S. (2003), *Investigations*, Oxford: Oxford University Press.
Kuhn, T. (1996), *The Structure of Scientific Revolutions*, 3rd edition, Chicago, IL: University of Chicago Press.
Maturana, H. and F. Varela (1980), *Autopoiesis and Cognition: The Realization of the Living*, Boston: Reidel (First published in 1973).
Maturana, H. and F. Varela (1998), *The Tree of Knowledge: The Biological Roots of Human Understanding*, revised edition, Boston, MA: Shambhala.
Mingers, J. (1995), *Self-Producing Systems: Implications and Applications of Autopoiesis*, New York and London: Plenum Press.
Moore, J.F. (1996), *The Death of Competition: Leadership and Strategy in the Age of Business Ecosystems*, New York: Harper Business.
Moore, J.F. (2003), *Digital Business Ecosystems in Developing Countries: An Introduction*, Boston, MA: Berkman Center for Internet and Society, Harvard Law School, http://cyber.law.harvard.edu/bold/devel03/modules/episodeII.html

Nachira, F. *et al.* (2002), *Toward a Network of Digital Business Ecosystems Fostering the Local Development*, http://www.europa.eu.int/information_society/topics/ebusiness/godigital/sme_research/index_en.htm, 15 September 2006.

Reinach, A. (1913), 'Die apriorischen Grundlagen des bürgerlichen Rechts', *Jahrbuch für Philosophie und phänomenologische Forschung*, **1**, 685–874 (English translation by Crosby, J.F. (1983), 'The A Priori Foundation of Civil Law', *Aletheia*, **3**, 1–142).

Rothschild, M. (1990), *Bionomics: The Inevitability of Capitalism*, New York: Henry Holt and Company.

Searle, J.R. (1979), *Expression and Meaning: Studies in the Theory of Speech Acts*, Cambridge: Cambridge University Press.

Steinmueller, W.E. (2000), 'Will new information and communication technologies improve the "codification" of knowledge?' *Industrial and Corporate Change*, **9** (2), 361–376.

Wenger, E. and J. Lave (1991), *Situated Learning: Legitimate Peripheral Participation*, Cambridge: Cambridge University Press.

Williamson, O. (1975), *Markets and Hierarchies: Analysis and Antitrust Implications*, New York: Free Press.

Winograd, T. and F. Flores (1986), *Understanding Computers and Cognition: A New Foundation for Design,* Bristol: Intellect Books.

PART II

The organizational dimension of digital
business ecosystems

3. The quest for new organizational forms: the strange case of open source software communities

Robert M. Grant

INTRODUCTION

Over a decade ago, Richard Daft and Arie Lewin (1993) asked: 'Where are the theories for the new organizational forms?' Their identification of the need for new theory was based upon their perceptions that: '. . . the new organizational revolution is sweeping one industry after another', and that 'quantum changes in manufacturing and computer mediated communication technologies have given managers radical new options for designing organizations'.

Before embarking on a quest for new theory, a prior step is to identify these new organizational forms and describe their major features. Certainly, management scholars have shown little reluctance in proclaiming discoveries of new types of business organization. Yet most of the novel organizational forms described in the literature – modular structures, ambidextrous firms, hypertext organizations, N-forms and 'inside-out doughnuts' – exist in the cognition of the observer. Empirical verification of their frequency or prominence is largely lacking. Indeed, one of the most noticeable features of today's business landscape is the persistence of conventional organizational forms – most notably the multidivisional corporation. This raises the issue of whether the longevity of the conventional corporate form is the result of its superiority in coordinating the complex processes of developing, producing and marketing goods or services, or whether it is simply a product of inertia and the absence of viable alternatives.

While the organizational revolution proclaimed by Daft and Lewin may exist more in the minds of management scholars than among the ranks of business enterprises, there is one organizational form that has long been an alternative to the integrated corporation. Extending back even before the industrial revolution, the networked organization – comprised of collaborating groups of firms, families or individual artisans – represents a means

of organizing complex productive activities that is substantially different
from the conventional hierarchies. Interfirm networks have been the subject
of considerable research interest. However, in recent years an entirely novel
form of network organization has emerged within the computer software
sector. Open source software (OSS) communities are made up of hundreds,
even thousands, of volunteers who collaborate to produce highly sophisticated software products. In several sectors of computer software, open
source products are either market leaders or are challenging commercial
software for market leadership.

It is precisely because the production of open source software challenges
so many of the accepted principles of management and organization
design that I choose to focus on them in this chapter. My goal is to identify
the principle organizational features of OSS communities, to establish how
coordination occurs within them and to compare them with the structures
and coordination mechanisms within conventional corporations. In the
process it should be possible to shed light upon the fundamental tasks and
processes of economic organization.

I begin by examining the principal features of conventional corporations
and the changing environmental conditions which are creating the need for
different types of organizational structures. I review the extent to which the
novel organizational forms identified by different management scholars
share common features, and the extent to which such organizational trends
are capable of empirical verification. I then focus explicitly upon network
organizations – both interfirm networks and then OSS communities.

THE TRADITIONAL CORPORATION

The dominant organizational form among most of the world's large corporations is that of the multidivisional firm. The typical structure is shown
in Figure 3.1. The diffusion of this structure from Du Pont and General
Motors to most of the leading corporations of the US (Chandler 1962,
Rumelt 1974), Europe (Whittington and Mayer 2000) and Japan (Kono
1984) was one of the most striking features of 20th century business
development and facilitated the processes of diversification, multinational
expansion and adaptation of business portfolios to technological and
market change. Yet the antecedents of the multidivisional form go back
further than Du Pont.

During the 1860s, Field Marshall Helmuth von Moltke systematically
restructured the Prussian army. The central feature of Moltke's new structure was the creation of a general staff that was responsible for strategic
decision making as well as specialist functions such as supplies, training,

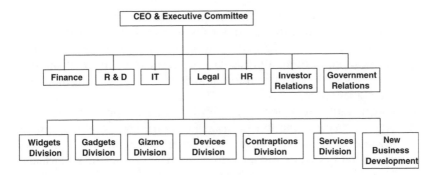

Figure 3.1   The traditional corporate form

intelligence, engineering and logistics. The bulk of the army was formed into a number of divisions, each comprising a number of units – infantry, artillery, cavalry and so on. Coordination and control were achieved by a common officer training system, rotation of officers between divisions and general staff, standardization of systems and equipment and rapid top-down communication of strategies and tactics. The swift and crushing victory of the Prussians over a larger and more experienced French army was a tribute to Moltke's organizational design. The superior coordination and more effective implementation of strategies by the Prussian army were the basis of its superiority in battle (Stark 1989).

The diffusion of the multidivisional form among large companies during the 20th century reflected the superiority of this model for organizing complex production activities in diversified companies serving multiple markets. Oliver Williamson (1981) identifies four key advantages of the divisionalized firm:

1. Adaptation to bounded rationality. Managers are limited in their cognitive, information-processing, and decision-making capabilities. Thus, the top management team cannot be responsible for all coordination and decision making within a complex organization, and the multidivisional corporation permits management responsibilities to be decentralized.
2. Allocation of decision making. Decision-making responsibilities should be separated according to the frequency with which different types of decisions are made. Thus, decisions that are made with high frequency (for example operating decisions) need to be separated from decisions that are made infrequently (for example strategic decisions).
3. Minimizing coordination costs. In the functional organization, decisions concerning a particular product or business area must pass up to

the top of the company where all the relevant information and expertise can be brought to bear. In the divisionalized firm, so long as close coordination between different business areas is not necessary, most decisions concerning a particular business can be made at the divisional level. This eases the information and decision-making burden on top management.

4. Global rather than local optimization. In functional organizations, senior managers tend to emphasize functional goals over those of the organization as a whole. In multidivisional companies, divisional heads, as general managers, are more likely to identify with the performance goals of the company as a whole.

CHANGING ENVIRONMENTAL REQUIREMENTS AND NEW ORGANIZATIONAL FORMS

Despite the ubiquity and resilience of the multidivisional corporate form, there is a widespread view that the changing competitive conditions of the 21st century business environment are requiring the adoption of new organizational structures.

The most notable features of the current business environment are intensity of competition – resulting, in particular, from the increasing pressure of international competition; market volatility – evident in the rapidly fluctuating process of commodities; and speed of technological change. All these have resulted in an environment characterized by turbulence and unpredictability. Technological changes – notably in information and communication technologies – and other developments increasing the stock of knowledge available to businesses have also increased the capacity of firms to respond to the increased demands of the business environment. Figure 3.2 identifies the principal changes occurring in the business environment, establishes the implications of these changes for the functioning and capabilities of business organizations, then proposes the changes in organizational structure required to support these new organizational requirements.

In response to these pressures for organizational change and structural innovations, management scholars have identified a number of new organizational archetypes that embody one or more of the structural features identified in the third column of Figure 3.2. For example:

- Bartlett and Ghoshal's 'transnational corporation' is a divisionalized form where standardized vertical relationships between national subsidiaries and the corporate centre are replaced by high levels of

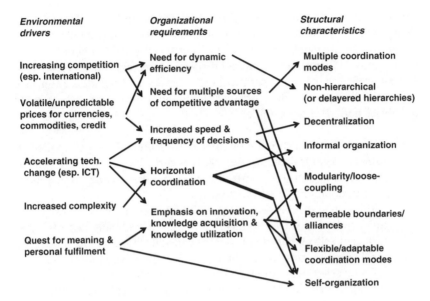

Environmental drivers	Organizational requirements	Structural characteristics
Increasing competition (esp. international)	Need for dynamic efficiency	Multiple coordination modes
Volatile/unpredictable prices for currencies, commodities, credit	Need for multiple sources of competitive advantage	Non-hierarchical (or delayered hierarchies)
	Increased speed & frequency of decisions	Decentralization
Accelerating tech. change (esp. ICT)	Horizontal coordination	Informal organization
Increased complexity		Modularity/loose-coupling
Quest for meaning & personal fulfilment	Emphasis on innovation, knowledge acquisition & knowledge utilization	Permeable boundaries/ alliances
		Flexible/adaptable coordination modes
		Self-organization

*Figure 3.2   Implications of recent environmental trends for firm
structure*

differentiation among subsidiaries and horizontal integration between them.

- Several 'revolutionary new structures' have been based on the idea that the organizational requirements for companies in today's 'knowledge economy' are fundamentally different from those in the former 'industrial economy'. Some of these knowledge-based structures include Quinn's (1992) intelligent enterprise, together with its special forms, including spider's web, starburst and inverted organizations, and Hedlund's (1994) N-form organization.

- Structures involving multidimensional coordination to develop and exercise diverse organizational capabilities. These include O'Reilly and Tushman's (2004) ambidextrous organization, Nonaka and Takeuchi's (1995) hypertext organization and Bushe and Shani's (1991) parallel learning organization.

- Organizations based upon radical decentralization and the displacement of top-down decision making by horizontal collaboration. These include Handy's (1990) federal organization and Volberda's (1999) flexible form.

- Organizations which coordinate outsourced operations and functions such as Davidow and Malone's (1992) 'virtual corporation' and Handy's shamrock organization.

While management observers such as Tom Peters and Gary Hamel have long proclaimed the old corporate model dead and emphasized the need for revolution and regeneration, the fact is that there is little evidence of new organizational forms appearing and thriving in the real world of business. Certainly there has been experimentation; however, the evidence suggests that most attempts at radical organizational innovation tend to survive for only brief periods. For example:

- Oticon, the Danish manufacturer of hearing aids, experimented in radical decentralization during the early 1990s – the so-called 'spaghetti organization'. After three years Oticon reverted to a more traditional management structure.
- Virginia-based AES, which by 2000 had become the world's largest independent power producer, adopted a radically-decentralized model of self-management which it called its 'honeycomb' model. By 2003, after a series of crises in the US electricity generation industry, AES reverted to a more traditional management system.
- In 1995, British Petroleum implemented radical decentralization involving the elimination of its major divisions and creating a new structure where each of its 150 business units reported direct to the corporate centre. While successful in encouraging flexibility, innovation and commitment to performance targets, by 2002 BP had reverted to a more conventional organizational structure within which the traditional sectors – upstream, downstream, chemicals and renewables – had been re-established.

The conclusion I draw is this: despite the organizational revolution proclaimed by business school academics and management consultants, new models of company organization are conspicuous by their absence. The most striking feature of today's corporate landscape is the similarity of organizational structures among large companies – whether American, European or East Asian – and the fact that the main characteristics of organizational structures in terms of boards, top management teams, functions, divisions, business units, the basis upon which organizational units are defined and the mechanisms for coordination and control have not changed radically over the past few decades. Equally striking is the recent history of new, innovatory organizational forms – most attempts by companies to introduce radically new organizational forms have met with little success. Not only did these companies fail to stimulate widespread imitation, but most abandoned their experimental organizational forms and reverted to more traditional structures. Indeed, since the adoption of the multidivisional structures by most large North American and European corporations during the first six decades of the 20th century (Chandler 1962), it is not apparent that any organizational innovation of comparable scope and impact has been widely adopted in the ensuing half century.

INTERFIRM NETWORKS

Yet if we view today's business landscape, there is one organizational form that, while not new, has certainly become more prominent in recent decades. This is the network form. Interfirm networks are clusters of primarily small and medium-sized firms linked by stable, long-term collaborative relationships. Most interfirm networks are geographically concentrated. In some industries interfirm networks are long-established – sometimes extending back before the industrial revolution. Examples include residential construction in most countries of the world and interfirm networks of Northern Italy – notably in clothing, shoes and furniture and also in some engineering products such as packaging equipment and motorcycles.

In other industries, interfirm networks have displaced integrated corporations – or at least, highly vertically-integrated companies have engaged in extensive outsourcing to the point where they increasingly resemble network forms. For example:

- In automobiles, Henry Ford's vertically integrated model ('iron ore in at one end, automobiles out at the other') has been comprehensively displaced by Toyota's lean production system, in which the automobile producer integrates a network of specialist suppliers of components and services linked by long-term collaborative relationships.
- In the Japanese textile industry, a vertically-integrated structure of the early 1970s gave way to fragmentation and stable long-term relationships between specialized spinning and spinning and weaving companies.
- In Hollywood, a highly integrated industry dominated by a handful of major studios became a network of increasingly specialized firms coming together for individual projects.
- In the US computer and telecommunications equipment sectors, the high levels of vertical integration associated with IBM and AT&T were displaced by the network forms represented by the production and supply systems of Dell Computer and Cisco Systems and closely associated with the Silicon Valley business model.

Networks of small and medium-sized firms have captured the interest of both management scholars and policy makers because of their apparent

ability to combine the flexibility and entrepreneurial drive of small firms
with the scale and scope advantages of large corporations – see, for example
Lorenzoni and Lipparini (1999) and Brusco (1982).

THE UNUSUAL ORGANIZATIONAL FEATURES OF OPEN-SOURCE SOFTWARE

For the purpose of studying alternative organizational forms, interfirm networks suffer from the disadvantage of combining two modes of economic
organization – firms and networks. For this reason it is particularly interesting that, during the past decade and a half, an entirely new type of
network organization has risen to prominence. Open source software (OSS)
communities are not only strikingly different types of organization from
those that have come to dominate the computer software industry – huge,
integrated, geographically-concentrated corporations such as Microsoft,
Oracle, and SAP – they also challenge many of the accepted principles of
management and organizational design. The fact that several OSS products
– most notably Linux and Apache – have successfully built substantial
market positions against strong competition from commercial software
products has accentuated interest in this phenomenon.

Thus, for the purposes of examining alternatives to the conventional corporate form, the novelty and distinctiveness of OSS communities makes
them particularly worthy subjects for empirical research. In particular, they
are particularly promising in terms of the insights they can offer into the
nature and role of structure and coordination in complex production
processes. To what extent and under what conditions can networks of vol-
unteering individuals outperform integrated corporations? And what is the
potential for organizations of this type to be successful in sectors other than
computer software?

Open source software communities are interesting because they seem to
contradict many of the most fundamental tenets of economic theory
and business practice. In particular, the communities are not-for-profit
organizations and the members who undertake the work of software development and bug reporting are volunteers who are not financially remuner-
ated by the communities. The apparent irrationality of computer engineers
incurring massive opportunity costs in creating public goods from which
they derive no direct benefit has attracted considerable commentary and
analysis – to many economists it is an affront to their dearly held concept
of 'economic man'. Hence, considerable efforts have been made to resolve
this apparent contradiction. Rewards from membership and contributing
may include learning, reputation effects, contacts with other members

(leading to future employment opportunities) and the ability to influence the development of an OSS project in the direction of that member's consumer interest (Lerner and Tirole 2002, von Hippel and von Krogh 2003). Raymond (2001) shows that the development of OSS constitutes a 'gift economy' (Boulding 1973). Exchange relationships are not bilateral but generalized. Each developer who contributes code recognizes that reciprocation is not necessarily from the recipient of his contribution but typically occurs through other members of the community. As Iannacci (2003) explains:

> to further clarify this point, consider a situation where a programmer volunteers an answer to a tricky programming question posted on the mailing list. He may have no expectation of being helped in return by the recipient of his contribution. However, he may expect to receive help from some other member(s) of the network who, in turn, might be reciprocated by yet some other actor(s). (p. 5)

However, for students of business organizations, some of the most interesting features of OSS communities are their capacity to create highly complex products that combine the efforts of large numbers of individuals while lacking the structures and systems that have conventionally been seen as essential to the effective management of such efforts. Indeed, in terms of reliability, security, speed of development and flexibility in adapting to different hardware platforms and national languages, OSS is often superior to competitive commercial software. As organizational forms, OSS communities have been viewed as embodying organizational principles that are diametrically opposed to those which underlie those of the business corporation. Thus, Mockus *et al.* (2000) point to the fact that – despite the involvement of hundreds, even thousands, of volunteers – individuals select what tasks they wish to perform and there is no allocation of individuals to particular tasks and no explicit system-level design. For some scholars, OSS communities embody the principles of emergence and adaptation associated with complexity theory. Thus, Iannacci (2003) states that the 'Linux development process is not the result of planned design but of retrospective sensemaking; not the result of ordered change but of random often chaotic enactments'. Muffatto and Faldani (2003) view OSS communities as complex adaptive systems:

> The open source community and its activities can be considered to have the characteristics of a complex adaptive system. The open source system is unique because it is not controlled by a central authority that defines its strategy nor is it completely chaotic. It can be placed in a middle position between a designed system and a chaotic one. In this position non-formal rules exist which allow the system to produce appreciable results. (p. 83)

To understand the extent to which OSS communities represent fundamentally new approaches to organization, let us examine some of the main features of organizational structure among a small group of successful, well-established OSS communities.

The Organizational Structure of OSS Communities

I examined some of the main features of organizational structure and management systems among 16 prominent OSS communities. The selection process was not systematic – essentially I chose communities responsible for OSS software products that were conspicuous through their widespread use and by the extent of media commentary. Table 3.1 shows a sample and some basic characteristics of the communities and their main products. The characteristics of organizational structure that I focused upon were legal structure, categories of membership, hierarchy, governance and leadership and the extent of vertical and horizontal specialization. Some of the most notable features of the communities are listed below.

Formal structure and governance

Most OSS communities are organized as non-profit corporations. In the US this means they are registered as charitable organizations under Internal Revenue Code Section 501(c) (3). This non-tax status requires the adoption of a formal governance structure and procedures including articles of association, a board of directors, elected officers and the submission of annual reports and financial statements. The principal exception is Linux, which lacks a distinct legal identity or formal organizational structure.

Boards of directors are elected by the members of the communities. However, despite the democratic constitution of most OSS communities, the most striking feature of the governing boards – and, in some cases executive officers – is their stability and longevity. For example, the nine-member board of Apache Software Foundation, which develops and maintains the Apache web server, includes six that were members of the original board when the foundation was founded in 1999. Several other communities have formal leadership vested in their founders or founding teams: the president of the Gnome Foundation is the same Miguel de Icaza who founded the project, while at Python Software Foundation, founder Guido van Rossum continued as chairman and president throughout 2004.

A key factor in the stability of many of the communities is that voting members of the foundations are typically a smaller group than those who are registered as users and developers. Moreover, new voting members join through the invitation of existing members – in some cases subject to board approval. Thus, at Apache, 'Individuals who have made sustained and

Table 3.1 The sample

Project	Functionality	Start date	Size*	Location of founder(s)	Legal form
Apache	Web server	1995	3m SLOC	US (mainly)	501(c)(3) corp
CLisp	Programming language implementation	Late 1980s	15m bytes	Germany	Informal
Debian	Linux distribution	1993	105m SLOC	US	501(c)(3) corp
Emacs	Text editor	1976	n.a.	US	501(c)(3) corp
Freenet	Software for anonymous internet publication	1999	n.a.	Scotland	501(c)(3) corp
FreeBSD	Unix operating system	1993	9.1m SLOC	US	501(c)(3) corp
Gnome	Desktop environment	1997	49.5m SLOC	US	501(c)(3) corp
GNU	Unix operating system	1983	n.a.	US	501(c)(3) corp
KDE	Desktop environment	1996	32.5m SLOC	Germany/Norway	Informal
Linux Kernel	Operating system	1991	2.4m SLOC	Finland	Informal
Mozilla	Web browser	1998	2.0m SLOC	US	501(c)(3) corp
Open Office	Office applications suite	2000	14.0m SLOC	Germany/US	Owned by Sun
Perl	Programming language	1987	15.5m SLOC	US	501(c)(3) corp
Python	Programming language	1990	n.a.	Netherlands	501(c)(3) corp
Sendmail	Email transfer agent	Early 1980s	n.a.	US	501(c)(3) corp
XFree86	Client-server interface	1991	1.3m SLOC	US	501(c)(3) corp

Note: * For comparison, Windows XP has approximately 40 million SLOC (source lines of code).

important contributions to one or more of the foundation's projects can be invited to become Members of the Apache Software Foundation'.[1] At Software in the Public Interest Inc., the community that supports the Debian project, there is a distinction between contributing and non-contributing members – only the former are allowed to vote. Eligibility for membership of the Gnome Foundation is also limited to 'contributors': individuals who have 'contributed to a non-trivial improvement of the Gnome project'.[2] At Free BSD Foundation new members may be proposed and seconded by existing members and are then voted on by the board of directors.

Hierarchy

The formal hierarchy of members, board of directors and officers relates to the legal organization of the OSS community, which is typically called a 'foundation'. The operational activities of OSS communities are typically undertaken in projects. Some communities may comprise a single project, but most involve several. These are also organized into the hierarchical structures within which there are three dimensions: the hierarchy of involvement, the hierarchy of integration and the hierarchy of decision making.

Hierarchy of involvement   All communities distinguish different categories of membership based upon length of membership and extent of involvement in the work of community projects. Some communities describe their structures as 'hierarchies of involvement'. Apache's categories of involvement are typical – project members begin as 'users', whose contributions are primarily reporting bugs and offering suggestions for future features; they may then graduate to being 'developers', who subscribe to project development mailing lists and contribute patches, and then to 'committers' – frequent and valuable contributors that are granted access to the source code repository. In most communities, only the most experienced and reliable developers are selected as committers, and their actions are governed by a committers' 'contract' or 'charter'. Committers are typically assigned to a specific area of the code tree. Mentors, themselves experienced committers, are often appointed to supervise new committers.

Hierarchy of integration   All the open source projects we studied are organized in a hierarchy of modules that corresponds to the structure of the software. The modular structure may take the form of separate projects within the community, or first level modules within a single project. Each module is typically comprised of several sub-modules. Thus, Gnome comprises eight projects, all of which are closely linked to developing and supporting the Gnome desktop environment for Linux and other Unix-like systems. These are:

- Gnome Accessibility Project – adapts the Gnome suite of software to the needs of people with disabilities.
- Gnome Art – provides designs and artwork to support the usability of Gnome.
- Gnome Bugsquad – quality assurance.
- Gnome Documentation Project.
- Gnome Packaging Project – provides binaries of Gnome to users and developers.
- Gnome Translation Project – supports internationalization and localization of Gnome.
- Gnome Usability Project – works to enhance the Gnome user experience.
- Gnome Webhackers – maintenance of Gnome websites.

The main Gnome project is organized into a large number of hierarchically-integrated modules. The Gnome libraries form 19 modules, core applications involve four primary modules, Gnome applications comprise 16 modules, while there are in excess of 30 modules that involve individual applications.

The Apache Software foundation comprises 17 projects in addition to the core Apache HTTP Server project. Some of these involve sub-projects. Each project is divided into a number of modules. For example Apache Ant, a Java-based build tool, has two modules, the main Ant module and the 'Ant-Antidote' module, which is a GUI front-end to Ant. PERL community comprises 33 projects which together amount to over 400 modules. At the heart of every module and sub-module is the source code tree. Coordinating the inputs of the different developers working on a module (or sub-module) is achieved through the CVS (Concurrent Versions System) tree which manages changes within the source code tree through storing the current version of the source code and recording all changes that have occurred (and who made those changes).

The hierarchy of integration is defined not only by the modular structure of the project code, but also by specific functions. For example, FreeBSD appoints individuals to a number of support teams. These include:

- The FreeBSD Documentation Engineering Team
- The FreeBSD Port Management Team
- The FreeBSD Donations Team
- The FreeBSD Security Team.

Hierarchy of decision making　The hierarchy of integration is paralleled by a hierarchy of decision-making power. At each level of integration there is an individual or group of individuals with decision-making power, the basis of which is the right to accept or reject submissions of code. In most OSS projects, the individuals heading modules and sub-modules are referred to as 'maintainers' – or in some cases (for example Mozilla) as 'module owners'. Overall integration and strategic guidance of a project is typically in the hands of a committee. For example, each Apache project has a Project Management Committee 'who take responsibility for the long-term direction of the projects in their area'. Each committee is chaired by a vice president who is an officer of the Apache Foundation.

The Linux kernel, as I have already noted, is characterized by its lack of formal organizational structure. Nevertheless, it shares a similar hierarchy of decision-making power. In the fall of 1998, Linus Torvalds, Linux's founder, decentralized decision making to a small group of 'trusted lieu-tenants', each responsible for particular modules of the Linux kernel. At the sub-module level, maintainers are responsible for coordinating code submissions. A key feature of the decision-making hierarchies both in Linux and in most other OSS projects is that, starting with committers and including module maintainers and project management committees, most of the individuals are appointed by more senior personnel rather than elected by community members.

Figures 3.3, 3.4 and 3.5 depict the organizational structures of several OSS communities and projects.

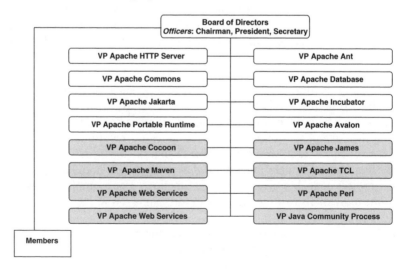

Figure 3.3　Apache Software Foundation: formal structure

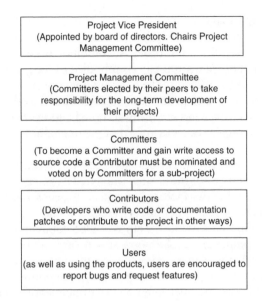

Figure 3.4 *The hierarchy of integration and decision making within an Apache project*

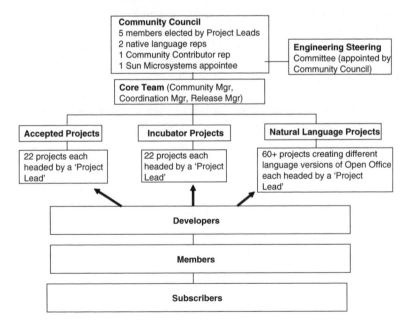

Figure 3.5 *Open office: organizational structure*

Authority and leadership

With the exception of the Linux kernel, whose organization is informal, most OSS communities and projects combine formal and informal authority. Formal or legal authority is embodied in the governance structure and mechanisms defined in the communities' constitutions, charters, articles of association and procedural rules. Informal authority is based upon norms of legitimacy as generally accepted within OSS communities and upon the characteristics and appeal of particular individuals' 'charismatic authority'.

In OSS communities, an important basis for informal authority is respect of community members for the most prominent developers within the community. This rests upon two factors – first, professional respect for the skills of the most capable software developers; second, a shared belief in the concepts of ownership rights. While the ethos of OSS communities is driven by the disdain for commercial exploitation of software and belief in software as a public good, these ideas coexist with the notion of the rights of authors. Eric Raymond argues that conventions regarding property rights in OSS projects closely parallel common law principles of land ownership. Thus, OSS developers achieve property rights through initiating new projects and functions (what Raymond refers to as 'homesteading the noosphere'), through founders transferring their ownership rights to another individual, or through taking possession of some area of activity that others have abandoned (Raymond 2001: 67–80).

In addition to Linux, several other OSS communities feature founders in leadership roles. These include Apache, where original founder Brian Behlendorf is a board member; Gnome, where founder Miguel de Icaza is president; and PERL, where founder Larry Wall exercises continuing powers of selection and direction. The role of these founder-leaders is often described as 'benevolent dictators' which Wikipedia defines:

> A 'benevolent dictator' (or Benevolent Dictator for Life) is the person who effectively holds dictator-like powers over that project, yet is trusted by other users/developers not to abuse this power. The term is used humorously, because the 'subjects' of the project leader contribute voluntarily, and the end-product may be used by everyone. A dictator in this context has power only over the process, and that only for as long as he or she is trusted. Examples include Linus Torvalds: Linux kernel, Guido van Rossum: Python programming language, Larry Wall: PERL, Alexandre Julliard: Wine. Many claim Jimmy Wales is the benevolent dictator for Wikimedia Foundation.[3]

Linus Torvalds is an exemplar of this leadership style, with its basis in legitimacy through ownership, individual competence and charisma. Torvalds's authority, like that of other 'benevolent dictators', derives ultimately from their status as founders of their communities and the implicit ownership rights associated with their authorship of much of the code that forms the communities' software products. Maintaining this authority depends critically upon the capacity of the leaders to embody and reinforce the values and beliefs of the community, while also being aware of and reflecting changes in the mood and norms of the community. However, day-to-day control is the result of the continuing operational role that these leaders play. Thus, Torvalds maintains control over accepting patches to the development branch of the Linux kernel and, as his comments clearly reveal, he feels under no obligation to accept submissions of code from other developers:

> I take stuff that I feel is good. Often that feeling of goodness comes from trusting the person who sends it to me, simply by past performance. At other times, it is because I think the feature is cool, or well done, or whatever. Hint: if you want stuff in my tree, make me trust you. Or work on things that I feel are innately interesting. Don't bother dragging me into your flame-wars and trying to convince me that I 'must' apply your patches.[4]

Similarly, Larry Wall occupies key operational roles at PERL, while Brian Behlendorf, one of the original founders of Apache, exercises continuing control over trees for several key modules, including apache-devsite, apache-search-site and http-test.

Management Systems among OSS Communities

I have shown that hierarchy forms the structure through which governance is exercised, the inputs of participants are integrated and decision-making powers are allocated, but what are the management systems through which community members are able to collaborate in order to integrate their activities? The organizational literature points to collaboration within organizations as involving two dimensions.

The first is cooperation. Different organizational members tend to have different goals and these tend to conflict with the goals of the owners of the organization. Overcoming goal conflict requires creating incentives and controls. The economics literature analyses goal misalignment in terms of agency problems. An agency relationship exists when one party (the principal) contracts with another party (the agent) to act on behalf of the principal. The problem of such a relationship is ensuring that the agent acts in the principal's interest. Within the firm, attention has focused on the agency problem that exists between owners (shareholders) and professional managers. The issue of what motivates software developers to participate in OSS communities and, once a member, what motivates them to continue donating their time and efforts to community activities has been the subject of considerable attention in the literature. In the absence of direct financial rewards, writers have identified several incentives, including indirect financial rewards (for example through career enhancement, skill development or entrepreneurial opportunities associated with for-profit activities that utilize OSS products), reputational and recognition rewards, and consumer interest (that is, most OSS products are tools used by developers) reinforced by networked reciprocity.[5]

The second problem is coordination. Even if organizational members are motivated to pursue the goals of the organization, unless individuals' efforts can be coordinated, production of the final product does not happen. In the case of computer software – highly complex products comprising millions of lines of code and the efforts of hundreds (sometimes thousands) of designers, developers, testers and quality assurance experts – coordination is a huge challenge. The conventional wisdom is that such software is best created through tightly-integrated teams of developers working at a single facility and engaged in intensive, face-to-face communication both within teams and between teams. OSS is developed in a very different way. Developers are dispersed globally, there are almost no face-to-face meetings and virtually all communication is electronic – via email and bulletin boards. The literature on OSS has emphasized the distinctive differences between OSS communities and commercial enterprises. Thus, Iannacci (2003) identifies software development within Linux as by an emergent, evolutionary process involving three principal stages: enactment, selection and retention. In contrast to the development process of commercial software that comprises a four-stage cycle – planning, analysis, design and implementation – in OSS the first three stages are absent. The result is a 'model where individuals act on intuition instead of following orders from above, a model that values retroactive strategies rather than proactive plans and admits novel actions rather than predetermined uses' (Iannacci 2003: 6).

The problem of coordination in OSS communities has received much less attention than that of incentives for cooperation and will be my focus in this section. In the sample of OSS communities which I studied, three principal modes of coordination could be identified: rules, routines and culture.

Rules
Given the geographical dispersion of OSS communities, it is not surprising that rules play a central role in facilitating coordination. Virtually every activity that occurs within OSS projects and communities is subject to rules. Rules may be categorized in terms of their purpose and nature. For example:

- Technical rules: relate to the specifications for code format, code architecture and documentation. Linux has 13 official Kernel-Hackerguides at its website that it recommends prospective developers to read before contributing.
- Procedural rules: relate to all aspects of community operations in terms of the process for bug reporting, approval of access to source code and mailing lists, procedures for code review, the processes for authorizing new projects and modules, procedures for releasing new versions.
- Infrastructure rules: code/data repository, bug system, tools, style guides.
- Organizational and constitutional rules and processes: these relate to a diversity of issues involving governance, rights of community members and processes through which the organization conducts itself. At the basis are fundamental constitutional rules for the community as set out in its charter and articles of association, the copyright that governs the intellectual property of the community,[6] the rights of members (including peer recognition), acceptance of funds, the role of outside business corporations within the community and activities such as meetings and conferences.

Routines
Activities such as bug reporting, mailing list discussions, approval of patches and managing new releases are defined by explicit rules and guidelines; ultimately, however, these activities become routinized. Organizational routines are 'regular and predictable behavioral patterns of firms' involving 'repetitive patterns of activity' that are 'ordinarily accomplished without conscious awareness' (Nelson and Winter 1982: 15, 97). Such routines are typically viewed as the basic building blocks of organizational capability. What we observe in OSS communities, therefore, is much the same as we observe in other organizations where organizational members have the advantages (in terms of ease of interaction) of co-location. Thus, in a McDonald's hamburger restaurant, although virtually all operational tasks are minutely documented in standard operating procedures, most tasks are performed without any reference to such rules and direction and are achieved through collaborative interaction involving limited communication and little conscious deliberation. In OSS communities routine tasks also become routinized to the point where they occur through semi-automatic patterns of interactions between organizational members. This routinization is facilitated by the fact that routines tend to be similar across different OSS communities. Figure 3.6 depicts a routinized set of interactions for the consideration and incorporation of a patch to the Linux kernel submitted by a developer.

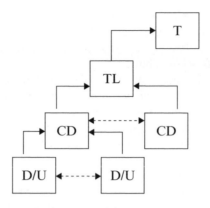

Note:
T – Linus Torvald
TL – Trusted Lieutenant
CD – Credited Developer
D/U – Developer/User

Source: Iannacci (2005).

Figure 3.6   Routine for approving and incorporating new patches to the Linux kernel

Culture
Finally, organizational culture represents an essential basis for coordination among all OSS communities. Organizational culture refers to the values and behavioural norms that are shared and accepted among organizational members. Their role as a coordinating device has been analysed by Kreps (1990), who regards culture as a substitute for contracting within the firm. A body of common values and norms is an efficient and flexible basis for coordination, especially under dynamic conditions, since they avoid the need for multiple contracting among organizational members.

To the extent that organizational members internalize the values and norms, culture facilitates smooth interactions between community members, it acts as a control on deviant or self-interested behaviour by organizational members and it lowers the risks that an individual's communications or actions will be misinterpreted by others. Among informally-structured organizations, culture is likely to be especially important in reinforcing trust relationships essential to decentralized decision processes. This point has been made clear by Linus Torvalds, responding to a proposal to systematize and decentralize Linux's patch approval process:

> The fact is, we've had 'Patch Penguins' pretty much forever, and they are called subsystem maintainers. They maintain their own subsystem, i.e. people like

David Miller (networking), Kai Germaschewski (ISDN), Greg KH (USB), Ben Collins (firewire), Al Viro (VFS), Andrew Morton (ext3), Ingo Molnar (scheduler), Jeff Garzik (network drivers) etc etc . . . A word of warning: good maintainers are hard to find. Getting more of them helps, but at some point it can actually be more useful to help the existing ones. I've got about ten–twenty people I really trust, and quite frankly, the way people work is hard-coded in our DNA. Nobody 'really trusts' hundreds of people. The way to make these things scale out more is to increase the network of trust not by trying to push it on me, but by making it more of a network, not a star-topology around me.[7]

The role of organizational culture as a coordinating device is enhanced by the commonalities in culture across the open source software movement as a whole. Eric Raymond (2001) has written intimately on the hacker culture that pervades OSS communities, which he shows involves not only values and behaviours (for example in relation to the 'gift culture') but also rituals and mysteries and expectations of new members. An important influence reinforcing the identity associated with this culture is antipathy to Microsoft (and to some extent to all large, powerful commercial software companies).

IMPLICATIONS AND CONCLUSION

The open source software community has been hailed as a radical, even revolutionary, new organizational form. Certainly OSS communities are very different from the large commercial enterprises that dominate most of the software industry. In particular, their reliance on unpaid volunteers who select the topics and issues that they work upon makes OSS communities more like charities, grassroots political movements and social clubs than economic organizations producing complex, technically sophisticated products. It is as organizers of complex production that OSS communities have attracted most attention. The ability of these loose-knit, geographically diffused organizations of thousands of individuals to produce computer software that can compete with the sophisticated products of Microsoft, Sun Microsystems, Oracle and other companies, yet without the management structures or planning systems of their commercial counterparts, is the most striking aspect of their operation for management scholars. As a result, OSS communities have been recognized as embodying the features associated with self-managing, complex adaptive systems.

Yet, when we look closely at the structures and management systems through which coordination occurs within OSS communities, it is apparent that they share many of the same characteristics of conventional corporations. In particular, OSS communities have clearly defined hierarchies.

These hierarchies comprise hierarchical governance structures, hierarchical integration of work through modular structures and hierarchical allocation of decision-making power. At the apex of several OSS communities are strong leaders whose authority rests upon tradition, ownership, competence and charisma. Second, OSS communities utilize the same coordination mechanisms – namely rules, routines and culture – that we observe in conventional corporations. Even some of the most distinctive features of OSS communities seem less different on investigation than has been claimed by observers. For example:

- The fact that individuals select the work they do is becoming less evident now that an increasing number of the developers contributing code for the leading OSS projects are employees of other IT companies who are assigned by their companies to working on open source projects.
- The widely distributed production model involving up to thousands of developers is true for some communities in terms of mailing list members – but for most open source projects the work of code writing tends to be concentrated into relatively few hands. Among the 100 most active, mature OSS projects listed on Sourceforge, the mean number of developers was 6.6 and the mean number of project administrators was 2.2 (Krihnamurthy 2002). In the case of one of the biggest and most successful OSS communities – Apache – the top 15 developers contributed 88 per cent of code – a larger percentage than at equivalent commercial software projects (Mockus *et al.* 2000).
- The processes of emergence and 'retroactive sense making' that some commentators have viewed as the hallmarks of strategy and development within OSS projects ignore the fact that in most projects there are individuals and groups (for example benevolent dictators and project management committees) who determine a guide strategy and product development. At the same time mailing lists offer forums for discussing strategic issues and influencing the direction of project development.

Looking at what, at first glance, appears to be a highly anomalous form of organization, may assist us in understanding those aspects of organization structure and management systems that are fundamental to the effective functioning of economic organizations.

The fundamental organizational challenge is the reconciliation of the efficiencies of specialization with the need for coordination. Organizations that comprise hundreds, even thousands, of members offer huge productivity benefits from allowing individual organizational members to specialize, but encounter the problems of, first, how they can achieve cooperation – the alignment between individual and organizational goals – and, second, how they will achieve coordination – the integration of individual expertise and individual efforts into the overall productive task of the organization.

While most analysis of organizational structure has focused upon problems of cooperation (for example goal alignment, agency and organizational deviance), important strides have been made in understanding issues of coordination, notably in drawing upon systems theory, cybernetics and information processing and knowledge-based approaches to the firm. The result has been insight into the role and nature of firms as organizers of production that extend well beyond the transactions cost and contractual models that have been at the centre of economic theories of the firm.

While OSS communities are interesting in relation to problems both of cooperation and coordination, my primary focus in this chapter has been coordination. A central theme of the knowledge-based view of the firm is that firms offer advantages over alternative organizational forms (markets in particular) in the coordination of economic activity. This advantage rests upon firms' ability to use mechanisms for coordination that are not available to markets or to other less tightly structured organizational forms. Firms are 'social communities in which individual and social expertise is transformed into economically-useful products and services by the application of a set of higher-order organizing principles' (Kogut and Zander 1992: 384). The literature points to two main mechanisms for achieving knowledge integration within firms: direction and routine. Direction provides a 'low-cost method of communicating between specialists and the large number of persons who are either non-specialists or specialists in other fields' (Demsetz 1991: 172). Firms convert sophisticated specialized knowledge into directives, rules and operating procedures that can be imposed through authority-based relationships.[8] Organizational routines involve complex patterns of coordination that permit different specialists to integrate their knowledge into the production of goods and services while preserving the efficiencies of knowledge specialization (Nelson and Winter 1982).

By contrast, market contracts for exchanging knowledge suffer not only from well-known sources of transaction cost, but also because they do not easily support either direction or routine. Costs of knowledge transactions are well known: explicit knowledge suffers problems of non-exclusivity and inalienability (Arrow 1962) and tacit knowledge transfers require a '. . . common language or . . . overlaps in cognitive frameworks . . . This requires time and effort: investments which are to some extent . . . transaction specific . . . [hence] yield issues of dependence and lock-in.' (Nooteboom 1996: 331). Within the firm, these problems are limited by a social context characterized by identification of organizational members (Kogut and Zander 1996) and the ability of the firm to appropriate knowledge rents through secrecy (Liebeskind 1996).[9]

Our most interesting finding with regard to OSS communities is replication of many of the same characteristics of organizational structure and management systems that we observe in the modern corporation. Thus, OSS communities are able to achieve coordination through rules and routines and integration by means of hierarchical structures even without much of the institutional structure of the firm – in particular employment contracts and conventional incentive mechanisms. This suggests that the features of organization that are common to both commercial firms and OSS communities may, in fact, be general to the attainment of efficiency and effectiveness in the production of complex goods. In particular:

- The ubiquity of hierarchy as an organizing structure for the production of complex products. In relation to static efficiency, there are advantages from grouping together those individuals whose interdependence is most intense and creating an organizational structure that economizes on interactions between different groups of individuals. In relation to dynamic efficiency, there are advantages from creating loosely-coupled modular structures that can allow decentralized adaptation. A key feature of hierarchy in OSS projects is the close correspondence between organizational hierarchy and the modular structure of the product.
- Commonalities in coordination mechanisms. In terms of management systems, we observe that OSS communities utilize several of the same mechanisms for coordination as conventional corporations. In particular, there is a heavy reliance on rules; in addition, organizational routines and organizational culture are also important coordination mechanisms. In comparison to business corporations, there is a different balance of coordination mechanisms. In particular, in OSS communities there is a greater reliance on rules and less on organizational routines. There is also virtually no role for direction in OSS communities – that is, the issuance of directives by managers to subordinates that is often viewed as the characteristic feature of organizational hierarchies based upon control supported by economic incentives. However, an important commonality of both types of organization is the reliance on organizational culture – a vital coordinating device especially in permitting adaptation to a changing environment.

In conclusion, studying what appear to be radical organizational forms such as open source software communities allows a better framing of the debate over organizational change within the corporate sector, as well as offering insights into some of the fundamental principles of organizational design.

NOTES

1. http://ftp.saix.net/pub/apache/foundation/roles.html
2. http://foundation.gnome.org/membership/
3. http://en.wikipedia.org/wiki/Benevolent_Dictator_for_Life (accessed 28 February 2006).
4. Quoted by Garcia and Steinmueller (2003).
5. See for example: Raymond (2001), Lerner and Tirole (2002) and von Hippel and von Krogh (2003).
6. Lanzara and Morner (2003: 34) suggest that the 'copy-left' rules that are common to open source licensing agreements are important because they 'provide a set of rules that regulate the distribution of knowledge and access to it', thus 'consolidating norms of reciprocity and mutual openness that belong to programmers' shared culture'.
7. http://www.ussg.iu.edu/hypermail/linux/kernel/0201.3/1070.html. Quoted by Iannacci (2005).
8. Conner and Prahalad (1996) use the term 'knowledge substitution' to describe the process of direction of an employee by a superior in the hierarchy. In practice, such direction is not simply a case of substituting the superior's knowledge for that of the subordinate. The essence of direction is that it permits different individuals' specialist knowledge to be integrated. Thus, the computer technician can give directions to the CEO as to what to do when his/her computer hard disk is infected by a virus.
9. A further advantage of firms is in overcoming the problems of metering and shirking to which team-based cooperation gives rise (Alchian and Demsetz 1972).

BIBLIOGRAPHY

Alchian, A. and H. Demsetz (1972), 'Production, information costs, and economic organization, *American Economic Review*, **62**, 777–795.
Arrow, K.J. (1962), 'Economic welfare and the allocation of resources for invention', in R.R. Nelson (ed.), *The Rate and Direction of Inventive Activity: Economic and Social Factors*, Princeton, NJ: Princeton University Press, pp. 609–626.
Bartlett, C.A. and S. Ghoshal (1998), *Managing Across Borders: The Transnational Solution*, 2nd edition, Boston: Harvard Business School Press.
Boulding, K.E. (1973), *The Economy of Love and Fear*, Belmont, CA: Wadsworth.
Brusco, S. (1982), 'The Emelian model: productive decentralization and social integration', *Cambridge Journal of Economics*, **6**, 167–184.
Bushe, G. and A.B. Shani (1991), *Parallel Learning Structures*, Reading, MA: Addison Wesley.
Chandler, A.D. (1962), *Strategy and Structure,* Cambridge, MA: MIT Press.
Conner, K. and C.K. Prahalad (1996), 'A resource-based theory of the firm: knowledge versus opportunism', *Organization Science*, **7**, 477–501.
Dafermos, G.N. (2001), *Management and Virtual Decentralized Networks: The Linux Project*, MA thesis, University of Durham.
Daft, R. and A. Lewin (1993), 'Where are the theories for the new organizational forms? An editorial essay', *Organization Science*, **3**, 1–6.

Davidow, W.H. and M.S. Malone (1992), *The Virtual Corporation: Structuring and Revitalizing the Corporation for the 21st Century*, New York: Harper Business.

Demsetz, H. (1991), 'The Theory of the Firm Revisited', in Williamson O.E. and S.G. Winter (eds), *The Nature of the Firm*, Oxford: Oxford University Press.

Garcia, J.M. and W.E. Steinmueller (2003), *Applying the Open Source Development Model to Knowledge Work*, INK Working Paper, number 2 (January), Brighton: SPRU.

Handy, C. (1990), *The Age of Unreason*, Boston, MA: Harvard Business School Press.

Hedlund, G. (1994), 'A model of knowledge management and the N-form corporation', *Strategic Management Journal*, **15**, 73–90.

Hock, D. (1999), *Birth of the Chaotic Age*, San Francisco, CA: Berrett-Koehler Publishers, Inc.

Iannacci, F. (2003), 'The Linux managing model', *First Monday*, **8** (12), URL:http://www.firstmonday.dk/issues/issue8_12/iannacci/.

Iannacci, F. (2005), *Coordination Processes in Open Source Software Development: The Linux Case Study*, Working Paper, London School of Economics, April, http://opensource.mit.edu/papers/iannacci3.pdf.

Kogut, B. and U. Zander (1992), 'Knowledge of the firm, combinative capabilities and the replication of technology', *Organization Science*, **3**, 383–397.

Kogut, B. and U. Zander (1996), 'What do firms do? Coordination, identity and learning', *Organization Science*, **7**, 502–518.

Kono, T. (1984), *The Strategy and Structure of Japanese Enterprises*, London: Macmillan.

Kreps, D. (1990), 'Corporate culture and economic theory', in J.E. Alt and K.A. Shepsle (eds), *Perspectives on Positive Political Economy*, Cambridge: Cambridge University Press, pp. 90–114.

Krihnamurthy, S. (2002), *Cave or Community: An Empirical Examination of 100 Mature, OSS Projects*, Bothell, WA: University of Washington.

Lanzara, G. and M. Morner (2003), *The Knowledge Ecology of Open-Source Software Projects*, Paper presented at the 19th Egos Conference, July 2003, Copenhagen.

Lerner, J. and J. Tirole (2002), 'Some simple economics of open source', *Journal of Industrial Economics*, **50** (2), 197–234.

Liebeskind, J.P. (1996), 'Knowledge, strategy, and the theory of the firm', *Strategic Management Journal*, **17**, 93–107.

Lipparini, A. and G. Lorenzoni (2005), 'Organizing around strategic relationships: networks of suppliers as knowledge generators in the Italian motorcycle industry', in K. Cool, J. Henderson and R. Abate (eds), *Restructuring Strategy: New Networks and Industry Challenges*, Oxford: Blackwell, pp. 91–114.

Lorenzoni, G. and A. Lipparini (1999), 'The leveraging of inter-firm relationship as a distinctive organizational capability: a longitudinal study', *Strategic Management Journal*, **20**, 317–338.

Mockus, A., R.T. Fielding and J. Herbsleb (2000), 'A case study of OSS development: the Apache server', Proceedings of the 2000 International Conference on Software Engineering (ICSE 2000), Limerick, Ireland, June, IEEE Computer Society Press, pp. 263–272.

Muffatto, M. and M. Faldani (2003), 'Open source as a complex adaptive system', *Emergence*, **5** (3), 83–100.

Nelson, R.R. and S.G. Winter (1982), *An Evolutionary Theory of Economic Change*, Cambridge, MA: Belknap Press.

Nonaka, I. and H. Takeuchi (1995), *The Knowledge Creating Company*, Oxford: Oxford University Press.

Nooteboom, B. (1996), 'Transaction costs and technological learning', in J. Groenewegen (ed.), *Transaction Cost Economics and Beyond*, Boston, MA: Kluwer Academic Publishers, pp. 327–350.

O'Reilly, C. and M. Tushman (2004), 'The ambidextrous organization', *Harvard Business Review*, April, 74–82.

Quinn, J.B. (1992), *Intelligent Enterprise*, New York: Free Press.

Raymond, E. (2001), *The Cathedral and the Bazaar*, revised edition, Sebastopol, CA: O'Reilly.

Robins, J.A. (1993), 'Organization as strategy: restructuring production in the film industry', *Strategic Management Journal*, Summer, 103–118.

Rumelt, R.P. (1974), *Strategy, Structure and Economic Performance*, Cambridge, MA: Harvard University Press.

Stark, R. (1989), *Sociology*, 3rd edition, Belmont, CA: Wadsworth.

Volberda, H.W. (1999), *Building the Flexible Firm: How to Remain Competitive*, Oxford: Oxford University Press.

von Hippel, E. and G. von Krogh (2003), 'Open source software and the private-collective innovation model: issues for organization science', *Organization Science,* **14** (2), 209–233.

Whittington, R. and M. Mayer (2000), *The European Corporation*, Oxford: Oxford University Press.

Williamson, O.E. (1981), 'The modern corporation: origins, evolution, attributes', *Journal of Economic Literature*, **19**, 1537–1568.

4. From a national to a metanational ecosystem: harnessing the value of global knowledge diversity

Peter J. Williamson

INTRODUCTION

Despite globalization of their supply chains, few companies have developed an ecosystem that harnesses the potential value of global knowledge diversity (Bartlett and Ghoshal 1989). Indeed, most companies still see the diverse knowledge that arises from the specific contexts of locations around the world as an impediment to their globalization strategies, rather than as a fount of new competitive advantage (Vernon 1966, 1979, Cantwell 1998).

The fact that most companies view knowledge diversity as a problem for globalization, rather than as an opportunity, stems from the very fundamentals of their internationalization mindset: the idea that building international strength comes from exploiting competitive advantages pioneered at their home base by transferring it into more and more locations around the world (Dunning 1996). From this standpoint, knowledge diversity is a problem, because it necessitates that the firm engages in a costly and uncertain process of adapting the business model and sources of competitive advantages it has perfected at home to fit diverse and different contexts in each new location (Hu 1992, Caves 1996).

This chapter explores companies that have taken an alternative approach to global knowledge diversity – by building an ecosystem that harnesses differentiated knowledge that is scattered around the world to fuel innovation that cannot be matched by competitors whose innovation process focuses on more restricted, local sources of knowledge around their home base (Johanssen and Vahlne 1977). My colleagues and I termed these companies 'metanationals' (denoting the idea of looking beyond national markets) because rather than considering the world as a collection of national markets in which to sell products developed at home, the metanational sees the world as a knowledge canvas, dotted with pools of distinctive knowledge about technologies and market behaviour (Doz et al. 2001).[1]

Metanationals build an ecosystem to identify and access this dispersed knowledge ahead of competition (a 'sensing network'). A metanational then links these distinctive pools of knowledge in original ways that yield innovations that competitors without an equally good access to the same pools of knowledge will find impossible to imitate (a process of 'mobilizing' knowledge). Finally, the metanational produces and sells the resulting innovations globally through a network of sales and marketing subsidiaries in large markets; it sources plants and back-office service operations in low-cost locations and specialized knowledge-intensive activities where the relevant knowledge is world-class (a more traditional global network that 'leverages' innovation for profit).

In what follows I describe this new type of metanational ecosystem and analyse the opportunities and pitfalls in building it. Examining the experience of pioneering metanationals like ST Microelectronics, ARM and Polygram Records, we will see that an effective network for digital communication is a necessary, but far from sufficient, element of an effective ecosystem for harnessing the potential of global knowledge diversity. Finally I describe the increasing use of this strategy by emerging multinationals from China – a trend that underpins the importance and urgency for global incumbents to re-evaluate their existing innovation ecosystems in terms of an ability to turn global knowledge diversity into a virtue.

THE METANATIONAL ECOSYSTEM

Imagine a company had created an ecosystem that could identify pockets of leading-edge technical knowledge around the world and access them before its competitors were even aware of their existence, a company that could spot emerging consumer trends and fashions anywhere they spring up worldwide, way before competitors even started to grasp their significance. Imagine that this company was then able to innovate by taking knowledge from all these sources and turning it into world-beating products and services it sold and delivered globally at lightning speed. Such a company would be an unbeatable global competitor. It would consistently trump rivals who tried to innovate using only the knowledge available around their doorsteps and thus merely projected internationally the business formula they had learnt at home. It would also out-innovate those who relied on 'centres of excellence' in a few of their biggest international subsidiaries for innovation.

Far fetched? A pipedream? Why is it so difficult to imagine a company doing this? An important part of the answer is that such a company would have to see the world very differently from the way most companies view it today: not as a set of markets to be served and cheap sources of labour, capital and material to be accessed, but as a canvas dotted with pockets of under-exploited knowledge. Once it began to look at the world as such a knowledge canvas, it would then have to learn how to exploit it for innovation by accessing, mobilizing, melding and leveraging this dispersed knowledge to create better products and services it could market and deliver globally.

Such a company would also have to think of the innovation ecosystem, not with nostalgia for the idea of a small, isolated team working in the proverbial 'garage', but as a process of ferreting out the best technologies and knowledge from every corner of the earth and learning to overcome the barriers of dispersion and distance. It would need a deep sense for what specific locations – or 'sites' – could uniquely contribute to its innovation and business processes and to get its people to combine intense pride in what the uniqueness of their local site could contribute with a deep desire to exploit these contributions globally. In short, its people would need to 'think local and act global'. This would require them to turn the old multinational adage of Percy Barnevik (former CEO of Asea Brown Boveri) fame: 'think global, act local', on its head. The metanational ecosystem does not come easily to most companies because it flies in the face of the traditional approach to internationalization that is deeply embedded in multinational organizations.

The challenge of building an ecosystem capable of sensing, connecting and exploiting complex knowledge that is scattered around the world is clearly formidable. To meet this challenge the winners in the knowledge economy must be able to outdistance their competitors at the three different levels depicted in Figure 4.1.

The first level of competition is the race to identify and access new and relevant technologies, competencies and knowledge of lead markets emerging in locations dotted around the world. Where, for example, is the next advance in biotechnology being hatched? Where are consumers experimenting with new uses for mobile phones?

The second level of competition is in the effectiveness and speed with which companies can connect these globally scattered pieces of knowledge and use them to create innovative products, services and processes (Kogut 1993). How effectively, for example, can a semiconductor maker marshal technologies scattered around the world to serve a customer need emerging elsewhere, thus creating a radically new 'system on a chip'? Which record company is most capable of turning an unknown artist from an exotic location into a global hit by fine tuning his/her repertoire to the tastes of consumers in major international markets?

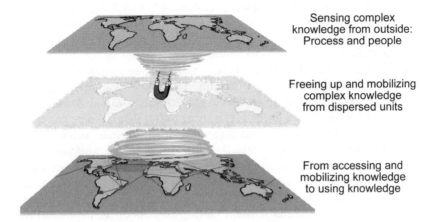

Sensing complex knowledge from outside: Process and people

Freeing up and mobilizing complex knowledge from dispersed units

From accessing and mobilizing knowledge to using knowledge

Figure 4.1   Levels of competition in a metanational ecosystem

The third level of global competition is optimizing the efficiency of the global sales, distribution, marketing and supply chain to leverage these product, service and process innovations across global markets rapidly and cost-effectively. How efficiently can the record company, for example, gear up to promote, produce and distribute its innovative album at the right price in the most markets? How efficiently can the semiconductor company adapt, produce and sell its new chip to customers around the world? Let us turn to consider what kind of ecosystem would be necessary to assist a company in succeeding in these three different, but interrelated, levels of competition.

BUILDING A SENSING NETWORK

It is instructive to begin by considering some of the companies which were able to build a metanational ecosystem successfully:

- ST Microelectronics, born from the merger of two struggling semi-conductor companies in France and Italy, was able to tap into innovative technologies and customer needs bubbling up in places like San Jose, Dublin, Helsinki and Singapore. This new knowledge enabled it to develop customized 'system on a chip' products. Armed with this innovative product line it was able to carve out a gap in the market between competitors like Intel and ASICS for applications as diverse as hard disk drives, mobile phones and car navigation systems. The fact that today it is the fourth largest semiconductor company in the world, having created more shareholder value than any of its competitors bar Intel itself, demonstrates the power of assembling a knowledge base that more myopic rivals simply cannot match.

- Shiseido, the Japanese cosmetics and skin care products company, found its market share and margins under threat as competitors used their exclusive perfume brands to gain loyalty from distribution. But the knowledge base around fragrance product development and marketing Shiseido needed was underdeveloped in Japan. Success came only from a sustained effort to internalize new knowledge from France – involving everything from starting production in Gien, close to other leading fragrance makers, through buying two prestige Paris beauty salon chains, Carita and Alexandre Zouari, to observe trend-setting customers first-hand, to hiring as CEO of its newly-starting perfume company in France a lady who was the marketing head of Yves Saint Laurent Parfums. Not only was Shiseido able to revitalize distribution for its cosmetics business, it has now become a leading and very profitable player in the perfume business with products like Eau d'Issey and the Jean Paul Gaultier range.
- Polygram, which became the world's largest record company prior to its sale to Seagram (and subsequently Vivendi Universal) for $10 billion, built an organization capable of identifying future global 'hit artists' from local talent in the bars and clubs of cities like Sao Paolo, Reykjavik, Naples, Paris, Athens and Hong Kong. While rivals like Sony Music, RCA and EMI fought over budding stars in New York and London – the time-honoured sources of global music talent – Polygram fished in a much larger talent pool. The result: more distinctive products, while bypassing head-to-head wars for talent.

One thing all these companies have in common is that they determinedly set out to improve their businesses by fishing for knowledge beyond their local ponds (Stopford 1995). To learn from the world, a company needs to engage with the international environment in new ways. It must become a 'global prospector' – looking for hotbeds of emerging technology or bellwether customers that foreshadow future trends. But tapping into new pockets of knowledge from around the world usually requires more than just short-term visits, 'study missions', searching the Internet or a visit to the Patent Office. Complex, subtle knowledge can only be accessed through:

- Partnerships with lead customers: Using its knowledge prospecting skills, for example, ST identified Seagate and Western Digital as 'strategic partners' from whom it could access the knowledge about hard disk drive (HDD) systems that it needed to create dedicated chips for controlling HDD. Through these alliances with such customers, it located the knowledge it needed in various customer sites in the United States and the Far East.

- Distributors: In their drive to improve their products, for example, Japanese and Korean consumer electronics firms often relied on US mass merchandizers, such as Sears and Wal-Mart, to specify features and performance for them. This allowed them to access knowledge that paved the way for later investments in building their own brands and distribution channels.

- Suppliers can provide access to new knowledge. The Taiwanese electronics giant Tatung, for example, used purchasing as a powerful engine to access technology and capabilities from the United States, Europe, Japan and Korea. This role was explicit – Tatung's purchasing heads report jointly to the heads of global purchasing and new product development.

- Collaboration with universities and public research centres can provide access to local scientific communities. Japanese pharmaceutical company Eisai, for instance, engaged in scientific collaboration with local research hospitals and medical schools, to prepare development and registration of promising new molecules it had discovered, particularly to fight Alzheimer's disease (Kuermmele 1997).

- Targeted acquisitions: When the pharmaceutical giant Glaxo-SmithKline (GSK) bought Affymax, a pioneer in solid-state combinatorial chemistry, it got more than a technology for speeding up its development pipeline. As a senior executive at GSK put it, 'There was a more strategic aim when GSK bought Affymax. It was to have a group of technologists and scientists in the San Francisco area, in the middle of the hive of innovation.'

In many multinationals, valuable knowledge also exists within existing subsidiaries. But it often remains locally imprisoned, underutilized by a global operation that either does not know about it, or local managers who cannot see its relevance outside their local market or facility. As Lew Platt, former CEO of Hewlett Packard (HP) put it: 'If HP knew what HP knows, it would be three times as profitable'.

Building an ecosystem to tap into new pockets of knowledge is the first stage of gaining competitive advantage by engaging with the world. In getting beyond this first stage, however, many companies fall into a deadly trap: creating a global debating society.

MOBILIZING DISPERSED AND DIFFERENTIATED KNOWLEDGE

We observed that even those companies that were effective in sensing a rich stock of potentially useful knowledge from the right locations frequently failed to exploit what they had learned (Szulanski 1997). They resembled prestigious debating clubs and learned societies: well-informed but ineffective in getting results. There were two common reasons for this failure. First, companies frequently failed to use the right channels to connect the nodes in their metanational ecosystem because they did not properly distinguish between flows of information and knowledge in their ecosystems (Kogut and Zander 1993). A second, key reason was the lack of effective innovation magnets. These magnets are an essential part of the ecosystem because they provide a focus to 'attract' dispersed knowledge and put it to work to solve a problem.

Magnets in the Metanational Ecosystem

We identified three types of magnets that proved effective in this role:

- Innovation projects built around a lead customer
- Innovation projects built around a common platform
- A repeatable innovation activity.

Which magnet was most effective depended on the characteristics of the innovation opportunity.

Innovation projects built around a lead customer proved most effective when the latent customer need being addressed was ill defined and where it was difficult to specify what the innovative product or service might look like at the outset. The effective use of a few leading global customers as magnets proved critical to ST's rise during the 1990s. ST's insight was to differentiate its offering by innovating 'systems on a chip' – such as the new chip it developed to replace the traditional circuit boards used to control hard disk drives. When ST began to develop this innovation, it understood neither the architecture nor the exact technologies and capabilities involved in data storage systems. To overcome these gaps, it needed to assemble relevant knowledge from different sites and product divisions scattered around its own international network, from competitors and from customers. It used an innovation project to develop a chip to control Seagate's hard disk drive as the magnet to bring this knowledge together, focused on a common innovation problem.

Innovation built around a common platform proved most effective where a reasonably tight specification of future customers' requirements was available rather than a vague notion of an unmet need or a fuzzy opportunity. An innovation project designed around a platform provides a more tangible magnet than a partnership with a lead customer. Early on, it is clearer what pieces of knowledge are required to further the innovation and how they might fit together. This, in turn, paves the way for a more predictable innovation process. A good example is the designer of Reduced Instruction Set Computing (RISC) chips, ARM Ltd – a company based in Cambridge, UK with around 600 people. ARM has a market capitalization of $5 billion dollars. It controls 70 per cent of markets for the RISC chip architecture inside mobile phones. The company draws knowledge from all of its hundreds of partners and produces a compromise architecture which it then licenses back to its customers. To sense the knowledge it needs, ARM has one hundred people situated full-time in customers' firms all over the world and not only customers, but also customer's customers. The magnet they use to bring this knowledge together for innovation is their product platform. We found, however, that breakthrough innovations were more likely to emerge when a lead customer performed the role of magnet. This was largely because the platform architecture typically imposed limits on the extent of innovation.

The use of repeatable innovation activity as the magnet worked best when it was possible to specify, in advance, the activities required to innovate. A good example is the record company, Polygram Records, now part of Universal Music Group. It built a dedicated organization charged with the activity of identifying future high-potential artists from local talent in the bars and clubs of cities like Sao Paolo, Reykjavik, Naples, Paris, Athens and Hong Kong and connected this new talent with Polygram's knowledge of international music markets and capabilities in creating, promoting and distributing new albums in markets around the world, to produce a stream of innovative hit records. Two immediate successes came from the marketing of Latin American stars to the Spanish-speaking population in the US, and by creating a market for Cantonese pop (or 'Canto') among the 60 to 100 million Chinese expatriates in the world. One of Polygram's most famous artists is Björk – a young female talent the company sourced in Iceland and helped develop into a global winner. The uniquely innovative strategy of identifying and developing musical talent and knowledge from unexpected locations proved critical to building the world's largest record company, which netted its owners a sale price of more than $10 billion.

Linking the Nodes of the Ecosystem

Consider the types of knowledge dispersed around the globe that ST has to bring together as part of its 'system on a chip' HDD project shown in

The digital business ecosystem

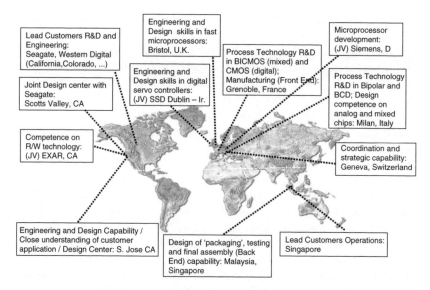

The following labels appear on the map:

- Lead Customers R&D and Engineering: Seagate, Western Digital (California, Colorado, ...)
- Joint Design center with Seagate: Scotts Valley, CA
- Competence on R/W technology: (JV) EXAR, CA
- Engineering and Design skills in fast microprocessors: Bristol, U.K.
- Engineering and Design skills in digital servo controllers: (JV) SSD Dublin – Ir.
- Process Technology R&D in BICMOS (mixed) and CMOS (digital); Manufacturing (Front End): Grenoble, France
- Microprocessor development: (JV) Siemens, D
- Process Technology R&D in Bipolar and BCD; Design competence on analog and mixed chips: Milan, Italy
- Coordination and strategic capability: Geneva, Switzerland
- Engineering and Design Capability / Close understanding of customer application / Design Center: S. Jose CA
- Design of 'packaging', testing and final assembly (Back End) capability: Malaysia, Singapore
- Lead Customers Operations: Singapore

Figure 4.2   Dispersion of different types of knowledge in ST's HDD project

Figure 4.2. For some types of knowledge – that which can easily be codified and readily interpreted even by those working in a different context far away from its source – mobilization is relatively easy. Technical blueprints or patents are a case in point: the knowledge they represent has been highly codified in a language that enables the message to be readily and unambiguously transferred to engineers or scientists with similar training, even if they are working in another corner of the globe. Other types of knowledge are easily mobilized because they can be embodied in machinery or equipment that can be physically transported. In the terminology of knowledge management, these types of knowledge are labelled 'simple' because they are easy to move (despite the fact that they are often incomprehensible to a lay person).

Much of the knowledge that is potentially most valuable for innovation, however, will have characteristics that make it very difficult to move, especially when the recipients who need to use it do not understand the local context in which the knowledge was originally generated. Imagine asking a Japanese car designer sitting in Nagoya to design an innovative vehicle that would perform well and be fun to drive on a German autobahn in the winter at high speed (Baumard 1999). You could provide the engineer with a mountain of reports concerning the behaviour of German car buyers, he could collect plenty of competitor data through the Internet, you could supply him with a wealth of technical data on alternative components from transmissions to braking systems. But would the transfer of all this sort of knowledge make you confident that the designer would come up with a winning innovation? Probably not! This is because, despite modern IT and communications technologies, key elements of knowledge required to do the design job would have been left behind in Germany – such as the behaviour of other drivers on the autobahn and what it feels like to be driving on a snow-covered road at high speed for considerable distances.

It would be very difficult to move this second category of knowledge to Japan in such a way that a local designer could successfully work with it. To really understand, you would need to experience driving a car in the context of a winter autobahn with German traffic. Even the experience of a test track in Nagoya with simulated snow would not come close to achieving a real appreciation of the market needs and how different technologies might perform in the German environment. We refer to this kind of tacit, context-dependent knowledge as 'complex', because it is difficult to move across the world.

Most innovation projects will require a combination of some knowledge that is simple to move and other pieces that are extremely complex to mobilize. To make a metanational innovation process work, therefore, will demand a mix of mobilization strategies. This means that while digital communications technologies can play an important role in connecting the nodes of an innovation network, this role is largely confined to knowledge which can be easily codified and that has only a low likelihood of misinterpretation when taken out of context. Clearly, the digital highways need to be augmented with other channels if a metanational ecosystem is to work effectively. One approach to finding the right ways to mobilize differently the types of knowledge required to make an innovation project fly is outlined in Figure 4.3. The starting point is to rate both the market and technological knowledge your innovation project needs to draw upon on a scale of complexity: from knowledge that can be readily codified and reliably interpreted by those working in the context of a different location, right through to knowledge that is tacit and difficult to interpret properly once taken out of context (Argyres 1999).

If both the required technology and the market understanding score low on the scale of complexity, the knowledge can be mobilized for innovation using IT and digital communications tools; the innovation team can interact with the various locations supplying knowledge at 'arms length' (the lower-left quadrant of Figure 4.3).

When the success of the innovation project is likely to depend on utilizing market knowledge that is high on the scale of complexity (such as a subtle understanding of customer behaviour), but technical knowledge required is readily codified, then it makes sense to locate your innovation

High	Move information about the technology to where the market knowledge is	Move knowledge by rotating people and by temporary co-location
Complexity of market knowledge	Exchange information ('arms length', digital transfer sufficient)	Move information about the market to where the technology is.
Low		

Low	*High*

**Complexity of
technological knowledge**

Figure 4.3   *Choosing appropriate channels to connect the nodes of a metanational ecosystem*

team near the key market knowledge (where they can experience the local context first hand). The technological knowledge, being much more readily mobile, can then be piped in (the upper-left quadrant of Figure 4.3).

By contrast, when the technological knowledge required to innovate is more 'black art' than science and procedure or requires spontaneous and close interaction with suppliers, universities or other local partners, but the necessary market knowledge can be fairly well represented through data and research reports, then the innovation team should spend most of its time working in the clusters from which the technology originates (the lower right quadrant of Figure 4.3).

Finally when both the market and technological knowledge required to innovate score high on the complexity scale, pockets of knowledge dispersed around the world will need to be mobilized by moving people (the upper-right quadrant of Figure 4.3). This was the situation that ST faced in designing its innovative 'system on a chip' to control Seagate's HDDs. The technological knowledge was in the heads of engineers scattered between multiple locations, while the 'market knowledge' (in this case knowledge about the performance requirements of each specific component and activity within an HDD necessary to create a fast and reliable final product) was part of the black art mastered by engineers in different Seagate sites. Mobilizing this set of knowledge involved forming a virtual innovation team with members working face-to-face for short periods to exchange knowledge that was otherwise difficult to move, before returning to various places dotted around the world where they could draw on specific types of local knowledge to push the project forward. ST recognized that simply bringing the innovation team together to work in one location would not have been effective, as divorced from the local context of the know-how they were meant to contribute, members of the team would have been proverbial 'fish out of water'.

In the examples that we researched we found that it was almost always necessary to bring key members of the magnet team together in one place to develop an initial knowledge architecture. In this early, 'creative' phase where most innovations remained uncertain and the respective knowledge required was unclear, melding by co-location of key individuals was required. As these meetings unfold, key members of the magnet team get to know each other personally, which enhances interpersonal trust and the effectiveness of technology-mediated communication later on. This process sometimes takes days, and sometimes weeks, of working together. Subjecting the innovation process to the tyranny of distance at this early stage is likely to end in failure.

Once the initial knowledge architecture has been agreed, there are advantages in dividing tasks among the magnet team. First, those with complex knowledge that is deeply embedded in a local context are likely to be more effective if they work together back in that local environment. Second, dividing into sub-teams that can work in parallel has the advantage of minimizing the amount of knowledge to be transferred between geographically dispersed locations. This is because only the knowledge that pertains to the interface between the modules needs to be passed across the world between teams.

Where the magnet was a global lead customer, we observed that fairly continuous rounds of face-to-face interaction were required throughout the entire process. Travel costs were generally high.

Where the magnet was a global platform, the melding problem can be effectively simplified by dividing into sub-teams which focus on a particular module within the knowledge architecture (such as producing the GPS module for a car navigation system).

Where the magnet is a global activity, the melding problem is best divided into a sequence of steps, with different team members assigned to work on each step. Consistency through the entire innovation process then needs to be assured by a single champion (such as the representative in charge of international repertoire in Polygram) or by designing 'rolling' teams where some members join and others retire during the process.

Once an innovative solution for a lead customer, a new product or service platform, or an innovative product variant (such as a potential hit record) has been created, its profit potential must be realized. This means transferring it to the day-to-day operations that can scale up the supply chain, improve efficiencies, make incremental improvements and engineer local adaptations necessary to leverage the innovation profitably. To reap the fruits of metanational advantage a company clearly needs a strong network of international subsidiaries capable of producing and selling the fruits of the innovation layers of the ecosystem. This part of the ecosystem is obviously a critical component and it is also where most assets and people are engaged. But given that it already forms the 'bread and butter' of multinationals' global operations, it is not the subject for detailed discussion here.

CHINA'S EMERGING DRAGONS AND METANATIONAL ADVANTAGE

It may seem paradoxical that one of the sets of companies that is most enthusiastically adopting this advanced, metanational form of ecosystem is the Chinese companies (often called the Emerging Dragons) that are starting to make their presence felt on the global scene (De Trenck 2000, Wai-Chung and Olds 2000). Part of the reason, however, is that they can more easily escape the legacy burdens, ranging from mindsets to existing asset bases, which can often impede established multinationals from taking advantage of this new way of harnessing the value of global knowledge diversity.

This development is best illustrated by a couple of actual examples. One of the most striking is the Pearl River Piano Group. To most of us, China and piano making may seem an unlikely combination. After all, the pianoforte, to use its full name, has quintessentially European roots. The first line of Pearl River's website acknowledges as much: 'If you have not heard of us' it reads, 'it may surprise you to know that we are a formidable competitor in the world piano market and we are growing fast'. In fact, with a capacity to produce 100 000 pianos per year, Pearl River is the world's largest manufacturer of pianos. As well as a 50 per cent share of the Chinese market it exports to 70 countries and since entering the US market in 1999 it has won a 15 per cent share. In upright pianos Pearl River's US market share is a staggering 40 per cent. It also makes baby grand pianos, along with a full-sized grand piano, both marketed under Pearl River's Ritmüller and Rudisheimer brands that it acquired from Germany.

A piano has 8000 components and 300 processing steps, and takes more than 200 hours of skilled labour to make. Before Pearl River appeared on the scene, 60 per cent of pianos were still largely handmade (80 per cent of high-end models were hand crafted). So how did a Chinese company master the arcane art of piano making, let alone build the capabilities to become a world leader in the business? The answer, in large part, is through building a metanational ecosystem.

The Pearl River Piano Group was actually established back in 1956 in the southern city of Guangzhou (know in the West as Canton). For decades it was just another Chinese state-owned enterprise. But in the early 1990s, as China's modernization gathered pace, Pearl River became aware that it was only earning one third the price for its pianos in China as foreign piano makers. It also came to the painful realization that its quality was, quite simply, dire.

With piano making hardly top of the priority list for government support, Pearl River's CEO, Mr Tong, recognized that he would have to upgrade. His first step was to search the world for expertise. His first hire was Charles Corey, former general manager of American Wurlitzer Piano's plant. Corey's background had been in quality control and he was regarded as a world expert. As Pearl River's first foreign consultant, he ended up working with the company for more than ten years, helping them, as Tong puts it: 'overcome dozens of technological problems'. In 1993 Pearl River hired two German experts to assist in improving the quality of their tuning process. The quality improvements they achieved allowed Pearl River to raise prices by 10 per cent. Over time, the company hired more than ten world-class consultants to assist in improving every aspect of piano making from design, through production to the final finish. Looking back, Tong observed: 'Without the help and guidance of these foreign experts there are some obstacles in piano making that we probably wouldn't have solved by ourselves in a life time!'

Despite China's low labour costs and his newly acquired knowledge of craftsmanship, Tong believed he would have to develop other layers of capabilities in order to succeed in the global market. The next capability he targeted was automated mass production. Here the acknowledged global experts were the Japanese. In 1995 Pearl River entered into a joint venture with Yamaha to invest $10 million in a state-of-the-art piano factory in Guangzhou. Yamaha announced that the joint venture was part of a two-pronged strategy to secure its foothold in the growing Chinese market and to provide a source of competitively-priced pianos that Yamaha could sell throughout the world. Under the terms of the joint venture, Yamaha would take 60 per cent of the output with the balance going to Pearl River. By 2000 the 200 000 square foot factory was producing 9000 pianos per year.

Having absorbed the application of automated, mass production technology to the problem of making pianos first hand over nearly five years, Pearl River brought its own sister plant on stream. The main difference: covering over three million square feet, with a capacity of 100 000 pianos per year, it was more than ten times the size of the joint venture facility operated with Yamaha.

Pearl River then turned its attention to timber processing, a critical stage in determining the ultimate quality of a piano. Working with the Guangzhou

Energy Research Institute of the Chinese Academy of Sciences it launched a major research project aimed at better understanding the science of drying timber. This resulted in proprietary technology that Pearl River used to develop state-of-the-art, computer-controlled kilns that significantly increase the quality of lumber used in the company's pianos and the introduction of climate control to ensure uniform conditions throughout the entire production process.

Through its dedicated campaign to build a metanational ecosystem, combined with large-scale investment and its own R&D, Pearl River had mastered the capabilities to become world class and, as Tong puts it: turn basic stuff into perfect products. It now makes 70 different models of piano – a product range unmatched by any of its competitors. In 2004 Pearl River decided to try to repeat this success in the market for guitars. One year later, it was producing 500 000 guitars annually. Its next target: the market for violins.

A second example is China's Chery Auto whose slogan sums up its goal of building a metanational ecosystem: 'Learn cost control from the Japanese, craziness from the Koreans, keen pursuit of technology from the Germans and market manoeuvres from the Americans'.

Chery got started down this path through knowledge spillovers from the joint ventures (JVs) between Chinese and foreign automakers such as the JV between Volkswagen and First Autoworks, makers of the popular Jetta brand in China. Chery's current CEO, Yin Tongyao, had 12 years' experience as the general manager of the assembly plant that produced the Jetta. When Chery was planning its first car, the Fengyun, in 1995 it modelled the chassis after the Jetta. The company took the decision to leverage the knowledge of suppliers in China to contract out those elements of a vehicle that it was difficult or uneconomic to produce. As Yin observed: 'We are very clear about what we can do and what we can't, and who to look to [as suppliers] when we can't'. Not surprisingly the component suppliers it leveraged were the same ones that had been nurtured by the global auto companies' JVs in China – a fact testified to by the bitter dispute between Chery and Volkswagen's other major joint venture in China, Shanghai VW, over shared suppliers. And as Volkswagen sought to leverage its global reach by centralizing the R&D in Germany, thereby offering early retirement to many of the engineers and technicians in its Chinese JVs, Chery promptly hired them.

Chery's Fengyun model was launched at two-thirds the price of the comparable Jetta. It was an instant success in the Chinese market, where many prospective buyers struggled to scrape together the funds to afford even a basic car. But Chery was aware that as competition in the market hotted up, it would have to sell on more than price alone. Its next step was to try to gain the ability to design attention-grabbing cars that set it apart from the competition. Chery therefore hired Italian design houses Bertone and Pinintarina along with other European and Japanese design firms to work on some of its new models. With stagnant demand in Europe, these design houses see exploiting their skills in China as their future. One third of Pinintarina's sales come from China. Tacit knowledge and experience that it takes years to build in high value areas like design used to be the sole preserve for established multinational companies. But in today's open global economy emerging dragons like Chery too can access those capabilities; there is no shortage of people willing to sell their experience – especially to a market of Chinese customers that is doubling in size year on year.

Another aspect of Chery's metanational ecosystem is to hire international experts directly into the ranks of its staff. At its research institute, 12 of the engineers were headhunted from Daewoo Motor. Its director, with a PhD from a US university and eight years' experience in Japan, is a Chinese returnee from Ford in America – recruited on one of Chery Human Resource Director's many trips to Detroit, where he regularly scouts for experienced talent who understandably wonder about their career prospects in the ailing auto capital and are seeking new frontiers. The head of cost management at Chery, meanwhile, is a German national who worked for Volkswagen – a company widely credited as being the best in the business at squeezing out excess costs – for 39 years. In total Chery has 20 foreign experts on its full-time research staff and dozens more foreign retirees on consulting contracts working on improvements at every stage of its assembly lines.

Other parts of Chery's ecosystem have been put in place through acquisitions of assets or companies. Chery got its start in engine technology by buying the equipment from a plant closed by Ford in the United Kingdom. Then in 2002 Chery launched an engine improvement project with the Austrian engineering company, AVL. Together they developed 18 different engines ranging from three cylinders to V8s and from a 0.8 litre gasoline engine to a four-litre diesel. All these designs meet the stringent Euro IV emissions standards. With the new technology in hand, Chery then invested $350 million in a new engine factory with capacity to produce 500 000 engines per year. The new plant's staff included 200 engineers, with individuals from eight countries across Europe, the Americas and Asia.

Meanwhile Chery has formed a joint venture with a leading Taiwanese company to manufacture moulds used in the pressing stages of automobile manufacture; its end goal: to develop proprietary technology for mould making. Another joint venture with an international partner aims to develop proprietary technology to manufacture transmissions.

By building an ecosystem capable of harnessing diverse knowledge around the world that comprises acquisitions, contracting international suppliers and designers, hiring foreign experts and establishing international joint ventures, along with complementary commitments to its own substantial R&D programme, Chery is relentlessly climbing the staircase towards a world-class capability set in the auto industry. Once in place, its next horizon will be the creation of an international brand, which it displayed at the Detroit Auto Show in 2005 and plans to launch in the US by 2007.

Pearl River and Chery are far from unique. More and more Chinese companies are systematically harnessing the diversity of global knowledge by building a metanational ecosystem to extend their sources of advantage beyond simply lower costs as they seek to develop as significant players in the global market (Williamson and Zeng 2003, 2004).[2]

CONCLUSIONS

The benefits gained by globalizing supply chains – lower costs and access to new inputs unavailable at home – have been immense. Globalization of the innovation process, meanwhile, has lagged behind. Yet competitive advantages gained by those companies that have taken steps toward globalizing their innovation activities have been every bit as impressive. By building an ecosystem that can harness the diversity of potentially relevant knowledge scattered around the world, these metanational innovators have been able to create more, higher-value innovation.

Building such an ecosystem obviously is not easy: it requires commitment to creating structures and processes capable of effectively prospecting the world for new sources of technology and novel market insight, establishing the right knowledge footprint to feed innovation in the company, and careful attention to mechanisms and organizational forms through which dispersed knowledge can be mobilized and integrated. Digital technology can play an important role in providing some of the connective tissue within a metanational ecosystem, but while it is necessary to help connect dispersed and differentiated knowledge, it is far from sufficient as a mechanism. Careful movement of people will still be required to make the ecosystem function effectively.

For many companies, building a metanational ecosystem also calls for a change in mindset. Most multinationals succeeded overseas by 'thinking global, acting local' – adapting products and services perfected at home to the differing needs of local markets around the world. But globalizing innovation requires the opposite mindset: 'thinking local, acting global' because to be effective metanational innovators, managers throughout the ecosystem need to ask themselves continually 'what distinctive knowledge do I see in this local cluster?' and 'how can it contribute to our global innovation effort?' Building an ecosystem capable of harnessing the diversity of global knowledge rather than seeing diversity as a costly impediment to global expansion, will require a different type of innovation process, organization and management. But the potential size of the prize, and the speed with which emerging competitors from the likes of China are adopting this strategy, means that more and more managers should be asking themselves how to equip their company for just this task.

NOTES

1. The core ideas on which this chapter is based are to be found in Doz *et al.* (2001) and the Web site www.metanational.net.
2. The rise of Chinese companies and their strategies is explored more fully in Zeng and Williamson (2006).

REFERENCES

Argyres, N.S. (1999), 'The impact of information technology on coordination: evidence from the B-2 "Stealth" bomber', *Organization Science*, **10** (2), 162–180.

Bartlett, C.A. and S. Ghoshal (1989), *Managing across Borders*, Boston, MA: Harvard Business School Press.

Baumard, P. (1999), *Tacit Knowledge in Organizations*, London: Sage.

Cantwell, J. (1998), 'The globalisation of technology: what remains of the product cycle model?' Chapter 12 in A. Chandler Jr. and L. Hannah (eds), *The Dynamic Firm*, Oxford: Oxford University Press, pp. 182–194.

Caves, R.E. (1996), *Multinational Firms and Economic Analysis*, 2nd edition, Cambridge: Cambridge University Press.

De Trenck, C. (2000), *Red Chips and the Globalisation of China's Enterprises*, Hong Kong: Asia 2000.

Doz, Y., J. Santos and P. Williamson (2001), *From Global to Metanational: How Companies Win in the Knowledge Economy*, Boston, MA: Harvard Business School Press.

Dunning, J.H. (1996), 'The geographical sources of competitivess of firms: some results from a new survey', *Transnational Corporations*, **5** (3), 12–23.

Hu, Y.S. (1992), 'Global or stateless corporations are national firms with international operations', *California Management Review*, **34** (2), 107–126.

Johanssen, J. and J.E. Vahlne (1977), 'The internationalisation process of the firm – a model of knowledge development and increasing foreign market commitments', *Journal of International Business Studies*, **8** (1), 23–32.

Kogut, B. (ed.) (1993), *Country Competitiveness: Technology and the Organizing of Work*, New York: Oxford University Press.

Kogut, B. and U. Zander (1993), 'Knowledge of the firm and the evolutionary theory of the multinational corporation', *Journal of International Business Studies*, **24** (4), 625–646.

Kuermmele, W. (1997), 'Building effective R&D capabilities abroad', *Harvard Business Review*, March–April, 61–70.
Stopford, J.M. (1995), 'Competing globally for resources', *Transnational Corporations*, **4** (2), 268–281.
Szulanski, G. (1997), 'Exploring internal stickiness', *Strategic Management Journal*, **17** (Special Issue), 27–44.
Vernon, R. (1966), 'International investment and international trade in the product life cycle', *Quarterly Journal of Economics*, **80**, 190–207.
Vernon, R. (1979), 'The product life cycle hypothesis in a new international environment', *Oxford Bulletin of Economics and Statistics*, **41** (November), 255–267.
Wai-Chung, H. and K. Olds (eds) (2000), *Globalization of Chinese Business Firms*, London: Macmillan Press.
Williamson, P.J. and M. Zeng (2003), 'China's hidden dragons', *Harvard Business Review*, October, 92–99.
Williamson, P.J. and M. Zeng (2004), 'Strategies for competing in a changed China', *MIT Sloan Management Review*, **45** (4), 85–92.
Zeng, M. and P.J. Williamson (2006), *Dragons at your Door: How Chinese Companies will Disrupt Global Competition*, Boston, MA: Harvard Business School Press.

PART III

Empirical studies on digital business ecosystems

5. Network of relationships in the Indian software industry: a novel business ecosystem?

J. Ramachandran and Sourav Mukherji

INTRODUCTION

Over the last decade, the Indian software services industry has grown at a phenomenal rate of 40 per cent. From a few hundred million in 1994–95, Indian firms exported software worth US$ 14 billion in the fiscal year of 2004. This success, especially coming from an emerging economy with little experience of export or globalization, has met with a lot of attention from popular press and management scholars. Many of them have tried to analyse the reasons behind such growth of the industry, either ascribing it to the demand for software all over the world because of increasing digitization in products, or to certain country-specific advantages that India enjoys, such as availability of a large pool of English speaking engineering graduates at a cost that is nearly a third of that prevailing in developed nations.

While the aforementioned factors contributed significantly to its success and growth, they are not sufficient explanations for the rapid scaling up that has been witnessed in this industry. Unlike software products, creation and delivery of software services is people-intensive. The organizational challenges of scaling up people-intensive operations are not trivial. On an earlier occasion, we have argued that rapid scaling up, as has been witnessed in the Indian software service industry, was a consequence of several managerial and organizational innovations (Mukherji and Ramachandran 2004). The software service firms created a unique governance structure, intermediate between a market and a hierarchy that facilitated customer acquisition and fuelled business growth from each customer account. Over a period of time, the value proposition of the software service providers evolved from 'resource augmentation' to superior resource leverage as well as risk diversification. In this particular chapter, we move from individual firm-level strategies and managerial innovations to analysing the collective behaviour of the industry. We explore whether the success of the industry can also be explained as a consequence of the network of relationships that emerged between the software service firms and other related industries.

Scholars have ascribed the success of organizations like Microsoft, Wal-Mart and IBM to their ability to create, manage and evolve a powerful network of business relationships. These firms organized their business networks into a powerful force by offering platforms on which others could build. These 'lead firms' emphasized the collective property of their business networks, rather than focusing exclusively on their individual profitability and spent considerable resources on orchestrating the network of relationships that exist among diverse firms within and across industries. Other firms, the 'niche players', make investments to leverage these platforms created by lead players to achieve high levels of productivity, resilience and innovativeness in the face of environmental shocks and turbulence. Lead firms like Microsoft or Wal-Mart are therefore conceptualized as the creator and nurturer of 'business ecosystems' (Iansiti and Levin 2004, Moore 1993) – an ideal organizational form for survival and rapid growth in a dynamic and competitive landscape. Analogous to natural ecosystems, business ecosystems are characterized by 'interconnectedness' and 'shared fate' among organizations that are diverse in nature, a structural property that contributes to their collective productivity and robustness.

The network of relationships among diverse firms and institutions that is witnessed in the Indian software industry leads us to conceptualize this industry as a 'business ecosystem'. Such relationships have led to the emergence of a collective robustness and resilience that far exceeds the capability or business acumen of individual players. In the following sections, we will analyse first the structural features and then the outcome measures of a successful business ecosystem that we argue is the Indian software services industry.

THE INDIAN SOFTWARE INDUSTRY AS A BUSINESS ECOSYSTEM

The structural features that characterize a business ecosystem are a web of interconnections between firms leading to 'shared fate' or interdependence, and diversity among the firms. The diversity of the Indian software services industry is borne out by the fact that most of the large service providers have a diverse set of clients and, as a consequence, are involved in developing a diverse range of software applications. The service portfolio of Wipro Technologies, a leading player in the industry, which caters to seven major business verticals, is a typical example, where their share of revenue from each of these industry verticals ranges between 17 per cent and 7 per cent, indicating a low degree of industry specialization. Wipro's case is even more interesting because historically, Wipro earned a significant portion of revenue by providing research and development services to global majors in the telecommunication industry. However, about five years ago, Wipro made a conscious decision to diversify its portfolio both in terms of industry domains and type of software services rendered.

Figure 5.1 provides the share of export revenues earned by the industry from multiple business verticals – highlighting the diversity of service provision that is witnessed at a collective level. Such diversity is also evident looking at the share of revenue that is earned from different kinds of software development activities, such as technology-intensive research and development outsourcing at one end of the spectrum or support and training services at the other end (Figure 5.2). Diversity in clientele and nature of services has also resulted in the diversity of revenue models that is witnessed here. While the bulk of the industry started with the 'time and material' model, where the client pays for a certain number of professionals for a defined period of time, regardless of the magnitude of work that the professionals undertook, today there is a large number of projects done on a 'fixed price' basis. Here, the service providers define the price at which they will undertake an assignment and commit to a specific date of delivery. In case of delays, the service provider absorbs the additional cost, as much as they enjoy the benefits if the assignment is completed before time.

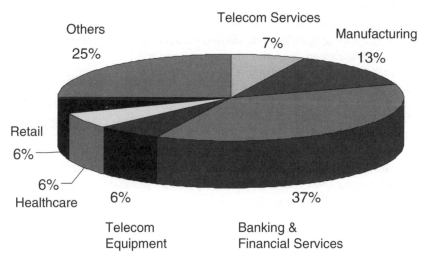

Source: NASSCOM

Figure 5.1   Percentage of software services revenue from different kinds of industries (2003–2004)

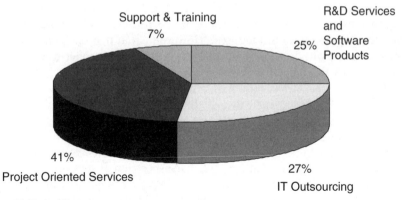

Support & Training
7%

R&D Services
and
Software
Products
25%

25%

41%

Project Oriented Services

- IT Consulting
- System Integration
- Custom Application
- Network Consulting & Integration

27%
IT Outsourcing

Source: NASSCOM

Figure 5.2   Percentage of revenue from different kinds of software services (2003–2004)

Increasingly one finds evidence of a 'risk work model', especially in the R&D outsourcing assignments. The service provider and the client jointly identify an investment opportunity for research in next-generation technology and agree upon a compensation model where both the parties share the profits in case of success with the new product.

For both natural and business ecosystems, diversity has been identified as a key enabler of ecosystem health. Diversity, it is argued, provides ecosystems with a portfolio of innovations and capabilities, which enable them to meet unexpected environmental shocks. Thus, even though individual members of the ecosystem who have not adopted or developed the necessary capability required to endure the environmental shock will perish, there would always be a requisite number of organizations that would possess the capability needed to survive the external shock. Since shocks by definition are unexpected, the coupling of a particular skill with an external shock is an unpredictable or random event. Given an organization's focus on efficiency and achieving 'unity of effort', it becomes very difficult to encourage such diversity within the organization boundary, given the unpredictability of utility of such diversity. The business ecosystem approach provides a way of creating and leveraging such diversity even though the diversity is not confined within the boundary of an organization, but is loosely dispersed within the ecosystem landscape.

As our examples illustrate, there is a high degree of diversity among the clientele, practice areas and business models of the Indian service providers. By catering to a wide variety of industries that are not necessarily correlated with one another, the service providers are able to diversify risks related to manpower requirement much more efficiently than their clients would themselves have been able to do individually. This is akin to mutual fund investors, where diversity in their portfolio provides them with more resilience against market shocks compared to investors focused on particular industries. Thus, diversity acts as a risk mitigator in this ecosystem not by inculcating innovations and creation of novel capabilities, but by the service providers' ability to handle a wide variety of clients and their application requirements with a similar production process and interchangeable skill sets. Under external shocks, business potential from a particular client or industry might deplete, but the diversity of portfolio enables the service provider to deploy the production process and human resources for servicing other clients who are less impacted by such shocks or not impacted at all. This makes the service provider resilient against technology and business volatility. We believe this is an important distinction in the conceptualization of business ecosystems, with respect to utility of diversity. In the context of emerging markets, where organizations rarely have the resources needed for investment in fundamental innovations, they can overcome the lack of technological innovation-led diversity by achieving diversity in their portfolio and thus become resilient to external shocks like the Indian software services industry.

Dense web of relationships and shared fate – the second structural characteristic of ecosystems can be witnessed in the industry at multiple levels. The relationship between clients and service providers in this industry is typically 'many to many'. While each Indian firm has relationships with multiple clients, the clients in turn have relationships with multiple service providers. The case of Nortel Networks can serve as an illustration. Nortel has dedicated software development centres in several Indian software service firms like Tata Consultancy Services, Wipro Technologies, Infosys Technologies and Sasken. Each of these relationships has been maintained for over a decade with the result that some of the core technologies of Nortel products are embedded in these development centres of Indian software service firms. Therefore, Nortel's success, in terms of competing in its markets, is significantly dependent on the competence and delivery capabilities of the Indian service providers. That is one level of shared fate.

Another dimension of this interdependency becomes apparent when we observe the business portfolio of a specific firm, for example Wipro, as an illustration. Wipro has close to 7000 software professionals involved with the development of telecommunication software for its global clients. It has possibly the largest pool of telecommunication software professionals employed by a single firm anywhere in the world. Wipro's client list includes almost all major global telecommunication companies. Therefore, it is possible to argue that the growth and evolution of the global telecommunication industry is, in part, dependent on how Wipro performs; just as Wipro's long-term prospects are determined by the fate of the global telecommunication industry. Industry data suggest that close to 80 per cent of the export revenue comes from repeat business, implying the enduring nature of the relationship between clients and service providers, which results in interdependencies and shared fate.

The third dimension of interdependence is witnessed in the relationship between the educational institutes and the software service firms. A large number of engineering colleges provide this industry with its most important input – skilled software professionals. However, the relationship does not end there – many of these firms have research centres and fund research projects in these engineering colleges and often work collaboratively with the faculty for designing certain course content, such that the students are better prepared to meet the demands of the industry. In summary, one finds the Indian software service industry engaging with a wide variety of industries, both locally and globally. These engagements are typically long-term in nature, leading to the creation and nurturing of a web of complex relationships. While the fate of the software industry, in myriad ways, is dependent on these diverse players, their fate is dependent upon how the Indian software service industry performs – which matches well with the web of interdependencies witnessed in natural ecosystems.

Even if there is similarity in structural features, how does one judge whether the industry is functioning successfully as an ecosystem? This is evaluated from the performance of the system in terms of its 'productivity growth' and 'robustness'. Figure 5.3 shows how the export revenue of the industry has increased more than the increase in number of employees, despite this being a people-intensive service business, which is a clear indication of productivity growth. Industry-wide data on internal cost structure suggest that while there has been a significant increase in employee costs[1] and costs of sales and administration,[2] the industry has managed to improve its operating margins.[3] Given that there has been an increased pressure on service billing rates during the same period due to a downturn in global business prospects in the markets of software service clients, the improvement in operating margins could only have been achieved from an increase in productivity.

The robustness and resilience of the industry is borne out by the fact that this period of rapid growth did witness several external shocks and business volatility. The industry growth was fuelled by one-off lumpy opportunities

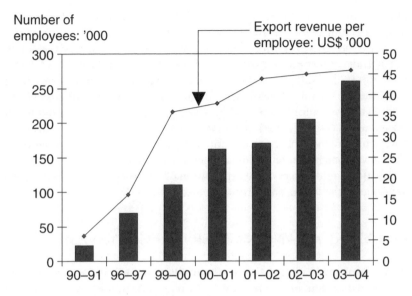

Source: NASSCOM and authors' analysis

Figure 5.3 *Growth in Employees and Export revenues of the Indian
software services industry*

such as the 'Year 2000' problem, or to a lesser extent, the opportunity for
'Euro conversions'. The industry had to cope constantly with the challenge
of smoothing such demand spikes even as they could not afford to let go
such one-off opportunities. This same period witnessed one major slump in
the information technology industry in the form of the 'dot.com bubble' as
well as several shifts in technology paradigms. Moreover, India as a destination faced sanctions from developed nations in terms of visa restrictions
to software professionals and an embargo by government institutions on
outsourcing services to India, because the developed world was concerned
with loss of employment opportunities in home nations as a consequence of
outsourcing.

Thus, the Indian software services industry can be conceptualized as a successful ecosystem. Over the past decade, it has shown rapid growth and
increased productivity in the face of environmental uncertainty. An important reason behind such robust growth, we have argued, has been the dense
web of relationships and diversity that is witnessed in this industry. However,
there is a significant difference in the industry structure from the existing conceptualization of ecosystem, which is the absence of any 'keystone' or industry dominator of the likes of Wal-Mart or Microsoft. In the absence of such
platform creators, it is interesting to find out who or what led to the creation

and development of this ecosystem – a role that has been ascribed to the lead firms in extant literature on business ecosystems. Multinational firms like Texas Instruments (TI), Motorola or GE were the first to identify the potential of India as a source for software services. They were the pioneers in creating the Indian software service industry when they set up fully owned or collaborative software development centres in India in the mid-1980s or early 1990s. However since that time, they have failed to achieve the magnitude of scale and success that the Indian software service providing organizations have achieved, most of which did not even exist when TI or Motorola set up their development centres in India. Their internal focus and logic of vertical integration could be a possible explanation of why they failed to become the keystone of the Indian software services industry.

CATALYST AS AN ENABLER OF ECOSYSTEM

Apart from the keystone, the other variety of organization mentioned in business ecosystem literature is the niche player. As and when the lead firm or the platform creator of the ecosystem decides to make its platform accessible to other firms, the niche player leverages the platform to create specialized products or services. While the niche player gains from accessibility to a privileged resource – the platform – which it would not have been able to create by itself, the platform creator gains from network externalities that are associated with any form of platforms – the greater the number of its users, the more its value to existing users, and as a consequence, the more valuable the platform. The relationship between a platform creator and the niche player is often transactional in nature, where each of them is aggressively pursuing self-interests and hedging against being too dependent on the other. It is not a trust-based collaborative relationship, as is talked about in the literature on network forms of organization, but a loose relationship akin to buyers and suppliers in the market, where the expectation of future transactions differentiates it from pure market forms.

The Indian software industry does not have niche players that match the description provided in business ecosystem literature. While there are pockets of specialization, there is little or no formal interaction between the large and the small players that would have been necessary for the niche players to leverage the platform created by large players. Moreover, the downturn of the global technology industry has adversely affected many of the specialized players, with the result that most players in the industry have diversified their portfolios and have emulated the larger firms in the industry. This has eliminated any formal interdependencies and created a high degree of competition among all players.

However, there are three institutions that have played critical roles in facilitating the development of the industry. They have acted as catalysts for the industry by creating reputation capital on the one hand and creating platforms for collaboration on the other. We define catalysts as those which create value for the ecosystem, but share most or all of the value that they create, rather than appropriating the value for themselves. The business ecosystem literature, possibly because it is focused largely on players from developed economies, does not mention the role that catalysts can play in the development of the ecosystem. Even though institutional mechanisms are sometimes mentioned in network literature, their roles are yet to be well researched (Powell 1990). The three catalytic institutions that played an important part in the growth of the Indian software services industry are the Software Engineering Institute (SEI) of Carnegie Mellon University, the software industry association NASSCOM and international stock exchanges like the New York Stock Exchange (NYSE).

SEICMM and International Stock Exchanges: Catalysts by Default

Carnegie Mellon University's Software Engineering Institute (SEI) came up with an evolutionary improvement path for software development, known as the Capability Maturity Model or SEICMM. It identifies specific practices to be followed during software development in 18 key process areas, which improve the ability of organizations to meet goals for cost, schedule, functionality and product quality (Paulk *et al.* 1993). By carefully managing requirements, using formal inspections on designs and codes and systematically practising risk management, organizations engaged in SEICMM improvement programmes experience significant productivity gains, schedule reduction and reduction in post-release defects (McConnell 1999, Harter *et al.* 2000). It has also converted the software development process, hitherto viewed as a craft form of production, into an engineering discipline amenable to various process control measures. Outsourcing is inherently risky for a client, especially for products like large-scale software applications that are knowledge-intensive and have a lengthy cycle time for production. Software engineering matrices mitigated these risks to a large extent, where the client could maintain control over the process of production even from remote locations. However, over and above reducing the technology risks, SEICMM reduced the perceived business risk that is associated with outsourcing from vendors in India.

Emerging nations from the third world, like India, often suffer from 'liability of origin' risks, implying adverse perceptions in developed markets about products and services from less developed nations due to an unfavourable image of less developed countries in the markets of developed nations (Cordell 1992). Nidumolu and Goodman (1993) describe how India was perceived as a land of conflict and corruption. India is ranked 116 out of 155 countries in terms of 'ease of doing business' by the International Finance Corporation.[4] All these would have made India an undesirable destination for doing business. However, the fact that SEICMM certification came from a renowned institution in the USA – the Carnegie Mellon University – helped to mitigate these risks. Beyond their own assessment of suppliers' ability, and the potential of resorting to contractual clauses in case of poor or non-performance, a third party certification that the supplier has the robust and high-quality internal processes necessary for software production, added to the confidence of the clients.

Recognizing the value of third party certification – especially from reputed institutions – Indian firms embraced the SEI framework, such that today over 95 software services organizations in India, the largest number in the world, have achieved CMM level 5 certification.[5] Moreover, for the Indian organizations the journey towards high-quality processes has continued beyond CMM level 5, to the extent that today many of them have obtained People CMM (PCMM), CMM integrated (CMMi) and Six Sigma certifications, ahead of software developing organizations from other parts of the globe. These new certifications extend quality standards to a host of other organizational processes, beyond software engineering. This relentless pursuit of quality certification, especially from renowned third party agencies, has enabled Indian service providers to mitigate, to a large extent, the liability of origin risks associated with India.

In March 1999, Infosys Technologies became the first Indian company to be listed on NASDAQ with an offering of over US\$ 2 billion. While the apparent reason for this listing was to raise capital for funding international acquisitions and provide international employees with stock options, the listing was also leveraged to create an international profile for the organization. NASDAQ listing enforced reporting of results according to the US GAAP, which was more rigorous than Indian accounting and reporting practices, thus ensuring an international standard of information disclosure and transparency. In fact, Infosys had started disclosing their results according to the US GAAP three years prior to the listing on NASDAQ to set norms of transparency for the industry and thus to distinguish the software services industry from other traditional industries in India.

Infosys's action was soon followed by other large software service firms like Wipro, so that as of mid-2002, software companies accounted for five out of eleven Indian organizations listed either on the NASDAQ or the NYSE. International listing also ensured that these organizations, as well as the entire Indian software service industry, came within the radar of international technology analysts like IDC and Gartner and investment bankers like Lehman Brothers and Goldman Sachs, all of which started tracking the performance of the industry and listed organizations, and thereby informed existing and potential clients. This has resulted in high visibility and credibility for the Indian software services industry and provides the industry with a cachet of being global and world class.

We view international stock exchanges like the NYSE or NASDAQ as one more critical enabler of the industry. While the primary function of the stock exchange is to be a market maker, rather like the SEICMM, they catalysed the journey of the Indian software industry towards instituting international standards of governance and financial management. If by embracing SEICMM, the industry players had opened up their software development process for external scrutiny and evaluation, listing on the international stock exchanges opened up their corporate governance practices before the global customer and analyst community. It is interesting to note that neither SEICMM nor the stock exchanges were mooted for the purpose to which they were used by the Indian software services industry. The industry, besides making use of their regular functions (quality certification and raising capital respectively) leveraged these institutions to raise the profile of the industry and in the process, overcame the hurdle posed by their liability of origin. Thus, these institutions played a facilitative role in improving the health of the industry, even though their own benefits from the system were marginal. Within the context of the Indian software service industry, they are prime examples of entities that distribute most or all the value they create – a new variety of species in a business ecosystem.

NASSCOM: Catalyst by Design

While SEICMM and the stock exchanges became catalysts by default, there was one more institution that performed a catalytic function by design. NASSCOM, an association of software organizations, was set up as the trade body and chamber of commerce of software and services industry in India. As an industry body, it was the first of its kind in India, set up with the aim of promoting the cause of the industry both at a national and international level, by means of lobbying and engaging in reputation building. Noteworthy among NASSCOM's various activities towards reputation building was a study instituted with international strategy consulting firm McKinsey, which highlighted the unique position of strength of the Indian software exports industry and predicted that the industry could grow to US$ 80 billion by 2008. This provided instant credibility to the industry and helped the software organizations to bid successfully for projects from

Fortune 500 customers, many of whom used McKinsey as their strategy adviser.

But NASSCOM's contributions went beyond the traditional role of industry associations' engagement with lobbying or reputation building. It started systematically compiling information about the industry and its players, which included not only financial performance but also information about the internal processes of the member organizations such as their client portfolios, revenue from different business segments and the quality processes they had instituted. While the information *per se* was valuable for potential clients and partners, NASSCOM also created a platform for exchange of best practices in the process. NASSCOM furthered this cause by organizing periodic seminars on a varied range of topics relevant for the industry. Leaders and the senior management of software service organizations used this forum for exchanging ideas on how to improve the overall health of the industry by learning from one another and presenting a collective face before the external world. While market forces made them fierce competitors in the global outsourcing marketplace, NASSCOM enabled collaboration, often at an informal level, to create an identity at an industry level.

Relationships between individuals and organizations are fundamentally premised on the notion of exchange. Business ecosystems are characterized by webs of loose relationships that exist between interdependent players. There are two kinds of exchange that take place in these relationships – exchange of products and services and exchange of information. It is the quality of information exchanged that distinguishes a market-based transaction between a buyer and supplier from other kinds of relationships found in the ecosystem. Catalysts like NASSCOM and SEI of CMU create value by establishing standards or by becoming platforms of information exchange and knowledge dissemination. This is platform creation of a different kind, compared to the ones created by the keystone. In the case of the Indian software industry, the platform creator does not appropriate anything of significance from the value it creates. This characteristic makes it a much more potent form of platform creator for the ecosystem than the keystones whose role of value sharing is only secondary to that of value appropriation.

CONCLUSION

In this chapter, we analyse the growth of the Indian software services industry from the perspective of an ecosystem. We argue that the industry exhibits all the characteristics of a successful business ecosystem because of the dense web of interrelationships that exist between diverse players – structural features that have contributed significantly to making the industry achieve high rates of growth and productivity in the face of external shocks and environmental uncertainty. However, this industry does not have any dominant player which had led to the creation or development of the ecosystem – a critical difference from the ecosystems that are described in the literature. The closest approximation of such an ecosystem that has no dominator is the open source ecosystem that has developed around the Linux operating system. Yet the open source ecosystem has a grand designer who orchestrates the development and maintenance of the Linux operating system platform. However, what makes the Indian software services ecosystem unique is its absence of either a dominator, or a grand design or a grand designer! Instead, the ecosystem leveraged the power of external and internal institutions to enable rapid growth and create resilience at a collective level. We believe such ecosystems can become a model for creating industries of a global scale and proportion from emerging nations.

NOTES

1. Employee costs as a percentage of revenue have increased from 22 per cent in 2000 to 37 per cent in 2004.
2. SG&A as a percentage of revenue has increased from 20 per cent in 2000 to 22 per cent in 2004. SG&A stands for Selling, General and Administrative Expenses. Income statement item which combines salaries, commissions, and travel expenses for executives and salespeople, advertising costs, and payroll expenses.
3. Operating margins as a percentage of revenue have improved from 20 per cent in 2000 to 24 per cent in 2004.
4. *Doing Business 2006*, Report by International Finance Corporation, 13 September 2005.
5. http://www.nasscom.org accessed on 2 May 2006. Statistics collected by NASSCOM in March 2005.

REFERENCES

Cordell, V.V. (1992), 'Effect of consumer preference for foreign sourced products', *Journal of International Business Studies*, **23** (2), 251–269.

Harter, D.E., M.S. Krishnan and S.A. Slaughter (2000), 'Effects of process maturity on quality, cycle time and effort in software product development', *Management Science*, **46** (4), 451–466.

Iansiti, M. and R. Levin (2004), 'Strategy as ecology', *Harvard Business Review*, March, 68–78.

McConnell, S. (1999), *After the Gold Rush: Creating a True Profession of Software Engineering*, Redmond, WA: Microsoft Press.

Moore, J.F. (1993), 'Predators and prey: a new ecology of competition', *Harvard Business Review*, May–June, 75–86.

Mukherji, S. and J. Ramachandran (2004), 'Complementary and continuous innovations: case of the Indian software industry', *Journal of Academy of Business and Economics*, **4** (1), 211–215.

Nidumolu, S.R. and S.E. Goodman (1993), 'Computing in India: an Asian elephant learning to dance', *Communications of the ACM*, **36** (6), 15–22.

Paulk, M.C., B. Curtis, M.B. Chrissis and C.V. Weber (1993), 'Capability Maturity Model version 1.1', *IEEE Software*, **10** (4), 18–27.

Powell, W.W. (1990), 'Neither markets nor hierarchy: network forms of organizations', *Research in Organizational Behavior*, **12**, 295–336.

6. The growing volatility of the global economy from a complex system perspective

Chuan-Leong Lam

INTRODUCTION

In this chapter, I would like to offer some observations on the properties of complex systems and use these properties to: 1) argue why simple cause-and-effect reasoning cannot adequately handle complex systems; 2) explain why the volatility of the global economy has increased; 3) point out some implications on the process of innovation; and 4) make some conjectures on the limits of the cognitive process and ask whether information technology (IT) can help humans extend their cognitive skills at sense making.

NEWTONIAN–CARTESIAN LOGIC

Over the last 300 years, Newtonian physics and Cartesian logic have been immensely successful in using a cause-and-effect type of reasoning to explain phenomena in the physical world. From the motions of the planetary system to the clever machines around us, the 'laws of physics' prevail marvellously.[1] This has led to an unquestioned assumption that reason holds the key to any phenomenon and its subsequent mastery. In our daily actions, we use this cause-and-effect reasoning implicitly without question. To paraphrase the economist J.M. Keynes ([1953] 1964)[2] we are slaves to the Newtonian–Cartesian logic system.[3]

However, cause-and-effect reasoning is best applied to simpler systems, for example rigid bodies or homogeneous gas or liquid systems. I believe that looking at issues in management or government through the framework of complex systems is more helpful in making better decisions.

COMPLEX SOCIAL SYSTEMS

Social systems are typically complex and have these following characteristics:

1. A network for exchanges amongst its elements (which, in turn, can be complex systems themselves);
2. Elements which are not similar to one another;
3. Interactions amongst the elements are not identical;
4. The elements can be autonomous, for example with human beings;
5. The behaviour of the elements changes with time even if other factors remain the same;
6. Usually, there is a central coordination system;
7. Systems containing humans can 'learn' through a feedback loop;
8. Social systems are nested within or overlapping one another.

The human body is an example of a system of tightly-coupled elements and central coordination of the nervous system. Companies, communities or entire nations can be regarded as complex systems with interconnections amongst the elements. These organizations also have a system of coordination in the form of their leadership ranks.

Complex systems therefore have an internal dynamic, which determines how the system will react to external stimuli. No two complex systems, not even the same system at different times, will necessarily react to the same external causes and produce the same effect.

An analysis based on simple cause and effect will not work without taking these properties into account. Often we confuse co-evolution with causality. That one thing follows another, even on a number of occasions, does not necessarily imply a causal relationship. This is a common logical fallacy.

Internal Properties of Systems

Some observations about complex systems are worth noting. First, systems can fail and die. In the long run, few escape this fate. History is full of companies, cities, countries, dynasties and entire civilizations that have faded away. Second, systems are seldom in equilibrium. The tendency of economics and management science to deal only with the steady state misses out much of the richness of the real world. Third, changes to a system need time to occur because new ideas, knowledge, attitudes and skills have to diffuse throughout the system. The speed of this diffusion, like the half-life of radioactive decay, varies from system to system and can seldom be hurried; it must ripen of itself. Fourth, system changes tend to be sudden or catastrophic rather than gradual. As this seems to contradict the idea of diffusion, let me explain. A new idea needs to diffuse itself through an organization. However, there comes a time when the new idea takes hold and then the system makes a very abrupt change. The collapse of the Soviet Union, the fall of the Berlin Wall, the sudden switch from communism to capitalism in China are examples of such sudden transitions. Fifth, the more complicated a system, the higher is the failure rate. This is because complicated systems have a more elaborate network of exchanges amongst the sub-systems and higher interdependencies. Disturbances to the exchange network or to a specific sub-system can render the system unworkable. I would now like to explore the two implications of complexity on the global economy and the process of innovation.

INFORMATION TECHNOLOGY REVOLUTION

The global economy is a very big and complex system. This short discussion will only touch upon the impact of IT. The IT revolution has extended man's ability to transmit information and control of machines over long distances. For the first time, with IT, human beings can control machines at a distance with greater precision and more 'intelligence' than ever before. One can even send a radio command to a vehicle on Mars to make it perform different actions.

In the past, when one stepped on the brakes of a car, a mechanical system linked the pedal to the brakes at the wheels. Today, this can be done by sending a digital signal to the brakes directly. The brakes can be made more 'intelligent' because sensors can tell if the wheels are locked and, if so, reduce the braking power to prevent skidding. In fact, the *Sunday Times* (Gadher 2005) reported that motorists can subscribe to a service whereby the maximum speed of their vehicles is controlled remotely by a satellite. The satellite will determine the speed of the vehicle and if the driver exceeds that speed, the satellite will override the driver's accelerator. Increasingly, such 'fly by wire' systems will become the means to control sophisticated machinery.

By extending man's ability to transmit information and control of machines over long distances, the IT revolution is as revolutionary as the industrial revolution, which extended human and animal muscle power by means of steam power. With IT and digital control machines, many manu-facturing processes can be highly automated. The consequence is that manufacturing has become more flexible and mobile. Entire production lines can be transferred to distant parts of the world at short notice. The learning time for undertaking complex production processes is shortened because the need to train highly-skilled machinists or craftsmen has diminished. Indeed some electronic components can only be made by machines.

The result is the globalization of manufacturing and one reason for the rapid rise of, for example, China as a manufacturing base. We can call this process the 'democratization' of manufacturing, which was once the exclusive domain of a few industrial powers.

The Spread of Information

The IT revolution has also radically changed the spread of information and knowledge. One can now access an unprecedented volume of information almost instantaneously through the Internet and the many search engines. However, a world tightly coupled through near instantaneous spread of information would be more volatile than a world compartmentalized. We are likely to lurch from one side to another more violently in response to information.

In addition, the ease and low cost of disseminating information due to the use of IT has helped to reduce the diversity of the sources of information. There is a danger that the information base is becoming too narrow. Many of us read the same reports and the same analyses, getting the same advice from the same few sources. This reduction in the diversity of sources of information can be very harmful. James Surowiecki (2004) points out that the best estimate of an outcome would be the aggregated estimate of the crowd as a whole provided that there is sufficient diversity of opinions and a good aggregator. If diversity of information is lost, the accuracy of our estimate or knowledge is reduced.

GLOBAL ECONOMIC VOLATILITY

In short, the global economy, businesses and governments are facing more volatility and risks because:

1. We are more connected through the globalization of business and thereby more interdependent;
2. We have become more specialized and hence more dependent on trade and the various systems supporting trade, for example, the financial and currency systems;
3. We are becoming more dependent on a narrower base of information; and
4. Technology has shrunk distance and time.

Hence, disturbances in any region or to the trading and financial systems can create severe and widespread disturbances. One example is the Asian Currency Crisis in 1997. This crisis spread with incredible speed; only the strongest economies or those whose currency regime was not open (and hence insulated) escaped the adverse effects. Another is the spread of the disease SARS in 2003. Had international travel been less convenient, the spread of the disease would have been slower.

A good example of the higher global interdependency today is China. Barely three decades ago, China's economy did not matter much to the rest of the world. Its goods hardly reached the shores of the advanced nations. Its trade was miniscule. China was not even a member of GATT, the predecessor of the World Trade Organization. Recently, however, the Chairman of the US Federal Reserve warned the US Congress not to impose tariffs on Chinese goods as 'it would lower' the standard of living in the US (*Asian Wall Street Journal* 2005). Such a statement would have been unthinkable just two decades ago. A Chinese oil company's proposal to buy an American one, Unocal, has raised security concerns. Haier, a Chinese electrical appliance maker, is proposing to buy Maytag (Dyer and Politi 2005). If the sale goes through, Haier will have, a 16 per cent share of the US market. This has raised competition issues.[4] Similarly, the exchange rate of the Chinese currency significantly affects global trade. How China handles its foreign reserves will affect the world's currency markets.

Undeniably, globalization has brought positive benefits in efficiency, economies of scale, new skills and new markets. What we need to note is the higher interdependencies that result from this. Business managers can no longer just look at their markets and corporate strategy in isolation. External events and unexpected shocks, which may spring from tiny, obscure sources, can shake their businesses to the core.[5] International events like the inevitable competition for energy, raw materials, markets and jobs between nations must figure in corporate decisions. Conversely, events in the corporate world, such as the collapse of Enron, WorldCom and Long Term Capital Management (LTCM) also have instant, worldwide repercussions.

On a larger scale, we have to ask whether the human system can live in harmony with the other systems on this planet. Can the Earth's resource system supply the ever-increasing demands of the consumer economy? Can it cope with its pollution and waste? Will mankind with its technological prowess drive other species of plant and animals to extinction? Can we prevent the spread of new emergent diseases within a tightly-coupled global system? These are new risks that accompany the globalized system.

INNOVATION

The properties of complex systems are also useful in explaining the advantage of being the first mover in innovation. Very often, the first-mover companies stay in and dominate their markets for a long time. Examples include Daimler-Chrysler and BMW in automobiles, IBM in mainframe computing, Intel in microprocessor technology and Microsoft in operating systems for PCs. Even entire localities and regions show this trait – for example, Silicon Valley in high technology, Switzerland in mechanical watches, New York and London in finance, Milan in fashion and so on.

This observation makes sense if we view innovation as a process of diffusion. Knowledge or creativity in a single person is not enough for a radical innovation to take root. That knowledge and idea must spread throughout the company or a region for the innovation to flourish. A whole ecology of new skills, talent, supplies and knowledge has to grow around the innovation. These factors cannot be acquired in a flash. It takes time for the people in the company or region to take to the idea, learn the new ways to make new things and for the new knowledge and technology to diffuse through the system. This process cannot be hurried.

However, once the first movers have institutionalized their skills and competencies into their system at large, they hold a very powerful advantage. It is very difficult for a challenger to dislodge them through a strategy of imitation or marginal improvements. The reason is that the challenger must also acquire the new skill sets over a period of time. His learning curve cannot be instantaneous, as he too must wait for the diffusion process to work. Meanwhile, the incumbent first mover will have moved further down the learning curve. A more promising way for the challengers is to seek a new idea in order to leapfrog the incumbent and seek a 'new market', as yet untapped. Then he would be the first mover in the new space and at the head of a new learning curve. Similar views can be found in Christensen and Raynor (2003) and Kim and Mauborgne (2005).

Isaac Ben Israel shared with me his observation that many systems are destroyed or transformed when only 20–25 per cent of its elements are destroyed or changed.[6] Innovators know however, how difficult it is to change even 20 per cent in the face of an entrenched, successful system. That is why change is often enforced catastrophically by the death of an existing system. It is highly attractive to think that systems, companies, nations or civilizations will always innovate and thrive. Unfortunately, history is full of dead systems, companies and so on. The process is more like that of Darwinian selection whereby a species less fitted to a particular environment dies out (or is reduced to a very small sample) and is replaced by another better fitted to the prevailing environment.

Schumpeter (1950) put it in more colourful terms. Innovation,[7] he argued, led to gales of 'creative destruction' as innovations caused old inventories, ideas, technologies, skills and equipment to become obsolete. The question, as Schumpeter saw it, was not 'how capitalism administers existing structures . . . [but] how it creates and destroys them'. This creative destruction, he believed, caused continuous progress and improved standards of living for everyone.

Singapore's Experience

At this stage, let me list some examples of innovations in Singapore, many of which were implemented in the 1960s and were contrary to the prevailing doctrines of that period:

1. Establishing a completely open domestic market and open competition, when the prevailing doctrine was one of infant-industry protection and import substitution behind high import tariffs;
2. Welcoming multinational companies when they were then shunned as exploiters of labour;
3. Maintaining an open-skies policy whereby other airlines are freely allowed to fly into Singapore in competition with Singapore Airlines. Not many countries are practising this even now;
4. Government taking an entrepreneurial role in setting up companies which, in turn, are allowed a free hand in their commercial transactions;
5. Implementation of rigorous pollution controls, anti-litter legislation, sophisticated urban planning and traffic management controls;
6. Early adoption of IT in the public and private sectors, which has resulted in a very high rate of IT literacy amongst individuals, companies and the government. Singapore is now ranked consistently amongst the top three countries in the world in terms of e-government and e-readiness in many surveys.

These examples illustrate the advantage of being a first mover in innovation and how the diffusion process through society at large offers a sustaining edge over subsequent followers of the same innovation.

THE PARADOX OF KNOWLEDGE

When it comes to understanding systems involving humans, there is a fundamental contradiction because humans are trying to understand a system of which they are members. In economics, business and human management, each new nugget of wisdom seems always to be replaced soon enough by a new one. For example, Keynesian style fiscal intervention was once thought to have defeated the business cycle. Now many economists think this idea is defunct.

Again and again, some 'solution' or 'key' to business or economic success is touted as the 'secret' of success or excellence. Subsequently, these novel theories are discarded quietly and unceremoniously. Not so long ago, the 'best' corporate strategy was to become a conglomerate. Mergers and acquisitions followed at a frenetic pace. Soon enough, the experts turned around and began to preach the virtues of being small and focused to 'unlock value'. Divestments became popular. This is not surprising if we note that human beings are both elements of the system under study and also the agent studying the system.

This impasse eventually led to Godel's Incompleteness Theorem (1962) which, loosely interpreted, implies that there can never be a last word on any human subject. For human systems, there is a parallel. Once a human being acquires a new insight into the very system of which he is an agent, he will use that new insight to his advantage. In doing so, he would almost certainly alter the properties of the system. This is like Heisenberg's Uncertainty Principle in the sub-atomic, quantum mechanics world where the very observation of a physical property destroys the property. We are caught in a self-contradictory logical loop.

This same conclusion was reached some 2000 years ago by the Chinese philosopher, Lao Tzu, with the cryptic phrase: 'The way that can be expressed cannot be the eternal way' (Lao Tzu, [1982]). My friend Ben Israel also drew my attention to the philosopher Ludwig Wittgenstein, who came to the same conclusion 2000 years later ([1921] 1974):

> 6.54. My propositions are elucidatory in this way: he who understands me finally recognizes them as senseless, when he has climbed out through them, on them, over them. (He must so to speak throw away the ladder, after he has climbed up on it). He must surmount these propositions; then he sees the world rightly.

> 7. Whereof one cannot speak, thereof one must be silent.

Harnessing IT for Sense Making

The use of simple cause and effect reasoning is widespread because it is relatively simple. Complex systems thinking is difficult because of the vast amount of data that has to be processed to make sense. Hence, a) complex systems create information overload; b) randomness and non-linearity create 'rare events', or risks more likely; and c) the incompleteness property implies that the search for answers must lead to more complexity.

Fortunately, much work is being done to harness new methods, including the use of IT for 'sense making' of complex data and systems by, for example, the Cynefin Centre under David Snowden, the company Systems Research and Development under Jeff Jonas, and the Arlington Institute under John Petersen. Their work may one day lead to the use of IT to extend human cognitive and mental processing power to handle very complex issues. It may even lead to an 'intelligence network' linking together the powers of many knowledge centres in the way that grid computing is exploiting the combined computing power of many machines for tasks that are beyond the power of a single computer.

CONCLUSION

To sum up, I would like to make five points:

1. Linear cause-and-effect reasoning is limited when it comes to complex systems. We need to liberate ourselves from the stranglehold of the 'Newtonian–Cartesian only' mindset.
2. The internal dynamics of social systems will determine how they respond to external stimuli. Decision makers have to understand such dynamics to have a chance of achieving their intended business or economic strategies. Merely imitating what others do usually results in failure.
3. Chance plays a very large part in the generation of new ideas. Innovation is not just about new ideas but also the diffusion of those ideas into social systems and their subsequent adoption or rejection. Radical innovation is often like Darwinian selection in that the old order or system dies away rather abruptly and is replaced by a new one.
4. There can never be a final word or 'solution' to issues concerning social systems because of the logical paradox of a human being understanding systems of which he is an element – a dilemma neatly captured in the saying: 'The way that can be told is not the way'.
5. We are seeking new ways of extending human cognitive powers through the use of IT and networks. This could well be the next cognitive revolution, following the trend set by the industrial revolution and the IT revolution.

NOTES

1. There are exceptions in the world of the very small (where quantum theory applies) and the very fast (where relativity applies).
2. Keynes J.M. ([1953] 1964), 'The ideas of economists and political philosophers, both when they are right and when they are wrong, are more powerful than is commonly understood. Indeed the world is ruled by little else. Practical men, who believe themselves to be quite exempt from any intellectual influence, are usually the slaves of some defunct economist.'

3. David Snowden, in the work on the Cynefin Diagram, has pointed out that much of the complex world is beyond simple cause and effect reasoning. See Kurzt and Snowden (2003).
4. Whirlpool subsequently won the bid for Maytag (see Kirchgaessner and Politi 2006).
5. Experts in chaos theory have suggested as an example that, in climatology, the fluttering of a butterfly's wings in one continent might eventually result in a severe hurricane in another, through non-linear effects.
6. Isaac Ben Israel derived mathematically that it takes a change of 25 per cent of the elements to have an 80 per cent probability of causing a system to lose its coherence and transform it. Even a change of 11 per cent of the elements has a 50 per cent chance of transforming the system.
7. Innovation here ranges from simple improvements to truly radical ones and includes the introduction of new means of production, new products and new forms of organization.

REFERENCES

Asian Wall Street Journal (2005), 'Greenspan warns against raising tariffs on China', 24–26 June.

Christensen, C.M. and M.E. Raynor (2003), *The Innovator's Solution*, Boston, MA: Harvard Business School Press.

Dyer, G. and J. Politi (2005), 'Maytag accepts preliminary offer', *Financial Times*, 22 June, p. 25.

Gadher, D. (2005), 'Forget cameras – spy device will cut drivers' speed by satellite', *Sunday Times*, 3 July, p. 4.

Godel, K. (1962), *On Formally Undecidable Propositions of Principia Mathematica and Related Systems* (Translated by B. Meltzer), New York: Basic Books Inc. (Reprinted by Dover Publications, 1992).

Keynes, J.M. (1953), *The General Theory of Employment, Interest and Money*, New York: Harcourt, Brace and Company [First Harvest/Harcourt, Inc. Edition 1964].

Kim, C.W. and R. Mauborgne (2005), *Blue Ocean Strategy*, Boston, MA: Harvard Business School Press.

Kirchgaessner, S. and J. Politi (2006), 'Whirlpool takeover of Maytag approved: Antitrust authorities give green light to $1.7bn deal', *Financial Times*, 30 March, p. 1.

Kurzt, C.F. and D.J. Snowden (2003), 'The new dynamics of strategy: sense-making in a complex and complicated world', *IBM Systems Journal*, **42** (3), 462–483.

Lao Tzu (1982), *Tao Te Ching (The Book of Changes)*, London: Random House (Translated by Gia-Fu Feng and Jane English, Wildwood House Ltd.).

Schumpeter, J. (1950), *Capitalism, Socialism and Democracy*, 3rd edition, New York: Harper.

Surowiecki, J. (2004), *The Wisdom of Crowds*, New York: Doubleday.

Wittgenstein, L. ([1921] 1974), *Tractatus Logico-Philosophicus*, New York: Routledge.

7. China and the new economy: a case of convergence?

Max Boisot and John Child

INTRODUCTION

China finally joined the World Trade Organization (WTO) in January 2002, following ten years of negotiations. The event was interpreted both inside and outside the country as a major step marking China's progress toward becoming a 'normal' open market economy, though reservations have been expressed about how quickly this can be achieved (Garnaut and Song 2002). In particular, the Chinese authorities are sensitive to the need to apply WTO provisions with discretion in order to prevent a major collapse of inefficient state-owned enterprises with the surge in unemployment and social unrest this would trigger (Solinger 2003).

Nevertheless, the prevailing assumption is that under its economic reform programme started in 1979, China has slowly been moving towards a market order that has become progressively more integrated into the global economic system through trading, foreign direct investment, the transfer of best practice and the spread of management education. The progressive development of such integration between economies and between their con-stituent firms is generally accepted as a defining characteristic of 'global-ization' (Dicken 2003). With globalization, more intensive social relations accompany economic integration and these in turn are seen to lead to growing similarities in cultures, behaviour and practices (Steger 2003). China's entry into the WTO is expected to accelerate its economic and social integration with the rest of the world. The hope is that the institutional and regulatory changes China's WTO entry should bring about will make it easier either to compete or to collaborate with Chinese firms. WTO entry has therefore been welcomed as a commitment to developing China's business-relevant institutions according to international norms. Pressures to conform to institutional norms and compete successfully under the same market conditions lead to the assumption that Chinese firms will gradually become more like their Western counterparts (Warner 2003). This process is therefore seen as a major boost to China's convergence with the West, both

in its economic and institutional environment and in the constitution and
behaviour of its firms.

The assumption that China, along with other transition economies, is
converging with the West has been further bolstered by a combination of
political, market and technological changes. Over a decade after the fall of
the Berlin Wall, many see the emergence of a 'new economy' as the
ineluctable technology-driven triumph of a capitalist market order over
competing alternatives.[1] By degrees, they then come to view a market order
as the natural order toward which, unless it is consciously impeded, all economic activity aspires and thus as something that everybody can intuitively
understand. A market order becomes, in effect, one of those taken-for-
granted assumptions that underpin all paradigmatic thinking (Berger and
Luckmann 1966, Kuhn 1962). For both its proponents and its detractors,
globalization and a market order turn out to be two sides of the same coin:
globalization leads to a market order and any move towards a market order
is a move into the global economy.

One variant of the globalization thesis invokes technological determinism as an explanation for the convergence of practices and of consumption
habits (Dicken 2003: Chapter 4). This regards technology as a driver of
convergence, arguing that the spread of modern technologies and the
resulting 'technological imperative' (Harbison and Myers 1959) leads both
firms and consumers in different parts of the world to adopt similar solutions to their respective problems. Evidence of how new information and
communication technologies (ICTs) have been applied has, however, failed
to support the notion of a technological imperative and instead, technology is seen as an enabler that opens up new possibilities without determining the choice between them (Child and Loveridge 1990, Castells 2002).

While China is undoubtedly moving towards a market economy, an
increasing proportion of which has capitalist ownership, this leaves open
the question of what kind of capitalist market economy China is adopting.
In a previous paper (Boisot and Child 1996), we challenged the assumption,
made both by the Chinese authorities themselves and by outside observers,
that China is inexorably moving towards a Western type of market
economy. We hypothesized that the country is moving towards an Asian
type of capitalism that other scholars as well as ourselves have labelled
'network capitalism' (Biggart and Hamilton 1992). This kind of capitalism
is characterized firstly, by a cultural preference for personalized face-to-
face relationships over impersonal relationships and secondly, by smaller
clan-like transactional structures over larger market-like structures.

Yet today, many Western economic actors are also seeking to build these
kinds of personalized networks – in global value chains, in outsourcing, in
strategic alliances, in the transnational firm, in social capital networks and

in trust-based networks (Child 2005). Evidence from surveys conducted in the USA, Europe and Japan suggests that many companies moved in these directions during the 1990s (Pettigrew and Fenton 2000, Pettigrew *et al.* 2003). This is an instance of networks operating in a capitalist fashion. But does it amount to network capitalism? If so, this would be prima facie evidence for the convergence hypothesis, but with convergence now taking place on to a network rather than on a traditional market order. It would imply that both Chinese and Western firms are tending to converge on to a set of 'best practices' that incorporate elements from each cultural region, rather similar to the selective melding of American and Japanese practices that Ouchi (1981) and others were urging 25 years ago.

The developments mentioned above – China's accession to the WTO, the emergence of a new economy based on trade liberalization and advances in ICTs and the huge Western involvement in China's economic development through inward foreign direct investment (FDI) and management education – would seem to support the convergence hypothesis. On the other hand, recent cautions on both technological determinism (for example Castells 2002) and the globalization thesis itself (for example Stiglitz 2002, Rugman 2005) indicate that these variants of the hypothesis are far from commanding universal support. Nor do the divergent institutional practices of developed capitalist countries suggest that convergence is imminent or even inevitable (Whitley 1999). Indeed, Guillen's historical analysis of organizational change in Argentina, South Korea and Spain turns the 'convergence through globalization' hypothesis on its head. For he concludes that global competition obliges countries to exploit their distinctive strengths and that this results in unique development trajectories rather than in convergence (Guillen 2001).

China provides a good case to test for the postulated convergent impacts of the new global economy as well as for the associated hypothesis that new technology is facilitating the process. On the one hand, it has engaged increasingly in international trade and investment and is rapidly acquiring the technological basis for a new economy with fast growth in ICT and telecommunications. On the other hand, it is characterized by a strong culture quite distinctive from that of the West and still preserves many of the institutional structures of a communist state. Both these features might be expected to give rise to a major divergence from Western countries in how business transactions are organized and new technology is used (Child 2000). In short, China provides a good opportunity to examine the convergence hypothesis afresh. Our argument so far suggests that such examination would benefit from an open mind as to the possible co-evolutionary relationships between developments at the macro level and those at the micro (firm) level (Lewin *et al.* 1999). In particular, if there are conflicting implications arising from the 'new economy' and from Chinese cultural embeddedness, these may encourage modes of management and organization that reflect both sets of contextual forces, rather than seeing them converge on to a universal model.

The aim of this chapter is to revisit the convergence debate with particular reference to China. The primary intention is to offer a conceptual advance by clarifying the meaning of the term convergence and by developing propositions on globalization and associated issues. The structure of the chapter is as follows: we first elaborate the problem and relate it to the theoretical literature. We then draw upon an augmented version of a conceptual framework that we used in our previous discussions of the issue: the Information-Space or I-Space.[2] The framework allows us to study agents' information processing and communications strategies as cultural and institutional phenomena. Next, we ground our discussion in empirical material. We then discuss our findings and put forward some propositions. A conclusion follows.

ELABORATING THE ISSUES

The phenomenon of globalization has rekindled the debate on convergence. Its detractors see globalization as a code term for the spread of American cultural practices and values across international borders and the concomitant suppression or extinction of local ones. They decry the elimination of cultural and institutional diversity in favour of 'McWorld' (Barber 2003) and the gradual homogenization of daily life across the globe. Others, by contrast, see the core values and beliefs that underpin cultural differences as irreducible and postulate a reaction to the encroachments of globalization that they label 'the clash of civilizations' (Huntingdon 1996).

The globalization thesis is a direct descendent of Enlightenment thinking concerning the spread of reason and light in a world of superstition and darkness. Marx himself subscribed to a variant of this thesis. His modes of production – specific combinations of forces and relations of production – saw pre-capitalist modes such as slave labour and feudalism giving way to capitalism and eventually to socialism. In Marx's scheme, an ever-expanding international bourgeoisie would sweep away the 'cobwebs of feudalism' and thus unwittingly prepare the ground for an international socialist order (Jessop 1987). Yet this order, in turn, came to be seen as a code term for Soviet domination and was resisted even by promoters of socialist values. In China, for example, the resistance to this variant of the globalization thesis was implicit in the expression 'socialism with Chinese characteristics'.

In discussions of convergence, technology and globalization are both implicitly taken to be drivers of convergence – in Marx's language they are forces of production. Technology offers practical and efficient solutions to shared problems. Globalization speeds up and facilitates communication so that what is thought and practised in one part of the globe can be made instantaneously available in others. When the best solution to a given technological problem emerges, it now spreads rapidly to others who grapple with it. It was not always so. Nineteenth century economic internationalism, for example, was largely based on trade and portfolio investment. At that time, there was little or no transfer of best practice. Contemporary foreign investment, by contrast, is much more direct. Companies actively manage their investment, making it a driver in the convergence process. Chandler showed that the telegraph and the railways brought forth the giant corporation and later the multidivisional structure (Chandler 1962, 1977). Within a short period of time, the organizational forms that made these giant structures possible spread to other countries (Franko 1976). The new economy has accelerated this mimetic trend. It has facilitated the standardization and spread of best practice across international borders and promoted international benchmarking – a stimulus to convergence in modes of management and organization. The internationalization of business and trade – through competition and the spread of best practice, accounting and managerial norms and the institutional technologies of governance – is therefore viewed as a driver of convergence.

And yet, arguably, there is a difference between the dynamics that were in force at the beginning of the twentieth century and those that are in force today. The concept of the technological imperative as a driver of convergence is built around three assumptions: (1) that there is a clearly defined technological efficiency frontier; (2) that only a limited number of technologies are available at the efficiency frontier – that is, there is typically one best way of doing things; and (3) that those who fail to adopt best practices available at the efficiency frontier do not survive – they are selected out. Clearly, to the extent that the technological imperative requires one to give up traditional practices for demonstrably more efficient ones, it is choice reducing. Equally clearly, in an expanding number of industries, technical change regimes have increased the number of different ways that we can produce goods and services, that is, they have been choice expanding rather than choice reducing. In this second scheme, globalization, far from imposing a limited number of solutions that dominate traditional approaches, actually extends the range of technical choices, many of which can be integrated with traditional approaches. The blending of Western and traditional Japanese practices in US-located transplants illustrates this process at work (Abo 1994).

The foregoing points to the possibility that technology can be both an enabler as well as a driver. If drivers lead to convergence, enablers, by expanding the choice set, lead to increasing diversity. In the language of an earlier discourse, drivers lead to increasing integration whereas enablers lead to increasing differentiation (Lawrence and Lorsch 1967). Whereas common technical standards, for example, would appear to act as drivers, the increasing number of technical options made possible through modular approaches to design (Sanchez 2001) act as enablers. The new information and communication technologies (ICT) extend choices and transmit them rapidly across the globe and some at least must be classified as enablers. For example, the UN plan to increase the number of personal computers and Internet access in emerging economies is a potential driver of globalization insofar as it forces the pace of literacy and Western computing practices. However, people in such economies are actually adopting an alternative communications technology much faster, for which literacy is not required – mobile phones (*The Economist* 2005). Mobile phone technology is in this way serving as an enabler of variation because it permits cultures to preserve differentiation, while at the same time enhancing communications. In short, whereas the liberalization of trade and opening of markets can be said to generate a driver of convergence, the part played by technology may also enable divergence to be preserved.

A further consideration is that while convergence, where it occurs, may reflect the influence of drivers, increasingly there is some choice in the way that one responds to drivers – that is, one has interpretative flexibility (Bijker 1987) and this is enabling. Technical change, and even globalization, thus navigate between a driving pole and an enabling one. The concept of the technological imperative focused on the first pole to the exclusion of the second.

Traditional research methodologies have also played a part in occluding the potential importance of enablers. As Ragin points out, in the social sciences, multivariate statistical analysis tends to eliminate systematically the variety that is latent in a variance in favour of the similarities that are latent in a mean (Ragin 1987). Arguably, enablers are more likely to be found in the former and drivers in the latter. In the same spirit, Mohr distinguishes between factorial or variance analysis versus configurational approaches (Mohr 1982). Variance analysis focuses on 'independent' variables as potential predictors of some focal phenomenon. The choice of these is normally guided by hypotheses that take one independent variable at a time. This runs the risk of obscuring exceptional but potentially interesting cases within the broad sweep of analyses based upon correlations and variances within the sample as a whole. Variance analysis is thus subject to certain limitations and tends to be mainly employed with generalized predictive models. Mohr (1982) identifies an alternative approach employing what he terms a 'process design', one that is oriented towards the discovery of the configuration and processes underlying patterns of association and change. Configurational analysis takes a holistic view, asserting that the different aspects of an organization make sense in relation to the whole and cannot be adequately understood in isolation (Meyer *et al.* 1993, Child 2002).

Variance and configurational analyses should be seen as complementary to each other. The first will pick up commonalities in a sample whereas the second will pick up differences. Yet since it is easier to achieve convergence in the values of a few variables than in the configuration of a larger number of variables, an exclusive use of the variance approach is likely to overstate the extent to which two populations are converging, treating any differences between them as so much 'noise' in the data.

The difference that we have just identified between drivers and enablers can be further explored by means of our conceptual framework, the Information-Space or I-Space.

A CONCEPTUAL FRAMEWORK

The I-Space takes the movement and processing of data as its point of departure for analysing computational processes within and between organizations. Data are transmitted and processed by multiple distributed agents who collaborate and compete on the basis of knowledge that they each possess (Carley 1995). The I-Space examines how data flows between intelligent data-processing agents vary as a function of how far such data have been structured and hence converted into information. Following Boisot (1995, 1998), we take data structuring to reflect an intelligent agent's attempts to make good use of limited data processing and transmission resources – that is, to economize on its bounded capacities for cognition and rationality (Williamson 1985). Data structuring consists of two distinct processes: codification and abstraction.

Codification tries to find economic ways of distinguishing between the categories of experience so as to assign phenomena to them speedily. Abstraction tries to economize on the number of categories that actually need to be activated in apprehending a given phenomenon. Codification and abstraction work in tandem to reduce an intelligent agent's data processing load. The positive effect of information structuring on information diffusion can be illustrated by means of a three-dimensional diagram in which we relate codification and abstraction on the one hand to diffusion on the other (Figure 7.1). The curve in the diagram indicates the proportion of some given population that can be reached per unit of time by a message as a function of its degree of codification and abstraction.

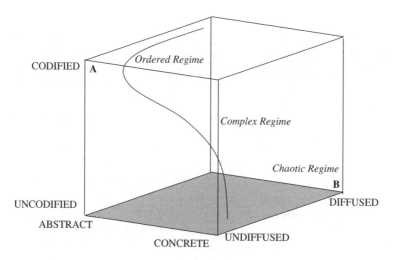

Figure 7.1   The diffusion curve in the I-Space

The I-Space describes a field of forces that creates distinctive informa-tion regimes as a function of the extent to which data are codified, abstract or diffused. Drawing on the literature of complexity theories, we can show that these regimes in varying degrees can be characterized as ordered, complex or chaotic (Boisot and Child 1999). In Figure 7.1, we can identify a region A where information is highly codified, highly abstract and little diffused and where in consequence, complexity will be at a minimum. We can also identify a region B where information is uncodified and concrete, and where diffusion will be at a maximum. In this region, complexity will be at a maximum and things will appear chaotic. In between regions A and B we find regions of varying degrees of complexity in which we hypothe-size that most organizational processes actually take place.

The information regimes to be found in different regions of the I-Space will affect the costs of any social and economic exchange taking place between agents in that region and hence the choice of institutional arrange-ments governing transactions in that region (Coase 1937, Williamson 1975). In Figure 7.2 we identify four generic institutional arrangements – markets, bureaucracies, clans and fiefs – that reflect the possibilities opened up to each by the information environment that they find themselves in. In Table 7.1 we briefly describe the transactional characteristics of each of these institutional arrangements.

A reciprocal relationship exists between these institutional structures and the cultural preferences of a group of agents engaged in recurring transac-tions with each other. Culture, whether taken at the national, industrial,

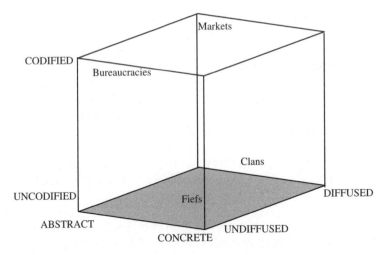

Figure 7.2   Institutions in the I-Space

Table 7.1   Four generic institutional arrangements

BUREAUCRACIES	MARKETS
• Information diffusion limited and under central control • Relationships impersonal and hierarchical • Submission to superordinate goals • Hierarchical coordination • No necessity to share values and beliefs	• Information widely diffused, no control • Relationships impersonal and competitive • No superordinate goals – each one for himself • Horizontal coordination through self-regulation • No necessity to share values and beliefs
FIEFS	**CLANS**
• Information diffusion limited by lack of codification to face-to-face relationship • Relationships personal and hierarchical (feudal/charismatic) • Submission to superordinate goals • Hierarchical coordination • Necessity to share values and beliefs	• Information is diffused but still limited by lack of codification to face-to-face relationships • Relationships personal but non-hierarchical • Goals are shared through a process of negotiation • Horizontal coordination through negotiation • Necessity to share values and beliefs

regional or corporate level, reflects what is shared, with whom, and under what conditions (Boisot 1986). The I-Space allows us to examine the information flows associated with cultural exchange under different assumptions of codification and abstraction.

The convergence hypothesis rests on an assumption that modernization consists of firstly moving up the I-Space through the codification of institutional and cultural practices and then of allowing decentralization to take place towards markets. The question is whether this is the only trajectory on offer. Taking into account the enabling properties of ICT and embedded cultural preferences suggests that variations are certainly possible.

Application of the new technology affects information flows in two ways that must be distinguished from each other:

- A diffusion effect: At any given level of codification or abstraction, it increases the speed and extent of data diffusion within a population of agents – that is, it increases the number of agents who have access to diffused data per unit of time. This effect reflects the dramatic lowering of communication costs over the past two decades and the rapid spread of inexpensive communication devices.
- A bandwidth effect: At any given level of diffusion, new technologies increase the potential volume of data that can flow between agents per unit of time. Data that used to be transmitted parsimoniously by telex can now move by e-mail, with high resolution photographs or video images attached. The bandwidth available has massively increased, and it has done so at an affordable cost.

These two developments have the effect of jointly shifting the diffusion curve downward and towards the right in the I-Space as indicated in Figure 7.3. Taken together, they increase both the reach and the richness of information flows (Evans and Wurster 2000)[3] while significantly increasing the computational capacity of transacting agents. As can be seen from Figure 7.3, the curve shift brought about by the ICTs of the new economy, by increasing the general availability of information within a target population, has the effect of increasing the relative costs of transacting in the ordered regime while simultaneously lowering the relative costs of operating in the complexity regime at the edge of chaos. Recast in institutional terms and as indicated by the horizontal and downward pointing arrows of Figure 7.3, the new economy appears to favour market and clan forms of governance over fief and bureaucratic ones. The horizontal component of the curve shift – expressing the diffusion effect and labelled D – by forcing information sharing and greater transparency, acts as a driver. The downward component of the curve shift, however – expressing the bandwidth

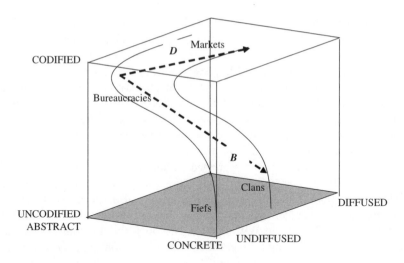

Figure 7.3   ICTs in the I-space

effect and labelled B – by expanding bandwidth and hence communicative choices, acts like an enabler.

The new technologies therefore sustain the viability of either a market or a clan form of governance or combinations of the two. They extend the range of strategic choice. If it is the case that the Chinese, and quite possibly other East Asians, have a culturally-informed preference for network capitalism rather than the pure market variant, then the question arises whether the availability of this choice is likely to sustain divergence between their modes of organization and those conventionally adopted in the West. At the same time, does the adoption by some Western firms of new organizational forms, including network ones, act in the opposite direction – to close the gap? We turn to these questions by reference to insights from empirical studies.

TRENDS IN WESTERN AND CHINESE BUSINESS PROCESSES

The Western Case

The shift in the diffusion curve of Figure 7.3 in a Western economic envir-onment is expected to reinforce both market and clan processes. Much of the discussion surrounding the application of ICT has been expressed in terms of a shift from hierarchical to market transactions, hence the popularity of organizational descriptors such as 'post-bureaucratic' and 'post-modern' (Clegg 1990). ICT has been used to reinforce market processes through the use of e-commerce and through furnishing the infrastructure for the de-structuring of composite hierarchical firms into outsourced and network value-adding systems (Child 2005).

The metamorphosis of unitary, bureaucratic firms into 'virtual' networked alternatives based on a combination of market contracting and ICT (information and communication technologies) has become a serious proposition. Dell Computers and some other companies successfully competing on the basis of speedy response to bespoke customer requirements under highly competitive conditions, have progressed a long way down the road to virtuality (Dell 2000). The 'dot.com' companies using the Internet to provide information that links consumers and producers also epitomize the introduction of a virtual form of organization that approximates to the efficient marketplace (Warner and Witzel 2004). Although the dot.com bubble has burst, the mode of doing business such companies pioneered is expected to grow rapidly. Even for 'old economy' firms, organization has been taking on a more temporary nature. In order to meet changing demands and retain their share of more competitive markets, firms came under increasing pressure to reorganize frequently in order to recombine or recycle their assets and key competencies, as well as to take advantage of the possibilities offered by e-commerce, especially in the area of procurement (Lewin and Volberda 1999, Pettigrew and Fenton 2000, Child and McGrath 2001).

The move towards a greater reliance on market processes does not, however, denote so much a substitution for bureaucracy as a complement to it. Two of its main components – hierarchy and a reliance on rules – are persisting among Western firms, though each is being modified with the assistance of ICT. For example, ICT has been used to facilitate the slimming down of hierarchies through delayering and outsourcing and it has supported the devolution of initiative within simpler structures. Hierarchy has been simplified and focused on to core activities, rather than abolished (Pettigrew and Fenton 2000). Similarly, ICT-supported systems of value-chain activities networked between partner firms rely upon agreed standardized rules (protocols) that permit codified data to be transmitted with speed and without ambiguity (Häcki and Lighton 2001). As Brunsson (1999) has noted, standardization remains an important vehicle for coordination in modern society. It does not necessarily imply hierarchical authority however, and indeed, it can be used instead to support the efficient operation of markets. Thus while the reliance on codified and abstract rules has not disappeared, in the new economy it has led to a re-balancing that has favoured markets at the expense of bureaucracies even while maintaining the latter in existence.

Western firms are also applying ICT to reinforce clan processes. They are doing so in response to increasing complexities in the business environment – such as the growth of hypercompetition, and the uncertainties associated with globalization – and the consequent need for trust building where complete contracts cannot be written. They are building up their clan processes in several ways, though again largely to complement or improve bureaucracy rather than substitute for it (Pettigrew *et al.* 2003). Business networks, for example, allow for partnerships between firms, but at the same time maintain those firms' control. The way that partners use ICT to exchange information about customers, products, schedules, inventories, costs and so forth more intensively than before enables them to extend the boundaries of the network without weakening their operational relationships. Many business networks are led, even dominated, by what has been called an 'orchestrator'. Dell is again a familiar example. The orchestrator decides on which other companies to invite into the network, on network protocols and operational plans. Such networks, however, thrive only if the leading partner looks out for the welfare of all the other companies on which it depends (Häcki and Lighton 2001). This combination of leadership and restricted (albeit often wide) membership with mutual dependence adopts clan-like features without losing all aspects of hierarchy.

Another example of how ICT is enabling the introduction of clan-like processes into Western business lies in the growing use of virtual teams. Recent advances in ICT are permitting new ways of structuring, processing and distributing work and communication activities (Boudreau *et al.* 1998). In particular, they are providing the means for work to be dispersed both physically and across time zones. In areas of work such as research and development, the use of ICT therefore permits a firm to bring together relevant specialized expertise from different parts of the world to work as a virtual team. A global virtual team is a group of geographically and temporally dispersed individuals who are assembled via ICTs to accomplish an organizational task (Montoya-Weiss *et al.* 2001). The use of global teams enables a firm to attract scarce knowledge workers from a wider range of sources. At the same time the incorporation of virtuality provides the means whereby they can work together in an integrated manner from dispersed locations. The richness and reach of information flows is clearly enhanced in a connectionist manner within what is a clan-like team setting. The virtual teams still operate, however, within a framework of goals and roles determined hierarchically by the mother corporation.

In the Western setting, then, the shift in the diffusion curve towards networks and clans is likely to act as a complement to bureaucracies rather than as a substitute for them. There are actually several factors in the West that limit substitution for bureaucratic norms and practices. One lies in the pressures for more effective corporate governance. This reinforces the maintenance of hierarchical lines of responsibility. Enron, for example, had been praised as an example of a firm in which the combination of devolved initiative and networking encouraged innovation and entrepreneurship. In the event, one of the reasons why the company ran into trouble lay in a failure of control associated with that same devolved initiative that the company's organization had encouraged. Many of Enron's new businesses, the failures of which were hidden through accounting manipulations, resulted from entrepreneurial initiatives made by middle managers rather than those at the top.[4]

Another constraint on the substitution of clans and networks for bureaucracies is that public opinion is no longer prepared to condone firms like Nike and Gap that orchestrate networks, sloughing off responsibility for the employment conditions and welfare of people employed by their subcontractors. It is recognized that however loosely coupled and disaggregated a value chain may be, it remains a system that enables and supports the proprietary brand of the leading firm in the system. This is obliging such firms to strengthen their control over network partners in a quasi-hierarchical manner.

A further limit to the substitution of clans or networks for unified hierarchies, particularly relevant to the comparison with China, stems from the individualistic cultures of Anglo-Saxon countries. The assumption of individual as opposed to collective responsibility can fragment the accountability structure and undermine the integration of diffused information that is required for effective coordination within a loosely coupled system. The events leading up to the 2001 rail disaster in Hatfield, England illustrate the problem (Child 2005). Due to a lack of coordination between the principal rail infrastructure authority and its three contractors, cracked rails were left un-replaced for ten months after the fault was first recorded. The delay gave rise to a fatal accident, the aftermath of which was a crisis programme of speed restrictions and disruption to the whole national system for several years.

The reliance placed in Western societies on 'credentialism' (Collins 1978) also preserves rule-orientation in transactions. It is expected that there will be strict adherence to professional and scientific standards. Confidence in transactional partners, and the trust placed in them, is therefore significantly based on competence attested by qualification. In the absence of credentialism and the institutional support for it, China has developed a cultural tradition that emphasizes the role of mutual obligation and personal trust as a safeguard in transactions (Xin and Pearce 1996).

The Chinese Case

Our earlier analysis of economic and institutional reform in China leads us to hypothesize that, in the absence of a large installed base of efficient bureaucratic or market institutions in that country, the shift in the diffusion curve brought about by the new ICTs will primarily favour the formation of clans and networks (Boisot and Child 1996). In contrast to the Western case, these will probably generate substitutes for bureaucracies and markets rather than complements to them.

The reliance of state-owned enterprises (SOEs) on network connections in order to cope with deficiencies in the bureaucratic allocation of supplies and other resources has been a long-standing one (Solinger 1989, Child 1994). More recently, the authorities in China have been encouraging the formation of networks between SOEs in the same sector, in the form of so-called 'business groups' (Keister 2000). While the rationale is ostensibly to secure economies of scale and other benefits of rationalization, an important reason has been to avoid the collapse of weaker SOEs and the unemployment that would follow given the extremely imperfect labour market in China.

There is other evidence that Chinese firms will rely on a network approach to absorb uncertainty rather than relying on bureaucratic and market mechanisms to reduce it (Boisot and Child 1999). Such a substitution of one institutional form for another is frequently adopted when it comes to the expansion of Chinese businesses abroad. The Chinese government has been active in encouraging specific types of outward FDI that it considers will generate benefits for the domestic economy and link in with its development assistance programmes. However, the government bureaucracy has not had the expertise to advise firms on profitable directions for expansion overseas nor on how to avoid the risks involved. Chinese firms have therefore preferred to form joint ventures, especially with overseas Chinese with whom they have prior connections, in order to reduce investment risk. They also rely quite heavily on ethnic and cultural links in deciding where to locate their overseas expansion (Cai 1999). These measures to reduce risk and psychic distance are an attempt to compensate for unfamiliarity with local business conditions and for a shortage of qualified staff with appropriate language skills and international business experience. To that extent, it is still a possibility that less reliance will come to be placed on personal connections once Chinese firms are able to reduce uncertainty by acquiring better informational and human resources. Some leading firms like Haier and Huawei have already moved in that direction (Kiran 2004, Harney 2005). Nevertheless, the approaches that Chinese firms have tended to adopt in dealing with uncertainty appear to express a culturally-informed preference.

This conclusion is reinforced by the way that both SOEs and private firms in China are highly dependent on personal relations in the form of *guanxi* to develop their external networks and to acquire business opportunities

(Park and Luo 2001).[5] This is especially true for private firms. They lack the institutional supports offered by government agencies, and good *guanxi* connections therefore provide an important substitute for gaining access to scarce raw materials, information and other resources (Luo 2000). Huang (2002) found that *guanxi* could play a helpful, even vital, role for newly-established Chinese private firms in terms of providing initial financing and access to markets.

Similarly, it has been traditional in China to rely more on the mutual obligations expressed by a relationship rather than on legal contracts. In fact, resort to a contract was taken as a sign of bad faith, a feature that many Western firms investing in China found hard to understand. This scene appears to be changing however, with more positive attitudes growing toward commercial law in general and the use of contracts in particular (Guthrie 1998, Luo 2002). Luo (2002) suggests from the results of his research that, while business transactions between local Chinese companies may still often be conducted on the basis of personal relationships rather than by arms-length contractual principles, the latter are significant in joint ventures with foreign firms and in such cases are accepted, even welcomed, by Chinese partners. Moreover, *guanxi* does not offer a guarantee of good results. In the experience of over 600 Hong Kong firms operating in Mainland China, reliance on special relationships with local government officials predicted poorer performance (Child *et al*. 2003). While one reason for this negative association could be that struggling firms tended to turn to government officials for assistance, there was little indication from the experiences related to the researchers that such a policy is fruitful.

Illustrations from Hong Kong Chinese firms
The Hong Kong family firm has been taken as representative of Chinese firms in general – more so than Mainland SOEs (Wong 1985). In the case of China, family firms reflect the cultural installed base, whereas SOEs are more reflective of the institutional installed base. Family firms also reflect the realities of small and medium private Chinese firms that today constitute the fastest growing sector of Chinese business.

The argument from cultural embeddedness would predict that Chinese firms will maintain characteristically Chinese modes of management in the course of engaging in the new economy, especially through overseas expansion. In this respect, they will continue to differ from their Western counterparts. Case studies of 16 Hong Kong Chinese family firms that have undertaken international expansion throw some light on the validity of this proposition. The firms were studied during the period 2000–2001. In each case, family holdings accounted for at least 30 per cent of their ownership and the family was the major shareholder. Nine were multi-generation family firms, while the other seven were first-generation family firms. They varied in sector, age, size and length of international experience. This variation reduces the likelihood that the identification of any culturally-preferred modes of management will be obscured by other contingent influences. The 16 firms also differed in their degree of internationalization, according to a number of criteria, as Table 7.2 indicates.

Forty-five managers were interviewed in these sixteen firms. A few respondents were interviewed twice and the number of interviews conducted therefore totalled 51. In each case, a top manager such as the company founder, chairman, executive or managing director was included among the respondents. Two other categories of respondent were (1) the senior manager in the Hong Kong head office who was responsible for managing overseas business units, and (2) the head of one or more overseas business units. These other categories of respondent were not present, or were not available, in every case. Among the subjects covered in the interviews were the formulation of internationalization strategy, choice of investment location, market entry mode, methods of managing overseas affiliates and other aspects of headquarter–subsidiary relationships.

Direct personal contact and networking by the firms' top managers were extremely significant in the process of deciding to diversify abroad and choosing the location to go to. Personal visits, primarily by the chief executive, were the most frequently used learning mode in each of the companies. The presence in a particular overseas location of a trusted friend or a loyal long-serving staff member was a major factor in enabling the heads of firms to opt to invest in that location. The top manager's personal networks were an important factor bridging the psychic distance between the familiarities of the home environment and the uncertainties of the overseas environment and hence reducing the perceived risk of overseas expansion. These personal networks were (1) external, based on a previous business relationship with other business people, and (2) internal, based on the ability to rely upon loyal and long-serving staff in the foreign location. Both relationships were essentially underpinned by trust rather than by formal guarantees such as contracts or qualifications.

Some examples illustrate the use of the top manager's external personal network. Case 3 is a knitwear manufacturer that has its own wholly-owned business units in 12 countries, but it entered into a joint venture in Thailand because that country presented it with an unfamiliar environment. The founder and head of the firm explained:

> In Thailand, most people speak Thai and all documents are written in Thai. I have known our local Thai partner, a Chinese man, for quite some time. He can act as a bridge between the Hong Kong management and the locally recruited

Table 7.2 Degree of internationalization of the 16 firms

Case no.	Ratio of foreign sales to total sales	Ratio of foreign employment to total employment	Number of business units outside Hong Kong	Number of countries outside Hong Kong in which firm operated	Psychic dispersion of overseas units[1]
1	90%	75%	4	3	3
2	95%	94%	100+	20	8
3	99%	98%	42	13	7
4	100%	98%	3	2	2
5	n.a.	19%	28	6	3
6	n.a.	1%	3	2	2
7	1%	3%	5	2	2
8	80%	47%	16	3	2
9	10%	35%	2	1	1
10	100%	95%	5	4	2
11	10%	70%	9	2	2
12	50%	39%	3	3	3
13	n.a.	55%	7	6	4
14	50%	60%	6	6	3
15	90%	95%	5	5	3
16	100%	97%	4	3	3

Note:
1. The number of psychic zones in which the firm's business units are located. The eleven zones applied included nine identified by Ronen and Shenkar (1985: 449), plus a zone named 'Mainland China' and a zone named 'Others'.

staff. He can also be relied upon to deal with the local government officials and businessmen. Hence, both parties are happy with the joint venture arrangement and this is a win-win situation.

The Executive Chairman and sole owner of Case 10 commented that 'the availability of suitable partners to enter into joint ventures is a very important factor facilitating the company's overseas expansion. So far, most of the partners are Chinese and they are all long time friends of mine.'

Case 11 is a diversified group engaged in construction, property development and construction materials. It has interests in Hong Kong, North America and Mainland China. Although the company has a research department of five to six persons to collect market information relevant to business development, the chairman articulated a number of ways in which his own network of personal relationships and personal visits had facilitated his firm's internationalization:

> I collect market information from other businessmen both through formal meetings and through informal occasions such as playing golf. They share their operating experience in various overseas locations with me. My friends are a major source of new business opportunities [gives specific examples, omitted for reasons of confidentiality]. I also visit different cities in order to understand their socio-economic background. For example, I visit local restaurants to see how much people spend on meals. I visit local department stores to see how they price their products. I even visit night clubs to see who are the people there.

Over half of the top managers relied on friends or business associates for information on new business opportunities. One third of them regarded the presence abroad of a trusted local business partner as a significant way to help them handle the differences between foreign conditions and those they were used to on their home ground.

The account given by an Executive Director in Case 6, a bank, illustrates reliance on an 'internal' network. It points to the role that the migration of a long-serving and trusted staff member can play in facilitating a Hong Kong firm's overseas expansion. In this example, a personal link internal to the organization actually triggered the bank to make its first move to the United States:

> I would say that trust is a more important criterion than competence for appointment of senior management positions. In fact, in the early 1980s, it was partially due to the migration of a staff member who had served our bank for more than 30 years, which triggered our first move to the United States. I still remember the Saturday afternoon when I talked to the staff member and invited him to head a representative office in the United States. This led to the establishment of our Los Angeles branch in 1984.

Once established overseas, the Hong Kong firms generally used a combination of formal Western-style practices and less formal methods in order to control and manage their foreign operations. Most of the firms had detailed policy guidelines, work procedures, job specifications and staff manuals prepared by the head office staff for use in the overseas business units. This was perhaps to be expected in the case of the two banks studied, for which external regulations and public accountability make it essential that standard procedures are followed. However, all but two of the other firms had also transferred their formal standard practices to foreign affiliates and attached considerable importance to so doing.

At the same time, respondents in each of the 16 firms also stressed the importance of personalized foundations for managing their overseas units. Two such foundations were most in evidence: the secondment of head office staff to the affiliate and the maintenance of frequent personal contact with it. The way that advances in ICT had eased the process of keeping in close touch with overseas operations was a constantly mentioned theme – it was clearly an important enabler. The most frequently employed technologies for communication between head office and overseas units were email and the telephone, with a growing use of video conferencing. This pattern of ICT utilization is, however, a general trend in business. What may point to a characteristically Chinese use of the technology is the virtually constant communication both by email and telephone reported in some of the firms. Another reflection of a traditional Chinese family business style (Redding 1990, 2000) was the heavy involvement of the top manager in communication with overseas units. When he (all were male) was not visiting the units in person, he was in many cases phoning their managers every day. Given that most of the companies studied were not small ones, this degree of personal involvement by the top executive is quite striking.

The following examples illustrate the significant reliance on a personalized approach in the operational management of the Hong Kong companies' overseas networks:

Case 3　　The CEO of this company is reported to spend about two-thirds of his time travelling around the world visiting its overseas operations and looking into new business possibilities. The company also stays close to its 42 overseas business units through (1) daily use of email and phone, (2) personal visits by overseas unit managers to head office at least once every two months and more when necessary, (3) visits by the directors and senior management to overseas factories, and (4) appointing at least one head office manager to take charge of each overseas unit.

Case 14 'The head of the overseas business division visits each unit outside Hong Kong very frequently [at least four times a year] in order to make sure that the Hong Kong head office practices have been transferred to the overseas locations. She will also visit the shops to check the set up and to collect information about the needs and other comments of customers. She carries information from the head office to the local shops and she also collects customer information from the shops. Effectively she is the bridge between the head office and the local shops.'

Case 16 This company has a factory in the PRC (People's Republic of China) and representative offices in Japan and the UK. The chairman (founder and sole owner) chose Xiamen to be the location for the firm's main factory because he was born there and 'I have all the necessary connections through my classmates, friends and relatives'. He spends much of his time there and he is the channel for most of the company's acquisition of knowledge about the market and operations.

IMPLICATIONS

We noted earlier the major changes that might be expected to propel China towards the Western model. However, judging by the cases just presented as well as other evidence, the reality appears to be more complex in two respects. First, Chinese firms continue to rely heavily on informal network relationships both for opening up new business opportunities as well as for ensuring necessary support for the smooth flow of current operations. This may reflect either continued uncertainties due to institutional imperfections or cultural embeddedness, in either case giving rise to behavioural path-dependence (Granovetter 1985). Competent 'clan-like' networking behaviour provides Chinese firms with social capital of considerable value. They are unlikely to discard it. Second, the potential benefits of a networking approach in terms of promoting innovation and achieving flexibility have been recognized for some time now in Western organizational theory – and latterly in practice too. Western thinking has come to place greater emphasis on the cultivation of trust-based relationships in order to build clan-like loyalties within organizations and effective partnerships between organizations. The growing interest in more organic organizational forms in the West implies that any convergence between the Western and Chinese business systems will not be a one-way progression.

WTO entry will expose the Chinese economy to greater competitive pressures as well as opening up new opportunities overseas. The use of ICTs is also being taken up rapidly in China. These factors will favour the use of clan-like networking as a metaphor of organization and the existing cultural orientation of Chinese firms might well facilitate such an application. If there is to be convergence around a new model of business organization, therefore, it may draw inspiration at least as much from China as from the West.

We suggested earlier, however, that institutional structures not only compete with each other for transactions in the I-Space, but they can also collaborate and complement each other – a point that has been largely over-looked by the literature on transaction cost economics. Many Western firms are now seeking complementary transactions throughout the space. Not either markets or bureaucracies or clans or fiefs, but rather markets and bureaucracies and clans and fiefs. They thus end up with configurations of institutions rather than with individual ones or hybrids. Similarly, we noted how Hong Kong Chinese firms are combining Western-inspired practices with behaviour patterns informed by traditional Chinese culture.

This simple point radically changes our conceptualization of the convergence hypothesis. Convergence on individual organizational practices under conditions of competition will be much easier than convergence on configurations of complementary practices. If we think of individual practices as components and of a given configuration of such components as an organizational architecture, then we see striking parallels between the problems of imitation in the field of organization and those in the field of technology. Research into enterprise-level innovation by Henderson and Clark (1990) showed how much easier it was to imitate technological components than to imitate a technological architecture. Discussion and research into the organization of multinational corporations similarly indicates a tendency to combine a convergence of some practices across countries with a tolerance of divergence in respect of other practices where adjustment to local environments is deemed to be appropriate (Bartlett and Ghoshal 1998, Malnight 2001). In other words, international business practice is built up on different convergent/divergent configurations. The question of convergence should therefore be asked with reference to both component dimensions and complete architectures; it is more likely to be found in specific component dimensions. We would suggest that the same applies to macro-level institutions.

We can now bring into the discussion our distinction between drivers and enablers to put forward the following four general propositions about convergence in the new economy:

Proposition 1   Technology is at least as much an enabler as a driver. The new information and communication technologies act as drivers when they promote and speed up the diffusion of information. They act as enablers when they increase the bandwidth available for interacting at a distance.

Proposition 2 Whereas drivers eliminate choice and promote convergence, enablers increase choice and favour diversity.

Proposition 3 Drivers are likely to force a competitive choice between organizational or institutional arrangements, whereas enablers are likely to allow a configuration of these to co-exist and collaborate.

Proposition 4 Convergence on individual practices is easier to achieve than convergence on complete organizational configurations. Similarly, at the macro level, convergence on individual institutions such as markets is easier to achieve than convergence on configurations of institutions. To the extent that ICTs act as enablers, therefore, they are likely to reduce the forces of convergence rather than increase them.

By focusing on technology and globalization exclusively as drivers of convergence, we overlook their parallel role as enablers of diversity. We then end up with a view of the world as an increasingly homogeneous place in which cultures are hard to distinguish from each other.

CONCLUSION

In this chapter we ask whether the 'imperatives' of globalization and modern ICT are inevitably destined to pull China toward a Western-type market order buttressed by associated institutions. Or alternatively, whether China will find ways of accommodating its own cultural and institutional preferences for those network forms of governance as put forward in the 'network capitalism' hypothesis. Even if in formal terms China adopts a more Western type of institutional order, as it is doing through its legal reforms and acceptance of the conditions for WTO membership, does this mean that its mode of business transacting and organization will move towards the Western model? If so, will it retain Chinese characteristics such as the heavy reliance on special connections and relationships known as *guanxi*? In a complementary manner, we also asked whether the Western order of transacting is moving to adopt certain network forms of a kind familiar to Chinese practice. The reality turns out to be complex and appears to be captured by affirmative answers to all these questions.

Behind the questions lies another issue concerning the potential connection between the effectiveness of the institutional regime and the use of networking in business. If the use of network capitalism is in part a compensatory mechanism for the uncertainties generated by a weak institutional regime, then it may be expected to decline as and when the institutional regime becomes more predictable and reliable. This would support the hypothesis of convergence toward a Western model. Although reciprocated relationships and mutual obligations are historically embedded into China's Confucian-inspired culture (Redding 2002), their intensive application in the form of *guanxi* started to spread only under special circumstances, some two or three years into the Cultural Revolution, in response to the need to secure everyday survival against the collapse of the social order (Yang 1989). This points to reliance on personal networks being a compensation for the lack of institutional reliability in the sense of providing predictable rules of the game (North 1990). If this is the case, as China continues to progress towards a transparent and non-arbitrary institutional order, encouraged by international agreements such as the WTO and enabled by the widespread dissemination of information through ICT, one might expect its modes of governing business transactions to change accordingly toward a legal-rational mode and away from a dependence on personal networking.

The counter possibility is that despite attempts to modify people's behaviour patterns through institutional change, the cultural preferences that inform such behaviour remain embedded in the social fabric as, arguably, they have in Japan (Dore 1973, Van Wolferen 1989). Thus Hong Kong's institutions are essentially Western in nature, deriving from the British legacy, yet the indigenous firms we studied appear to exhibit cultural embeddedness in their behaviours. If this is the case, embedded cultural preferences can be expected to re-emerge in Mainland China under a more liberal institutional regime. Chinese cultural characteristics were submerged for the best part of half a century under communism by newer layers of institutional change in the social archaeology of people's mindsets. However, the increasing openness of the system under the post-1978 reforms may have permitted such cultural characteristics to reappear in recent decades. The neoliberalism underpinning WTO provisions might, on this argument, even allow greater scope for Chinese culture to shape economic and business behaviour into an idiosyncratic form. The rules of the game may be neoliberal but their interpretation and the institutional co-evolutionary dynamics that they give rise to will then remain distinctly Chinese.

Historians like Fairbank and Goldman (1998), while recognizing the diversity in Chinese culture, bring out its high level of persistence over a long chain of evolution. Various authorities have identified the values underpinning Chinese culture that are relevant to management and organizational behaviour (for example Shenkar and Ronen 1987, Lockett 1988, Redding 1990, 2002, Bond 1996). These values are commonly expressed in a number of forms that are of particular relevance to business behaviour in China. For example, respect for position and experience mean that long-serving senior figures in organizations are readily accorded leadership status. Family-based collectivism manifests itself in the rapid development today of family business, often securing finance and early opportunities through family or close connections. We have already noted how the importance placed upon personal relationships readily gives rise to 'relational networking' based on interpersonal connections. This traditional Chinese behavioural pattern is ascriptive, communitarian and particularistic. Such *Gemeinschaft* legacies make it quite distinct from the *Gesellschaft*[6] legal-rational type of social integration often associated with Western ways of doing things and with 'modernization' (Tönnies 1957, Weber 1964).

Our discussion of the Chinese case leads us to reconceptualize the meaning of convergence. China may well end up adopting the whole panoply of Western institutions and organizational practices and yet configure and operate these in a way that remains distinctly Chinese and thus hard for others to imitate. There would then be a convergence on the components but not on the architecture of a Western institutional order – if, indeed, there is such a thing. At heart, the globalization debate is one about the future of cultural identity, both at a national and at a regional level. Our conclusion is that if the process of modernization profoundly modifies cultural identity, it certainly does not abolish it.

NOTES

1. In this chapter we use the term 'new economy' to cover more than just Internet-based firms.
2. In an earlier paper (Boisot and Child 1996), the model was labelled the Culture-Space or C-Space.
3. Evans and Wurster (2000) argue that the new economy has abolished the trade-off that existed between richness and reach. Figure 7.3 suggests that the new economy has shifted the trade-off rather than abolished it.
4. *Financial Times* (2001), 4 December, 16; *Financial Times* (2002), 23 August, 21, 26.
5. The term *guanxi* in a general sense simply means 'relationship' or 'connection'. In the sphere of business relations, *guanxi* usually signifies an informal personal relationship based on reciprocity of assistance or favour, and incorporating a high level of trust.
6. Ferdina and Tonnies (1887) first conceptualised the distinction between *Gemeinshaft* (community-traditional community of personal relations) and *Gesellshaft* (society-modern contractual society of impersonal relations) that has been for a long time a significant, if not the most significant strand of modern social science scholarship.

REFERENCES

Abo, T. (ed.) (1994), *Hybrid Factory: The Japanese Production System in the United States*, New York: Oxford University Press.
Barber, B. (2003), *Jihad vs. McWorld: Terrorism's Challenge to Democracy*, London: Corgi Books.

Bartlett, C.A. and S. Ghoshal (1998), *Managing Across Borders*, 2nd edition, London: Random House.

Berger, P. and T. Luckmann (1966), *The Social Construction of Reality*, New York: Doubleday.

Biggart, N.W. and G. Hamilton (1992), 'On the limits of a firm-based theory to explain business networks: the Western bias of neoclassical economics', in N. Nohria and R.G. Eccles (eds), *Networks and Organizations: Structure, Form, and Action*, Boston, MA: Harvard Business School Press, pp. 471–490.

Bijker, W. (1987), 'The social construction of bakelite: toward a theory of invention', in W. Bijker, T. Hughes and T. Pinch (eds), *The Social Construction of Technological Systems*, Cambridge, MA: MIT Press, pp. 159–187.

Boisot, M. (1986), 'Markets and hierarchies in cultural perspective', *Organization Studies*, **7**, 135–158.

Boisot, M. (1995), *Information Space: A Framework for Learning in Organizations, Institutions and Culture*, London: Routledge.

Boisot, M. (1998), *Knowledge Assets: Securing Competitive Advantage in the Information Economy*, Oxford: Oxford University Press.

Boisot, M. and J. Child (1988), 'The iron law of fiefs: bureaucratic failure and the problem of governance in the Chinese economic reforms', *Administrative Science Quarterly*, **33**, 507–527.

Boisot, M. and J. Child (1996), 'From fiefs to clans and network capitalism: explaining China's emerging economic order', *Administrative Science Quarterly*, **41**, 600–628.

Boisot, M. and J. Child (1999), Organizations as adaptive systems in complex environments: the case of China', *Organization Science*, **10**, 237–252.

Bond, M.H. (1996), *The Handbook of Chinese Psychology*, Hong Kong: Oxford University Press.

Boudreau, M., K. Loch, D. Robey and D. Straud (1998), 'Going global: using information technology to advance the competitiveness of the virtual transnational organization', *Academy of Management Executive*, **12**, 120–128.

Brunsson, N. (1999), 'Standardization as organization', in M. Egeberg and P. Lägreid (eds), *Organizing Political Institutions: Essays for Johan P. Olsen*, Oslo: Scandinavian University Press, pp. 109–128.

Cai, K.G. (1999), 'Outward foreign direct investment: a novel dimension of China's integration into the regional and global economy', *China Quarterly*, **160** (December), 856–880.

Carley, K. (1995), 'Computational and mathematical organization theory: perspectives and directions', *Computational and Mathematical Organization Theory*, **1**, 39–56.

Castells, M. (2002), *Internet and the Network Enterprise*, Plenary address given to the 18th European Group for Organizational Studies Colloquium, Barcelona, 4 July.

Chandler, A.D. Jr (1962), *Strategy and Structure: Chapters in the History of the American Industrial Enterprise*, Cambridge, MA: MIT Press.

Chandler, A.D. Jr (1977), *The Visible Hand: The Managerial Revolution in American Business*, Cambridge, MA: Belknap Press.

Child, J. (1994), *Management in China During the Age of Reform*, Cambridge: Cambridge University Press.

Child, J. (2000), 'Theorizing about organization cross-nationally', *Advances in Comparative International Management*, **13**, 27–75.

Child, J. (2002), 'A configurational analysis of international joint ventures drawing upon experience in China', *Organization Studies*, **23**, 781–815.

Child, J. (2005), *Organization: Contemporary Principles and Practice*, Oxford: Blackwell.

Child, J., L. Chung and H. Davies (2003), 'The performance of cross-border units in China: a test of natural selection, strategic choice and contingency theories', *Journal of International Business Studies*, **34**, 242–254.

Child, J. and R. Loveridge (1990), *Information Technology in European Services*, Oxford: Blackwell.

Child, J. and R. McGrath (eds) (2001), Special Research Forum on 'New and evolving organizational forms', *Academy of Management Journal*, **44**, 1135–1322.

Clegg, S.R. (1990), *Modern Organization: Organization Studies in the Postmodern World*, Thousand Oaks, CA: Sage.

Coase, R.H. (1937), 'The nature of the firm', *Econometrica*, **4**, 386–405.

Collins, R. (1978), *The Credential Society*, New York: Academic Press.

Dell, M. (2000), *Direct from Dell*, New York: HarperBusiness.

Dicken, P. (2003), *Global Shift: Reshaping the Global Economic Map in the 21st Century*, 4th edition, Thousand Oaks, CA: Sage.

Dore, R. (1973), *British Factory, Japanese Factory*, London: Allen and Unwin.

The Economist (2005), 'The real digital divide', 12 March, 9.

Evans, P. and T. Wurster (2000), *Blown to Bits*, Boston, MA: Harvard Business School Press.

Fairbank, J. and M. Goldman (1998), *China: A New History*, Cambridge, MA: Harvard University Press.

Franko, L. (1976), *The European Multinationals*, Greenwich, CN: Greylock.

Garnaut, R. and L. Song (eds) (2002), *China 2002: WTO Entry and World Recession*, Canberra: Asia Pacific Press.

Granovetter, M. (1985), 'Economic action and social structure: the problem of embeddedness', *American Journal of Sociology*, **91**, 481–510.

Guillen, M.F. (2001), *The Limits of Convergence: Globalization and Organizational Change in Argentina, South Korea and Spain*, Princeton, NJ: Princeton University Press.

Guthrie, D. (1998), 'The declining significance of *guanxi* in China's economic transition', *The China Quarterly*, **154**, 254–282.

Häcki, R. and J. Lighton (2001), 'The future of the networked company', *McKinsey Quarterly*, **2001** (3), 26–39.

Harbison, F.H. and C.A. Myers (1959), *Management in the Industrial World*, New York: McGraw-Hill.

Harney, A. (2005), 'The challenger from China: why Huawei is making the telecoms world take notice', *Financial Times*, 11 January, 15.

Henderson, R.M. and K.B. Clark (1990), 'Architectural innovation: the reconfiguration of existing product technologies and the failure of established firms', *Administrative Science Quarterly*, **35**, 9–30.

Huang, Q. (2002), *Social Capital and China's Private Enterprise Start-ups: An Examination with Special Reference to the IT Sector*. Unpublished PhD thesis, University of Bristol, June.

Huntingdon, S. (1996), *The Clash of Civilizations: Remaking of World Order*, New York: Simon and Schuster.

Jessop, R. (1987), 'Mode of production', in J. Eatwell, M. Milgate and P. Newman (eds), *Marxian Economics*, London: Macmillan, pp. 289–296.

Keister, L. (2000), *Chinese Business Groups: The Structure and Impact of Interfirm Relations during Economic Development*, Hong Kong: Oxford University Press.

Kiran, V.B. (2004), *Haier: Developing a Global Brand. Case #304-264-1*, Hyderabad: ICFAI Business School Case Development Centre.

Kuhn, T. (1962), *The Structure of Scientific Revolutions*, Chicago: The University of Chicago Press.

Lawrence, P.R. and J.W. Lorsch (1967), *Organization and Environment*, Boston, MA: Harvard Business School Press.

Lewin, A.Y., C.P. Long and T.N. Carroll (1999), 'The coevolution of new organizational forms', *Organization Science*, **10**, 535–550.

Lewin, A. and W. Volberda (eds) (1999), Special issue on 'Coevolution of strategy and new organizational forms', *Organization Science*, **10**, 519–690.

Lockett, M. (1988), 'Culture and the problems of Chinese management', *Organization Studies*, **9**, 475–496.

Luo, Y. (2000), *Guanxi and Business*, Singapore: World Scientific Publishing.

Luo, Y. (2002), 'Partnering with foreign firms: how do Chinese managers view the governance and importance of contracts?' *Asia Pacific Journal of Management*, **19**, 127–151.

Malnight, T.W. (2001), 'Emerging structural patterns within multinational corporations: toward process-based structures', *Academy of Management Journal*, **44**, 1187–1210.

Meyer, A.D., A.S. Tsui and C.R. Hinings (1993), 'Configurational approaches to organizational analysis', *Academy of Management Journal*, **36**, 1175–1195.

Mohr, L.B. (1982), *Explaining Organizational Behavior*, San Francisco: Jossey-Bass.

Montoya-Weiss, M., A. Massey and M. Song (2001), 'Getting it together: temporal coordination and conflict management in global virtual teams', *Academy of Management Journal*, **44**, 1251–1262.

North, D. (1990), *Institutions, Institutional Change and Economic Performance*, Cambridge: Cambridge University Press.

Ouchi, W.G. (1981), *Theory Z*, Reading, MA: Addison-Wesley.

Park, S.H. and Y. Luo (2001), 'Guanxi and organizational dynamics: organizational networking in Chinese firms', *Strategic Management Journal*, **22**, 455–477.

Pettigrew, A.M. and E.M. Fenton (eds) (2000), *The Innovating Organization*, London: Sage.

Pettigrew, A.M., R. Whittington, L. Melin, C. Sanchez-Rundes, W. Ruigrok and F. Van den Bosch (eds) (2003), *Innovative Forms of Organizing*, London: Sage.

Ragin, C.C. (1987), *The Comparative Method: Moving Beyond Qualitative and Quantitative Strategies*, Berkeley, CA: University of California Press.

Redding, S.G. (1990), *The Spirit of Chinese Capitalism*, Berlin: de Gruyter.

Redding, S.G. (2000), 'What is Chinese about Chinese family business? And how much is family and how much is business?' in H.W-C. Yeung and K. Olds (eds), *Globalization of Chinese Business Firms*, London: Macmillan, pp. 31–54.

Redding, S.G. (2002), 'The capitalist business system of China and its rationale', *Asia Pacific Journal of Management*, **19**, 221–249.

Ronen, S. and O. Shenkar (1985), 'Clustering countries on attitudinal dimensions: a review and synthesis', *Academy of Management Review*, **10**, 435–454.

Rugman, A.M. (2005), *The Regional Multinationals*, Cambridge: Cambridge University Press.

Sanchez, R. (2001), 'Product, process and knowledge architectures in organizational competence', in R. Sanchez (ed.), *Knowledge Management and Organizational Competence*, Oxford: Oxford University Press, pp. 227–250.

Shenkar, O. and S. Ronen (1987), 'The cultural context of negotiations: the implications of Chinese interpersonal norms', *Journal of Applied Behavioral Science*, **23**, 263–275.

Solinger, D.J. (1989), 'Urban reform and relational contracting in post-Mao China: an interpretation of the transition from plan to market', *Studies in Comparative Communism*, **23**, 171–185.

Solinger, D.J. (2003), 'Chinese urban jobs and the WTO', *The China Journal*, **49**, 61–87.

Steger, M.B. (2003), *Globalization: A Very Short Introduction*, Oxford: Oxford University Press.

Stiglitz, J. (2002), *Globalization and its Discontents*, London: Allen Lane Penguin Press.

Tönnies, F. (1957), *Community and Society (Gemeinschaft und Gesellschaft*, translated by C.P. Loomis), East Lansing, MI: Michigan State University Press.

Van Wolferen, K. (1989), *The Enigma of Japanese Power: People and Politics in a Stateless Nation*, London: Macmillan.

Warner, M. (2003), 'Introduction: Culture and Management in Asia', in M. Warner (ed.), *Culture and Management in Asia*, London: RoutledgeCurzon, pp. 1–23.

Warner, M. and M. Witzel (2004), *Managing in Virtual Organizations*, London: Thomson.

Weber, M. ([1947] 1964), *The Theory of Social and Economic Organization* (Translated by A.M. Henderson and T. Parsons), New York: Free Press.

Whitley, R. (1999), *Divergent Capitalisms*, Oxford: Oxford University Press.

Williamson, O.E. (1975), *Markets and Hierarchies: Analysis and Antitrust Implications*, New York: Free Press.

Williamson, O.E. (1985), *The Economic Institutions of Capitalism: Firms, Markets, Relational Contracting*, New York: Free Press.

Wong, S. (1985), 'The Chinese family firm: a model', *British Journal of Sociology*, **36**, 58–72.

Xin, K.R. and J.L. Pearce (1996), '*Guanxi*: connections as substitutes for formal institutional support', *Academy of Management Journal*, **39**, 1641–1658.

Yang, M.M.F. (1989), 'Gift economy and state power in China', *Comparative Study of Society and History*, **31**, 25–54.

PART IV

Tools and frameworks for digital business ecosystems

8. The management of intellectual property in the digital business ecosystem[1]

Puay Tang and Jordi Molas-Gallart

INTRODUCTION

Information technology (IT) has increased the capacity to capture, store, process and transmit data. These features have enabled a wide array of applications and its pervasive use today is observed in all realms of activity – business operations, public sector services, educational facilities, the household and so on. Indeed, the use of IT is widely acknowledged to bestow an assortment of benefits, such as cost savings and other forms of efficiencies. Yet IT can be a double-edged sword. Its ability to capture and transmit information at the click of a key can just as easily facilitate information loss and leakage (advertent and inadvertent) with the same easy action. As companies increase their use of digital networks to manage their internal and external processes, the potential for such losses increases, despite attempts by organizations to protect against them. The use of IT and electronic networks thus increases the risk of all forms of intellectual property (IP) to misappropriation or leakage, inadvertent or otherwise. Enhancing the security of networks is now a thriving business. Yet network security is more than just adding more IT-based solutions. Instead organizations must know and address appropriately the risks that such use engenders.

This chapter analyses the nature of the problems posed by IP management in shared digital environments (SDEs), which form an integral element of the digital business ecosystem. The chapter discusses a range of approaches to their solution. Our main concern here is the management of information and data whose disclosure or unauthorized use can generate a loss of commercial advantage to its owner. Although strictly speaking, not all IP falls within this category,[2] we retain the use of the term IP for convenience, as it is also the term commonly used to refer to departments, groups and experts dealing with the formal (intellectual property rights – IPR) and informal protection of commercially sensitive and proprietary information.

The chapter is based on an in-depth analysis of the use of SDEs in the UK defence industries. In this area an exceptional effort is taking place to develop precise codes of practice and procedures affecting all aspects of the contractual process and project management, including, IP management. In collaboration with industry, the UK Ministry of Defence (MoD) has developed extensive guidelines and sets of contractual conditions for the management of IP in SDEs. This situation provides a unique test bed for analysing the impact of formal regulations and processes for the management of IP, and the challenges faced when explicitly addressing IP management issues in inter-organizational networks and systems. Further, existing MoD procurement policies emphasize the use of inter-organizational IT networks to improve project performance and have established detailed IP regulations to develop and implement large SDEs.

THE CONTEXT

Until recently, the management of IP and its associated IPR was treated as a specialized function within a company. Corporate strategy would concern itself mainly with the management of tangible and financial assets, and IP management would be left to specialist lawyers who deal with patents and other forms of formal IP protection as needed. Similarly, IT managers who dealt with corporate systems for data access control rarely consulted with the legal or commercial departments on IP issues such as the potential data leakage inherent in the treatment and transfer of electronic data. This situation is changing. Towards the late 1990s, analysts were underlining the importance of IP and IPR management as a key element of corporate policy (Teece *et al.* 1997, Teece 1998, Ruggles and Holtshouse 1999, Shapiro and Varian 1999, Chesbrough 2003, Rivette and Kline 2000, Davis 2004, Reitzig 2004). IP is now seen as a strategic intangible asset influencing corporate performance (Quinn 1992, Nonaka and Takeuchi 1995, Davenport and Prusak 1998, Buigues *et al.* 2000, Rivette and Kline 2000, Chesbrough 2003).

Important as IP is for the modern corporation, scholars have found it a difficult concept to define accurately.[3] The American Heritage Dictionary defines IP as a product of the intellect that has commercial value. The Oxford English Dictionary defines it as property which is the product of invention or creativity, and which does not exist in a tangible physical form. In short IP refers to intangibles that are commercially valuable. Yet IP can be expressed in many different tangible forms: books, blueprints, designs and trademarks are all expressions of IP which can be made available to other parties.

As the recognition of the commercial value of IP deepens, its protection increasingly becomes an important managerial challenge. Simultaneously, as noted above, data replication and transmission is becoming easier thanks to rapid development in IT, thus augmenting the risk of data conveying valuable IP leaking to competitors. An Irish survey conducted in 2005 reported that 138 US companies suffered a loss of from US$35–39 billion in 2004 from IP theft and corporate information leaks (Business Wire 2005). This seems to be an improvement on a US survey undertaken in 2002, which estimated that between $53 and $59 billion were lost to 138 responding firms (coincidentally the same number of firms who responded to the 2005 Irish survey!) through incidents in which proprietary information was disclosed. Over two-thirds of the firms surveyed 'strongly agreed' with the statement 'The Internet, networks, computers and related technologies have created significant new threats to sensitive proprietary information'. This threat has become the most important source of concern, particularly among large companies (ASIS International *et al.* 2002). Similarly, in the UK, a 2004 survey of 203 companies conducted by the National High Tech Crime Unit, reported that 12 per cent of the firms had experienced instances of data theft through the Internet, causing losses amounting to approximately £7 billion (Lyons 2004). Such realization of the risks posed by the growing use of electronic data networks as constituents of the digital business ecosystem, suggests the need for specialized IP and information management strategies addressing data control and access issues.

So far, corporate responses and academic analyses have focused on IP management within the firm (Grindley and Teece 1997, Tang 1998, Chesbrough 2003, Reitzig 2004). Five years or so ago, firms built fortress-type IT systems and imposed tight controls on their database administrators. But as companies extend their enterprise outwards to third-party access, such as suppliers, the line between the internal and external network becomes fuzzy, and securing the network from a plethora of users becomes correspondingly more difficult. Indeed, an important benefit of digital 'networking' of firms for competitive advantage has been well discussed by economists (Krugman 1986, Boisot 1998), although one needs to note that the state of IT applications has advanced markedly since the mid-1990s, hence facilitating the development of more sophisticated data and communication networks. Still, little on the management of IP in these 'networked' arrangements had been addressed in these studies.

We argue that the problems and challenges faced are further exacerbated when managing IP in the context of inter-firm collaborative projects in which groups of firms, often competitors, and sometimes their customer organizations share in the design, development, manufacture and operation of complex products. Here, large amounts of technical data (including designs, product specifications, manufacturing processes and so on) can be shared through the use of advanced IT tools – SDEs. These involve electronic networks, software platforms and electronic data management systems used by project partners to manage and share technical data. SDEs are being proposed as a tool to assist large design, engineering and manufacturing projects in a wide variety of sectors, for reasons of efficiency and improved project management, among others. Thus, the management of IP in SDEs poses problems that are different in nature and scope from those of IP management within the firm or even with suppliers.

The chapter is structured as follows. We first discuss our approach. We then introduce the main relevant traits of present UK defence procurement practice, in particular the way it deals with IP, and analyse the specific IP management problems encountered when conducting collaborative ventures in the defence industries. We follow with a discussion of the strategies for responding to these challenges, and an analysis of the ways in which two specific SDEs have been implemented. We find that they have adopted different implementation models. We conclude with generic lessons for IP management in collaborative ventures conducted in a digital business ecosystem.

OUR APPROACH

We adopted a case study methodology to address the IP corporate management practices in the main British defence-related corporations and the way they relate to the IP practices of their main customer, the MoD. This choice does not limit the relevance of our study to the UK defence industries. We justify the choice because the UK defence sector has invested a special effort in developing precise codes of practice and procedures affecting all aspects of the contractual process and project management, including IPR procedures and the use of SDEs (see below). This situation provides a sterling opportunity for analysing the impact of formal regulations and processes on the management of IPR. Further, the 'Smart Acquisition' initiative launched by the UK MoD Smart Procurement Implementation Team (1999) emphasizes the use of e-commerce and advanced IT to improve project performance, that is, to promote the development of a digital business ecosystem. Accordingly, the MoD has established a catalogue of detailed IPR regulations to support the development and implementation of sophisticated IT systems for product development, manufacture and maintenance. The experience of the UK defence sector is significant for other sectors. Although there are unique aspects to the regulatory environment of the defence sector, there is nothing inherently unique in the contractual procedures and guidelines for IP management for this sector. For instance, the guidelines on how to develop a contractual structure for a 'shared data environment' (discussed below) are equally applicable to any other industry. It could be argued that the IP environment in which defence customer agencies and their industrial suppliers operate is characterized by a cosy relationship derived from a long-term customer–supplier relationship in what is a comparatively closed and trusted environment. If this was ever the case it is no longer so now. New suppliers are entering the defence market, the defence industrial structure is in the midst of potentially profound changes (Gholz 2003) and changes in procurement practices have heightened the tension between large defence suppliers and their customers.[4] The UK defence sector is therefore becoming more open and akin to other commercial environments.

The first step in our study was a documentary study of the IP practices and regulations used in defence contracting laid out in the 'contractual conditions' used by the MoD procurement agency (the Defence Procurement Agency – DPA). We followed with a programme of semi-structured interviews using two different interview protocols, one addressing corporate policies and activities, and another oriented to the analysis of IP management practices within specific projects. The main objective of the interview programme was to determine the ways in which firms addressed IP management in a digital environment both within the corporation and in collaborative programmes.

To guide the interviews we designed a protocol structured according to a list of IP management topics with potential effects on firm and corporate performance. We based the list on IP management issues identified by the extant literature on IP management within specific sectors and firms (Grindley and Teece 1997, Tang 1998, Hall and Ziedonis 2001, Shapiro 2001, Tang and Paré 2003, Granstrand 2004, Guilhon *et al.* 2004). A panel of academic, industrial and government IPR experts validated the interview protocol, which we then piloted through a six-hour long interview with two IPR and commercial managers of a major UK defence corporation. Following the pilot we adapted the protocol and used the two different formats, as noted above.

We then carried out a programme of formal interviews and informal meetings with UK defence manufacturers, industrial associations and the Defence Procurement Agency. During a period of nine months ending in July 2004, we carried out interviews with 33 senior officials and executives, covering, among others, the largest UK defence systems manufacturers.[5] The participating companies selected interviewees with direct experience in IP management, IPR and contractual issues, and the implementation of IT

tools, either at corporate level, or within the context of specific collaborative projects. Finally, we organized a conference in March 2005 in which the
results of our study were validated. The event was attended by some 50 IP
management experts, lawyers and executives from the defence industries,
the MoD and the Department of Trade and Industry. Because of the sensitivity of the issues explored we will not attribute the information used in
this article to any individual or organization.

THE CASE: MANAGING IP IN THE UK DEFENCE MARKET

All the firms and organizations involved in this study are simultaneously
using different network technologies and inter-organizational systems.[6]
These are usually for large complex projects involving a number of suppliers, coordinated through a prime contractor, to provide a system or a service
for use by the UK armed forces. Under the current UK defence procurement
approach, most of the above stakeholders participate in Integrated Project
Teams (IPTs) set up by the DPA (Ministry of Defence Smart Procurement
Implementation Team 1999). The IPTs bring together representatives from
the client organization, final users and industrial producers, and play a
complex interface role between suppliers, the MoD client and military users.
Each IPT has a 'leader' who is the line manager for most core members of
the IPT, and the formal point of contact with the MoD representative (final
customer). The leader is responsible for meeting the agreed cost, performance targets and milestones, and for facilitating communication among all
main project stakeholders throughout the project's life cycle, from concep-
tion, through research and development, production, operation, maintenance and upgrading, and ultimately disposal. In practice, every project
establishes its own set of network technologies and inter-organizational
systems, and its contractual conditions and procedures. This means high set-
up costs for every project (there is an element of reinventing the wheel and
limited cross-project learning). Consequently, defence firms work with a
wide variety of network environments and under varying contractual conditions. For instance, one interviewed firm is running 300 separate projects
supported by different IT networking arrangements and contractual conditions to manage and share data with often the same customers and suppliers. Such a situation engenders not only additional costs but also a situation
in which it is difficult to control and monitor the information flows through
the variety of inter-organizational systems.

That every project sets up its own IT system and IP rules and practices is
also explained by the 'alarming' lack of detailed corporate IP policies,

a finding also reported by a study commissioned from DLA, a London-based law firm (Nunan 2004, Tait 2004). Companies are familiar with the process of formally protecting their IP: it is common for large firms, including those in this study, to employ patent attorneys, copyright specialists and so on, within an IP department. For instance, the firms interviewed for this project either focused their IP management approaches on patenting strategies or relied on trade secrets.

Yet a concentration on formally protecting firm IP does not amount to a fully-fledged corporate IP management policy. First, not all formally protected IP yields economic rewards and the costs of building a patent portfolio can be substantial. A corporate IPR audit could reveal where formally protected IP is yielding direct economic benefits, both in terms of licensing income and, more importantly, protecting key technologies ('crown jewels') that underpin the competitiveness of the firm. An audit should record where and how the company's IPRs are or have been used, and who uses them. These practices could also help a corporation identify what parts of its IP (not formally protected) are important to the company. Second, internal and external enforcement practices of controlling the use and sharing of IP and monitoring of infringement form an integral part of a company-wide IP management policy, whether they be formally protected or not.

Instead, we have observed that the IP management 'ethos' is biased, in the main, towards the formal protection processes – deciding whether or not to patent. The often informal practices that determine, for instance, when and how to share proprietary information with clients and partners are not instituted as part of a corporate IP policy.[7] The rest of this section discusses some of the problems that the defence companies and their customers have encountered when addressing IP issues in this context.

IP Issues in Collaborative Environments

The protection of information within SDEs
The first key problem with an SDE is the protection of 'background information'. This refers to the wide range of pre-existing proprietary information that a company brings to a collaborative project, from technical data and components and subsystems to manufacturing processes and design techniques. These will need to be integrated with technology brought by other firms or developed for this project, and therefore other firms may need to have access to such background information. By sharing background information through SDEs, companies run the risk of inadvertent leakage of commercially sensitive information; not only technical data about specific components, but also designs, design techniques or other processes that are not usually patented, but rather kept secret.

The second potential problem relates to the early release of 'foreground information', information developed during the course of the project. Although the MoD (as in our case study) will have rights of use over such foreground information where it has funded its development, the concern for contractors relates to the possibility that, through an SDE, the customer may access data that are still being worked upon. First, work-in-progress foreground information may include commercially sensitive information on company techniques and processes that will not be included in the final data packs delivered to the customer. Not all data in the foreground information is necessarily funded by the MoD as it could be privately ventured, a situation which is not uncommon in defence projects. Furthermore, firms are concerned about liability issues that may be derived from the customer accessing and using data that are still in draft form and not ready, or not intended, for delivery to the customer.

Shared digital environments generate concerns in relation to both of these problems. Because digital data are easy to replicate, systems to monitor and track the information shared through the SDE must be established together with strict procedures on data sharing. The establishment of such systems and procedures is more than a technical problem, as alluded to above. Although approaches exist or have been suggested for strict data access control, there is a palpable fear among the staff responsible for IP policy in all the companies interviewed that engineers do not adequately appreciate the importance that misappropriation of background information may have for their firm. Anecdotes abound of engineers who were only too happy to share proprietary and commercially sensitive technical details with their peers in other companies when involved in collaborative projects. An example of this is an incident in which an engineer blithely shared the software architecture of the firm's proprietary process with an engineer of a collaborating firm. Interviewees attributed such behaviour to 'cultural' traits within the engineering community that drive individuals to share their work with their partners across organizational divides, much in the same way that academics are widely known to do. Although most of the anecdotes involved instances in which such exchanges were not always facilitated by electronic networks (sometimes in conversations and data exchanges in paper form) concerns were expressed about what would happen when the digital systems for collaboration are in place and its use enforced that could allow a loquacious engineer to send reams of technical information across to project partners at the click of a button.

All companies were concerned about this problem, albeit in different degrees, depending on the extent to which they saw their competitive advantage as depending upon codified technologies that could be transferred to potential competitors, or on being 'first to market'. They all agreed, however, that there is a need to 'educate' their engineering staff about the importance of protecting their IP appropriately, particularly as inter-organizational collaboration is increasingly being supported by advanced IT.

Convergence of product and process data
An effect of the use of IT in systems design is the confluence of product and process data within the same data sets. This is the case, for instance, in the manufacture of specialized components for aero-engines or for aero-structures, which is driven by unique software-based processes. Naturally companies do not wish to reveal these processes to third parties, but sharing product data in electronic format could imply also sharing software-based processes when product and process data are inextricably linked. Companies that base their competitive advantage on the uniqueness of their manufacturing processes fear that an SDE could make them vulnerable to disclosure of their trade secrets.

Divergent approaches to IP management and data control among collaborators
To complicate matters even further, defence projects will often involve foreign partners operating within different legal and regulatory environments. This means, for instance, that an SDE will require data control access systems able to cope with the export and technology control regulations in each of the participating countries. As technical data, IP is covered under the export control regime of most NATO countries, so sharing of IP would invariably come under export control considerations. Collaborating companies have to ensure that data mounted in an SDE does not violate each collaborating partner's national export control regime. IP management methods will have to be coupled with the technical and regulatory structure emanating from the need to adhere to different export control regulations.

Equally, coping with different approaches to IP management across countries is problematic. Firms may question the IP management practices of their foreign partners and may decide to withhold information. We were offered examples of firms involved in international collaborative research programmes that were not contributing their best IP to the project, thus resulting in the joint research project performing at a suboptimal level.[8]

A related problem is the lack of consistency in the meaning of the terms used by firms and governments to class the different levels of information protection and access. For instance, terms like 'restricted' are interpreted differently among firms. Varying interpretations were feared to result in inadvertent misuse or leakage of important IP. Although we found no cases in which these differences led to identifiable financial losses or leakage of vital IP, our interviewees were adamant about the need for consistency and common use of terms, particularly when structuring an SDE for collaborative projects.

The Solutions

The issues and difficulties presented above, however, need not pose an insurmountable barrier to the introduction of SDEs in collaborative defence projects. In fact, both customers in the defence agencies and their industrial suppliers have been seeking solutions to address the aforementioned problems through four different but interrelated areas:

1. The definition of codified procedures to enable the assured identification of all individuals accessing the system, together with their rights of use across all stakeholders;
2. The establishment of procedures and rules regarding the management of the SDE, and the marking and segregation of the data the SDE contains;
3. The network technologies and inter-organizational systems they support;
4. The underlying training necessary to raise awareness of the importance of IP management among stakeholders and to explain the nature and implications of the tools and procedures in place.

The first two areas or aspects, can, in principle, be addressed through contractual conditions and associated commitments.

Contractual conditions
The uncertainty on the use and sharing of IP and IPRs that follows from the collaboration of diverse partners in the development and production of large complex systems can be addressed through the inclusion of detailed contractual provisions. In the UK, the MoD has formulated a wide choice of DEFCONs ('Defence Conditions') and DEFFORMS (templates for annexes that can be appended to contracts) for contract officers to include in contracts (Ministry of Defence 2004). These provide detailed contractual clauses and provisions applicable to a wide set of situations.

Although it is not mandatory for IPTs to include specific DEFCONs within a contract, explicit guidance documents recommend the adoption of some DEFCONs in specific contractual conditions. For instance, DEFCON 14 is commonly included in contracts and its use is recommended whenever the contracted work is likely to generate IP. This and other generally used DEFCONs provide, in practice, an established contractual framework that defines the MoD negotiation policy for key aspects of defence procurement, including IPR.

While some DEFCONs are relatively straightforward and are applauded by the defence companies for their necessity, there are others that have given rise to serious contention between the MoD and defence suppliers. In part, the differences emerge from the difficulties of covering all possible future events through generic contractual provisions. For instance, many defence systems are used for long periods, extending over three or more decades during which they will be subjected to several planned and unplanned upgrades and changes – for instance, the customer may require improvements in system capabilities to meet new challenges. Managing these complex systems over such long periods of time gives rise to difficult IP problems.

We distinguish two main sets of difficulties. First, when there are several units of such systems operating side by side (for instance, a squadron of fighter aircraft), it is common that the individual systems will have slightly different configurations although they may be formally identified as the same model. In practice, different sub-classes of each model may be identified *ex-post* by 'working backwards' through the different modifications to which the planes have been subjected. In this situation, it is often difficult to identify and monitor the ownership of the IP that may be involved in each small change, as well as the components that were part of the initial system, but have been superseded by new ones. A line-by-line definition of the different IPR contained within a complex system may not be possible and therefore it may remain preferable to stipulate IPR conditions in generic terms.[9]

Second, ownership of product data can generate problems with long-term system maintenance and repair needs. Contractual conditions try to address this situation. For instance, the application of DEFCON 15 will require from a contractor the supply of a 'manufacturing data pack' to which the MoD will have rights of use. DEFCON 15 is only to be applied when the development of a system has been fully funded by the MoD. Yet today's highly complex defence systems are likely to include subsystems or parts, or involve processes whose development has been privately funded, a point already discussed above. The leading prime contractors we interviewed pointed out that it is very likely that some of the IP that the client requests to be included as part of the manufacturing data pack will be the result of private investment. They are therefore anxious not 'to give away' data that could be and are likely to be commercially sensitive, particularly if the (subsequent) support and maintenance of the system is not to be undertaken by the prime contractor, but by a third party.

Furthermore, there is a cost to the provision of a data manufacturing pack that DEFCON 15 does not appear to address. As product components and subsystems are constantly updated, updating a manufacturing data pack entails refreshing the data over the life cycle of the system to take account of the changes introduced by the prime contractor and its supply chain. This cost, coupled with the IP problem addressed above, does not appear to be thoroughly recognized by the MoD, according to the interviewed companies.

The preceding examples show some emerging tensions in the application of IP conditions by the UK MoD. The root of the problem is that it is almost impossible to foresee and track all the contributions, changes and new requirements that will take place during a complex system's long life. Nonetheless, there was a consensus among our interviewees, shared by officials at the DPA, that it is necessary to codify procedures for the protection of IP when dealing with the procurement of complex, long life cycle systems. In fact some DEFCONS, such as DEFCON 15 referred to above, have been developed in collaboration with industry.

Relevant to our chapter is the '687 family' of DEFCONs and DEFFORMs, which establish how a 'shared data environment' should be operated. For instance, DEFFORM 687c provides a detailed 'Electronic Information Sharing Agreement' setting out the obligations and responsibilities of the SDE operator as well as user rights and obligations. DEFFORM 687c was finalized in 2001, after about 18 months of preparation in which both representatives from industry and from the MoD participated. In addition, the MoD developed a set of guidance notes to these DEFCONs and DEFFORMs at the request and with the collaboration of the Confederation of British Industry. These contractual tools can therefore be seen as the outcome of a consensus-seeking process between industry and the MoD, which formally endorses their use.

On the whole, UK defence prime contractors regard the use of most IPR DEFCONS positively and many of them have worked well. But they also insist that DEFCONS must continue to abide by a principle of equity in which the MoD may not assume ownership of company IP without adequate terms of compensation. A continually evolving defence procurement policy, which, in turn, is driving changes in the content and application of contractual conditions, is perceptibly stirring up tensions within the main defence contractors. These issues remain the sticking points between suppliers and the MoD.

Supporting network technologies and inter-organizational systems

The technological foundations and the strategic rationale for deploying IT systems to conduct collaborative working across geographically dispersed sites have been in place for some time. From the early 1990s communities of practice developed around concepts like TDI (Technical Data Interchange) and CALS (Continuous Acquisition Life-Cycle Support) among others. TDI focused on the development of common standards for exchanging the electronic files used by different Computer-Aided Design and Computer-Aided Manufacturing (CAD/CAM) systems (Donnington 1995). CALS was a more ambitious set of initiatives developing guiding principles and associated standard- and technology-developing activities aimed at creating a new type of relationship between customer and supply network that would use advanced IT to integrate the different phases in the procurement of a complex system (design, production, support and so on) into a continuous relationship. A key element in the implementation of the CALS vision was the creation of a 'Contractor-Integrated Technical Information System': a full technical data set that would accompany a complex system through its life cycle, from conceptual design to system decommissioning, and would be delivered to the customer together with the system. In an SDE this data set would be available to partners during the system's design and production.

Initial applications of these principles proved problematic.[10] During the 1990s, the civilian Boeing 777 became the best-publicized case of collaborative design and production across different locations for an aircraft system. Not only was this example heralded as an innovative programme for its team management approaches, but it was also lauded for representing the first use of digital computers to design and electronically pre-assemble an entire plane.[11] Further, joint design was achieved through a distributed computer network, consisting of mainframes and workstation installations in Japan, Kansas, Philadelphia and other locations.

Yet for all its achievements, this IT system fell short of constituting a full-blown SDE in the way defined above. Instead of offering a centralized product database available online to project partners under various access control conditions, the communication between suppliers and Boeing was often carried out using more rudimentary techniques, which in the opinion of an interviewee was because 777 is 'old technology' and the prime contractor did not see the need to introduce a more sophisticated IT system for data transmission. According to our interviewees, suppliers would e-mail their designs to the prime contractors' sites and vice versa, a process that was often slow and cumbersome given the size of the file attachments and the low speed of the modem links used. The slowness also caused project participants' design deadlines, for instance, to be delayed because the IT network could not always cope with the volumes of data being transmitted. This meant that file attachments were left sitting 'on hold' until the system could clear the backlog of data transmission.

In practice, the diffusion of SDEs using centralized databases accessible to project partners is still very limited. The US-led Joint Strike Fighter (JSF) and the British 'Type 45' Destroyer, described in more detail below, are the main examples of involvement by UK defence firms in programmes in which an SDE is being used.

Training

The third contemplated solution to the problems arising from the management of IP in collaborative projects is the need to inculcate in the engineering personnel a staunch sense of the importance of corporate IP. While training is a frequent measure undertaken by corporations in various areas, training in the case of IP management does not appear to be widely adopted or considered as a core part of training. As noted above, all the firms interviewed expressed concern about the allegedly casual attitude of engineers towards the protection of company IP. The ease by which data can be transferred electronically makes this concern more pressing. To combat a laissez-faire attitude towards the appropriate treatment of corporate IP by project personnel, some companies have issued guidelines about sharing data across companies, warning employees about inappropriate sharing of data. Penalties for misappropriation of data can include dismissal, fines and even imprisonment. Others have introduced induction briefings on the management of IP and export control regulations, especially for those who are involved in international collaborative projects. However, these training sessions are conducted on a project-by-project basis, rather than as part of a corporate IP management policy. Such a measure signals potential ineffectiveness for IP management on a corporate level.

Interviewees unanimously agreed about the need for systematic training of engineers on the importance of corporate IP and the handling of these assets, as part of a company-wide IP policy. The need for such training was also highlighted by ASIS, whose report also found that there was little evidence of training and awareness of information security in the US (ASIS International *et al.* 2002). The report also found that proper labelling or marking and handling of classified information are not the norm among companies, nor are employees typically trained to safeguard proprietary information in the office or while travelling.

Two Implementation Models

This section describes the two models of SDEs. These examples will show how Internet standards have been central to the implementation of SDEs in the defence sector, despite the need to tailor the combination of off-the-shelf software technologies and Internet access to the specific needs of each complex project. As we will see below this still represents a difficult challenge for which no ready-made solution exists and that can be addressed using different implementation models.

As already discussed above, we found few defence programmes with British participation in which an SDE system has been put in place. Here we show that the two main cases responded with dissimilar implementation models. They are different in the way the two major constituents of an SDE solution as discussed in the previous section (the contractual framework and inter-organizational systems) are defined and combined. We can distinguish them accordingly:

1. A 'regulated approach' as applied in UK contracts using elements of the 687 series of DEFCONs and DEFFORMs. These contractual conditions were defined by a group of experts from defence suppliers and the DPA and relate to the way in which the SDE will work.
2. A 'prime-led' approach as applied in the US-led JSF transatlantic collaborative programme. Here the prime contractor controls the definition of the inter-organizational system and imposes it, together with its associated IP conditions, to its international supply chain.

Regulated approach: Type 45 and contractual conditions
The Type 45 Anti-Warfare Destroyer is a large 7350-ton ship designed to provide fleet defence. Six platforms have already been contracted out of a total planned requirement of eight. This is the first fully-fledged development and production programme to implement an SDE following the approach laid out by the '687 family' of defence contractual conditions (DEFCONs) and forms (DEFFORMs). Type 45 draws upon DEFFORM 687a, which places obligations on the prime contractor to create and manage a central database of project information and make it accessible to users. DEFFORM 687b establishes a 'database information agreement' that sets out mutual obligations for all parties accessing it. These forms include IP clauses establishing, *inter alia*, that uploading data into the database does not imply the granting and unauthorized use of any IPR and an obligation on the contractor to grant a user licence to the customer (MoD) to operate and maintain the database system once this is transferred from the contractor.

The Type 47 SDE is based on Internet architecture, can be accessed through a Wide Area Network or dial-up connections, and uses a suite of off-the-shelf software applications. In some cases the applications have had to be modified in-house to adapt them to the specific needs of the programme; this is the case, for instance, with Windchill, a set of software tools to enable a shared, Web-based configuration and document management system.

BAE Systems Electronics Limited is in charge of setting up the SDE. This is one of the responsibilities of the 'Prime Contract Office' (PCO), but it has involved other partners and stakeholders in the development of the system through the application of DEFFORMs that are themselves the result of a process of negotiation among many industry stakeholders and Government. Also, the PCO drew on the input from main stakeholders, which include five main supplier firms and the programme client, the Defence Procurement Agency, in the definition of the SDE, its applications and management, and the user practices. This process, conducted through an 'Enterprise Integration User Group' comprising representatives of all the main stakeholders, is responsible for overseeing the system implement-ation across stakeholders, and reviewing and updating the enterprise inte-gration strategy. The resulting 'Enterprise Integration Implementation Plan' affirmed that IPR previously owned by a stakeholder will not 'nor-mally' be published in the SDE, and that if it is, such 'background IPR' will be protected by access controls and made accessible only to the required stakeholders.

The Type 45 SDE is however limited in the extent of the applications and data exchanges it supports. The system carries extensive information on project management tasks and provides a tool for sharing project informa-tion across several participating firms and the client representatives. Yet the use of the system is limited to information that does not have a classification of 'Confidential' or higher national security restriction, a classification which is not unusual in defence projects. Technical data pub-lished in the SDE include graphical representations of the 'product geom-etry' and result in a 'product model' that can be used to guide the evolving design within the collaborating firms. However, detailed design data, as for instance the CAD files used for the design of the different elements, are not shared through the SDE.

Despite these limitations the Type 45 SDE presents a new stage in the extent to which collaborative tools based on IT have been implemented to facilitate the collaboration across organizations involved in the develop-ment, production and operation of a complex product and the manage-ment of stakeholders' IP. The system has now been in place for almost five years, has become a key tool in the management of the programme and is delivering the services to the PCO and its client.

Still, it is worth noting that an important reason for the relative simpli-city and success of this SDE is that it is a domestic project and that no foreign suppliers may access the system. The main reasons for the added complexity when dealing with international programmes, as noted above, are the need to deal with complex export control legislation and to accom-modate different national regulations on issues like IPR and privacy. Given its relatively 'smaller' size and national character, it is questionable whether this type of SDE would be 'scalable' for larger international projects.

The JSF case discussed below provides an example of the challenges faced when international collaboration is organized around an SDE.

Prime-led approach: the case of JSF

The prime contractor for JSF is Lockheed Martin Aeronautics (LMA), which is both the final assembler and systems integrator, and also a sub-systems and parts manufacturer for the aircraft. LMA has implemented an SDE which again rests on Internet standards and a combination of off-the-shelf software tools, including 'Metaphase' (a Product Data Management programme enabling access to an extended supply network) and again, Windchill (providing a web access to programme management data). LMA controls access to these facilities. This is a mandated system for suppliers, imposed as a condition for collaboration, in which LMA manages and controls the SDE, and defines and establishes architecture and procedures.

The SDE revolves around a Joint Data Library (JDL) that serves as the node for the sharing of technical data across project participants. Ownership of data in the JDL is indicated by restrictive agreed legends, which are included in the footer of all data and drawings. Access to the JDL is established through formal agreements, so-called Technical Assistance Agreements (TAAs) between LMA and its suppliers. TAAs provide the formal approval mechanism enabling stakeholders to post and access data in the SDE and specify the kind of data that can be accessed and used by the supplier. TAAs have become a very complex tool to operate, particularly when they involve foreign (non-US) suppliers. Often, several TAAs are signed with each supplier covering different sets of data for which the supplier acquires rights to upload and download. In particular, when the suppliers are foreign nationals, such TAAs have to take into account existing US export control regulations and establish the relevant data access control accordingly. On the one hand, this has a positive effect: as access to the JDL requires a TAA it therefore takes into account export control regulations. Data accessible by a partner through the JDL is, in practice, approved for transfer abroad in accordance with existing US export control regulations. On the other hand, the system has become cumbersome to operate. For instance, a British firm participating in the programme has signed over 160 TAAs covering, among other things, different requirements relating to the export and re-export of the technical data in different components and subsystems.

Furthermore, any data communication between two suppliers has to be approved by LMA, regardless of the TAAs signed between it and the two suppliers. Accordingly the JDL is partitioned: suppliers cannot access the project data of other suppliers; only LMA as prime contractor has access to all data and information in the JDL. Furthermore, when a supplier is involved in different subsystems it will access different and separate folders under different TAAs. This means that different parts of a corporation working on other sections or aircraft subsystems will not have access to each other's data sets within the JDL. Again this has positive and negative effects. On the one hand, each supplier has its own set of folders containing its own information, which acts as a means of IP protection, avoiding potential confusion as to what information belongs to whom. On the other hand, the system slows down collaboration across suppliers. If a company needs data from another supplier, it will have to request it from the prime contractor, who will then 'post' the information in a common folder available to both companies, after checking that the requested information is available and indicated on the TAAs signed by both companies.

Last but not least, management of the access control at individual level is even more cumbersome. Any supplier employee wishing to access JDL data will have to request permission from LMA, which then manually checks whether a TAA and the rights cover the individual. Once this information is ascertained LMA provides access to the relevant project folder or folders. Yet the onus is on the individual to ensure that the information or access rights it needs are listed on the relevant TAA. Participating companies have had to train the employees working on this system on the complex operating procedures by which it is regulated.

The JSF SDE clearly diminishes the chances of data leakage but apart from slowing down collaboration and being operationally cumbersome, it could cause data replication across folders. Data replication carries with it the risk of data fracture; that is, unless configured appropriately, the data in one folder could be updated without the same data being changed in another folder, thereby ending in two versions of the same document.

Still, the rather elaborate but awkward control systems of the JSF SDE represent the collective means for managing the IP of participating international collaborators. Unwieldy as they may appear to be, it becomes apparent that in international collaborative projects, the issues of export controls and IP are co-mingled and that an SDE to support such collaboration will need to consider these dimensions, bearing in mind that export-controlled items also contain an array of IP and IPR. These considerations return us to the observation that an international collaborative SDE will be complex, but one whose difficulties may not be insurmountable.

MANAGING IP IN COLLABORATIVE SDEs: SOME LESSONS

Despite the burgeoning literature on the development and implementation of IT applications to support business activities, there is a noticeable paucity of studies on how firms use IT to manage their IP in a digital business ecosystem. This chapter has analysed the IP issues that arise in inter-organizational collaborative projects using SDEs, extending as well the current literature on corporate management of IP which has so far focused mainly on IP management within the firm.

Our study focused on defence projects typically involving the development and production of large weapons systems that consist of thousands of components and subsystems delivered by large supplier networks. This environment increases the complexity of managing IP and of setting up an SDE affording protection, security, confidentiality, privacy, authenticity and integrity of data, and identity management for access control. Yet, 'mass/consumer market' collaborative projects, such as of the auto industry, also involve a large number of parts and components, and so the lessons we offer for IP management in conducting business activities in a digital business ecosystem may not be exclusive to the defence sector.

So how can the scope of an SDE be extended so that the potential offered by IT to organize and coordinate complex design and engineering tasks across organizations is fully exploited while minimizing the risks of IP misappropriation and leakage? The problems that our study has unveiled suggest actions that can expand the scope and functionality of future SDEs, and collectively, for a digital business ecosystem.

We divide our suggestions into (1) technical; and (2) strategic and/or managerial.

Technical

As we have seen, an approach to prevent unauthorized data access is the data segmentation approach used in the JSF SDE, which is unwieldy. The alternative here is to administer the system by tagging each data element with information including its origin, security, commercial confidentiality markings and access restrictions, and then linking the access rights of individuals to the markings. This requires a parallel identity and access management system, in which all individuals must have proof of identity to log on to the system. Access will depend on the individual's organization, role within the organization and any other factors like nationality, with a bearing on the definition of his or her access privileges.

Such a 'data level' management system would allocate access rights automatically, thus eliminating the need for a manual management of access privileges. The technologies and procedures to set up such a system exist. For instance, proposals have been put forward establishing detailed procedures to tackle security concerns and export control regulations in transatlantic arms collaboration programmes. An example of this is the Transatlantic

Collaboration Program, an initiative of a group of US and UK defence firms to develop frameworks for secure transatlantic collaboration. The Program commissioned Booz Allen Hamilton to produce a framework and then a design for building secure IT collaborative environments, including the required processes, mechanisms and technologies for collaborating partners (Booz Allen Hamilton 2003, 2004). The SDE is currently being piloted by a few of the US defence firms involved in the Program.

Strategic and/or Managerial

The establishment of a robust IT system underpins a secure digital business ecosystem for the management of IP. However, we argue that managerial issues can overshadow the technical aspect. Specifically, an SDE able to deal adequately with IP issues has to rest on five key foundations:

1. A commitment by participant companies to a corporate IP policy laying out guidelines and codes of practice on the treatment of corporate IP, including training of research personnel;
2. A recognition that a corporate IP policy entails integration of input from the IT, legal and commercial departments into its definition;
3. A commitment to allocate the necessary resources for managing the SDE system throughout the collaborative partnership;
4. An agreement on the ICT tools to monitor and track the information shared through the SDE;
5. The establishment of procedures to ensure continual robustness, security and functionality of the SDE system.

Most of these foundations relate to non-technical issues. Our study revealed that commercial and IP managers were particularly concerned about those aspects of IP management that are more difficult to control through contractual or technical measures. To reiterate, disquiet was evident among all firms interviewed about the way in which engineers and designers were believed to be treating the information they were working on and the results of their work. The capacity to copy and transmit data afforded by IT amplified the ability of careless employees to transfer commercially sensitive data outside the firm. Under these circumstances the lack of guidelines on the treatment of information assets can emerge as a barrier to the establishment of an SDE. Corporate-wide IP management policies and procedures can be seen as a precondition to the establishment of project-specific SDEs.

Furthermore, although technical approaches exist to deal with this problem, such as the incorporation of 'data level' access management controls to prevent unauthorized access, there is a need for a corporate IP management policy to address training and raise awareness of the importance of heedless sharing of data. A corporate policy needs also to consider company-wide processes and procedures for the treatment of company IP that is not formally protected, and not focus on the protection mechanisms themselves, for instance, to patent or to keep a particular IP a trade secret.

Moreover, as different SDEs are created for different projects, there is a possibility that in the future, the same company will be involved in several SDEs using different systems, contractual conditions and IP sharing rules. Such complexity also calls for better training of research personnel in the treatment and management of IP, lest it result in incoherent IP management practices. Therefore, training on IP management in a collaborative environment needs to rise above its current project-by-project approach. A corporate IP management policy should systematically address these issues and establish procedures and behavioural guidelines with respect to the treatment of IP and information.

Importantly, a corporate IP management policy sits at the interface of IT strategy, commercial and contractual policies, and engineering and design practices. While it is necessary for commercial and legal personnel to 'steer' the policy, it is the engineers and technical personnel who will eventually be responsible for their implementation. We have often found the interaction tenuous between these two groups of people. For instance, the Type 45 Enterprise Integration Plan establishes mechanisms to request the opinions of SDE users on the operation of the system. This is an example of a good management principle: such a policy provides an information channel between engineers using the SDE and those in charge of its management. Yet despite following 'good practice', Type 45 SDE falls short of bringing together engineering, IT personnel, commercial and legal communities in the definition of an IP management policy approach. It must be noted that in ensuring that IP is properly protected and used, and data access effectively controlled in an SDE, contractual obligations, IP practices and IT architecture must be inextricably linked. This requires close collaboration between the commercial and/or legal and IT departments and therefore needs to be led from the corporate executive level. Lapses in this collaboration would probably lead to an inadequate IP management policy.

In more general terms the establishment of inter-organizational networks needs to account for the legal and regulatory environment within which SDEs operate in a digital business ecosystem. Again, for instance, the requirements imposed by export control regulations will also affect the architecture of an international SDE. It is important to note that these constraints are not unique to defence projects; many high-technology programmes will deal with controlled technologies and will be subject to the same constraints regardless of their military or civilian character. The influence of regulatory constraints on the nature and structure of SDEs is crucial, as discussed above, although this has often been overlooked in the literature on inter-organizational networks.

CONCLUSION

In sum, our study has argued that the nature of the IP management challenges posed by the implementation of SDEs requires commitment and support at the corporate executive level. Yet we found that IT implementations are viewed by project directors as additional costs rather than investment for the future, as it is often difficult to attribute specific monetary benefits to the introduction of these technologies. When in 1995 one of us carried out a study on the diffusion of CALS principles in the UK, an expert in a major firm stated that the industry displayed 'a file transfer rather than an open database mindset' (Molas-Gallart 1996). This state of affairs appears to continue today, even as SDEs appear to be a useful tool for collaborative working. We cannot, however, ascribe this situation to the impossibility of IP management within collaborative IT networks; neither can we attribute it to technological difficulties in establishing open database architectures to underpin collaboration. The procedures and underlying technologies to establish the networks and protect IP exist. Their slow diffusion could be ascribed to the detachment with which corporate executives deal with the details of IT systems to be used in specific projects.

A clearly defined corporate IP strategy, therefore, is instrumental for effective and successful IP management throughout the organization, within and beyond SDEs, regardless of the sector. Importantly, a strong executive drive is needed to bring together the commercial, IP and IT functions within the company and across the different partners in a collaborative project. It is also needed to support an increasing trend, albeit differently configured, of 'networked' and 'shared data environments' – the digital business ecosystem – to ensure that corporate IP strategies can ably function within and beyond collaborative projects.

NOTES

1. The research for this paper has been jointly funded by the UK Economic and Social Research Council 'E-Society Programme' and the UK Ministry of Defence under the Joint Grants Scheme (ESRC Award Reference RES-335-25-0017). The authors

gratefully acknowledge the comments of the executives of the defence companies inter-viewed, and Prof. J. Adams and Robert Shields. Responsibility for errors is solely ours.
2.   Some IP, like brands and designs, needs to be 'disclosed' to be valuable.
3.   For a clear discussion of the IP concept and the different forms of IP see for instance Weil and Snapper (1989).
4.   We explored elsewhere the mistrust between defence suppliers and the MoD generated by the way in which IPR was handled in the privatization process of the British defence research establishments (Molas-Gallart and Tang 2006).
5.   Except for six telephone interviews, the rest were all face-to-face interviews carried out by both of us.
6.   Here we use the term 'network' to refer to a group of organizations collaborating within a specific large project. 'Network technology' is the technical information and commun-ications infrastructure that supports the network, and an 'inter-organizational system' refers to the applications shared by the network through its network technology (Volkoff, Chan and Newson 1999).
7.   Only one firm interviewed had a clearly articulated IP management policy supported by an IT system. This is used to track which patents were used in each of the firm's prod-ucts, so that the firm can monitor where and how patents are used and also to identify infringements.
8.   The practice of holding back one's best technology when contributing to international collaborative programmes has long been pointed out as a major problem in international arms collaboration.
9.   However, there is a debate in the field of relational contractual theory as to the extent to which contracts can and should be written to address all possible eventualities in a complex, long-term project. Contract theorists have argued that a contract is not an abstract formalistic mechanism, but one that typically involves development of rela-tionships that go beyond the terms of a contract and evolve through the course of the project (MacNeil 1980, 1999). The practice in defence contracting, however, has tended towards the detailed specification of conditions and deliverables trying to cover for all possible eventualities.
10. For an early discussion of their application to Eurofighter, the European fighter aircraft project, see Spinardi, Graham and Williams (1995).
11. However, a very sophisticated IT system for technical data sharing across US partners, project design and engineering has been described and analysed for the B-2 Stealth Bomber, an aircraft design and manufacturing project that predated the 777 by several years (Argyres 1999).

REFERENCES

Argyres, N.S. (1999), 'The impact of information technology on coordination: evi-dence from the B-2 "Stealth" bomber', *Organization Science*, **10** (2), 162–180.
ASIS International, PricewaterhouseCoopers and American Chamber of Commerce (2002), *Trends in Proprietary Information Loss: Survey Report*, Alexandria, VA: ASIS International.
Boisot, M.H. (1998), *Knowledge Assets: Securing Competitive Advantage in the Information Economy*, Oxford: Oxford University Press.
Booz Allen Hamilton (2003), *A Framework for Secure Collaboration across US/UK Defence*, UK Council for Electronic Business.
Booz Allen Hamilton (2004), *Transatlantic Secure Collaboration Programme (TSCP): How-To-Guide*, UK Council for Electronic Business.
Buigues, P., A. Jacquemin and J.-F. Marchipont (eds) (2000), *Competitiveness and the Value of Intangible Assets*, Cheltenham: Edward Elgar.

Business Wire (2005), *Intellectual Property Still Remains a Huge Difficulty for US Companies* 2005, 11 November. Available from http://www.intellectualsecurity.com/2005/11/intellectual_property_still_re.html#more

Chesbrough, H. (2003), 'The logic of open innovation: managing intellectual property', *California Management Review*, **45** (3), 33–58.

Davenport, T.H and L. Prusak (1998), *Working Knowledge: How Organizations Manage What They Know*, Boston, MA: Harvard Business School Press.

Davis, L. (2004), 'Intellectual Property Rights: strategy and policy', *Economics of Innovation and New Technology*, **13** (5), 399–416.

Donnington, J. (1995), *Electronic Data Interchange in the Automotive Industry: Managing Information Flows for Greater Profitability*, Financial Times Management Reports, London: Pearson Professional.

Gholz, E. (2003), 'Systems Integration in the US Defense Industry', in A. Prencipe, A. Davies and M. Hobday (eds), *The Business of Systems Integration*, Oxford: Oxford University Press, pp. 279–306.

Granstrand, O. (2004), 'The economics and management of technology trade: towards a pro-licensing era?' *International Journal of Technology Management*, **27** (2–3), 209–240.

Grindley, P.C. and D.J. Teece (1997), 'Managing intellectual capital: licensing and cross-licensing semiconductors and electronics', *California Management Review*, **39** (2), 8–41.

Guilhon, B., R. Attia and R. Rizoulières (2004), 'Markets for technology and firms' strategies: the case of the semiconductor industry', *International Journal of Technology Management*, **27** (2–3), 123–142.

Hall, B.H. and R.H. Ziedonis (2001), 'The patent paradox revisited: an empirical study of patenting in the U.S. semiconductor industry, 1979–1995', *Rand Journal of Economics*, **20** (1), 101–128.

Krugman, P. (ed.) (1986), *Strategic Trade Policy and the New International Economics*, Cambridge, MA: MIT Press.

Lyons, J. (2004), *Internet Investigations: International Standards and Co-operation*. Paper read at UN/ECE Advisory Group for the Protection and Implementation of Intellectual Property Rights for Investment, 1–2 April,Warsaw.

MacNeil, I.R. (1980), *The Social Contract*, London: Yale University Press.

MacNeil, I.R. (1999), 'Relational contract theory: challenges and queries', *Northwestern University Law Review*, **94** (3), 877–907.

Ministry of Defence (2004), *Guidelines for Industry: 10: The Intellectual Property Rights (IPR) DEFCONs, Part B*, Defence Procurement Agency [cited July 2004]. Available from http://www.ams.mod.uk/ams/content/docs/toolkit/ams/buttons/modind/gfi10.htm, 17 September 2006.

Ministry of Defence Smart Procurement Implementation Team (1999), *The Acquisition Handbook: A Guide to Smart Procurement 'Faster, Cheaper, Better'*, First edition, Bristol: Defence Procurement Agency.

Molas-Gallart, J. (1996), *Telematics in Life-Cycle Management*. Paper presented at the International Conference on Management and New Technologies, Madrid, 12–14 June.

Molas-Gallart, J. and P. Tang (2006), 'Ownership matters: intellectual property, privatization and innovation', *Research Policy*, **35** (2), 200–212.

Nonaka, I. and H. Takeuchi (1995), *The Knowledge-Creating Company*, Oxford: Oxford University Press.

Nunan, J. (2004), 'Strategy? What strategy?' *Copyright World*, **146**, 9–10.

Quinn, J.B. (1992), *Intelligent Enterprise*, New York: Free Press.

Reitzig, M. (2004), 'Strategic management of intellectual property', *Sloan Management Review*, (Spring), 35–39.

Rivette, K. and D. Kline (2000), 'Discovering new value in intellectual property'. *Harvard Business Review*, **78** (1), 59–64.

Ruggles, R. and D. Holtshouse (1999), *The Knowledge Advantage*, Oxford: Capstone Publishing.

Shapiro, C. (2001), *Navigating the Patent Thicket: Cross-Licenses, Patent Pools and Standard Setting*. Available from http://faculty.haas.berkeley.edu/shapiro/thicket.pdf, 17 September 2006.

Shapiro, C. and H. Varian (1999), *Information Rules: A Strategic Guide to the Network Economy*, Boston, MA: Harvard Business School Press.

Spinardi, G., I. Graham and R. Williams (1995), 'Technical data interchange in the Eurofighter project', *Science and Public Policy*, **22** (1), 29–38.

Tait, N. (2004), '"Alarming" findings on intellectual property', *Financial Times*, 28 October, 5.

Tang, P. (1998), 'How electronic publishers are protecting against piracy: doubts about technical systems of protection', *The Information Society*, **14** (1), 19–31.

Tang, P. and D. Paré (2003), 'Gathering the foam: are business method patents a deterrent to software innovation and commercialization?' *International Review of Law Computers and Technology*, **17** (2), 127–162.

Teece, D.J. (1998), 'Capturing value from knowledge assets: the new economy, markets for know-how and intangible assets', *California Management Review*, **40** (3), 55–79.

Teece, D.J., G. Pisano and A. Shuen (1997), 'Dynamic capabilities and strategic management', *Strategic Management Journal*, **18**, 509–533.

Volkoff, O., Y.E. Chan and E.F.P. Newson (1999), 'Leading the development and implementation of collaborative interorganizational systems', *Information and Management*, **35** (2), 63–75.

Weil, V. and J.H. Snapper (1989), *Owning Scientific and Technical Information: Value and Ethical Issues*, New Brunswick and London: Rutgers University Press.

9. MAP-STEPS: a framework for opportunity assessment and development of a sustainable business model for eBusiness

Swapan Kumar Majumdar

INTRODUCTION

Globalization of trade and the rapid evolution of Information and Communication Technology (ICT) are compelling organizations to redefine their business models. This chapter examines the features of emerging digital business ecosystems (Majumdar 1999, Peltoniemi 2004), identifies the macro and micro variables of eBusiness models (Majumdar 2005), and proposes a framework for comprehensive analysis of eBusiness opportunity and the development of fitting business models to reduce the risks of extinction, and to gain sustainable competitive advantage.

ICT is changing the construct, boundaries and rules of competition (Porter 2001), but not the core intent of business. It is consistently opening up new ways of reaching and collaborating directly with customers and business partners and eroding age-old barriers of geography and traditional methods of doing business. ICT is empowering customers and competitors alike and creating equal opportunity for all. To survive and thrive in these diverse and hypercompetitive digital business ecosystems (DBEs), organizations and entrepreneurs have to examine and explore the options for creating superior values for their customers and shareholders and for maintaining a competitive edge in their chosen market places. They have to develop strategies to win the minds and trust of demanding customers and one cannot do this unless one knows how the minds of the masses are moving and how the market opportunities are changing.

The intent of eBusiness is to develop cost-effective and user-friendly business and information exchange processes across the extended value chain (Porter 2001), and to lower the risks of failure (Kaplan 2002). Corporate governance is the management of organizations' activities to create and reap values for the stakeholders of the business. The heart of corporate governance is its business model – its strategy for creation and delivery of superior value. The 'bricks and mortar' business models do not fit the digital business ecosystems, where ICT is the new enabler and differentiator of business, distance is dead, work never sleeps and the value chains and boundaries of industry are blurring. The new business ecosystems are compelling organizations to rethink their directions and reinvent their business models.

Digital business ecosystems raise hopes as well as uncertainties. The rise and fall of many 'dot.com' businesses (Kaplan 2002) demonstrate that one can hardly shine in tomorrow's world with yesterday's solutions. Absence of empirical evidence inspires researchers to find the answers to several fundamental questions like: What are the fundamental issues in creating sustainable organizational improvement? How can we determine the right eBusiness opportunity? How can an organization move from where it is to where it wants to be? What are the transitional issues? Why do some organizations execute successfully, while other organizations fail to do so? What are the key factors that make the most difference?

To avoid the costly mistakes of the past and steer through the tunnel of uncertainty, it is necessary to have a framework, which in effect would guide eBusiness organizations and entrepreneurs to renovate and reinvent their business models under the changing standard and context of DBEs. The development of one such framework requires an understanding of the key features and keystones of the eBusiness model.

ARTIFACTS OF THE eBUSINESS MODEL

The aim of any eBusiness initiative is to improve its performance. This is measured by market share, operational efficiency and profitability. However, not all of us live in the same business ecosystem. Diversity is reality. A digital business ecosystem is a conglomeration of different interlinked business entities in a given environment.

The development of effective, forward-looking eBusiness models requires visualization of external and internal entities and elements of eBusiness that affect the performances of the business. Once these major entities and elements are identified, keystones are revealed, on which an effective eBusiness model can be built. The four keystones of the eBusiness model are technology, market, digital business ecosystem and performance. Figure 9.1 shows the key features of the keystones and their significance in the development of the effective eBusiness model.

A successful business model radiates from its business strategy, which can create and deliver unique value to its customers and shareholders in a given market within a given business ecosystem by using the right technology and resources, aligning people and the processes to achieve the desired level of performance. Formulation of eBusiness strategy has to pay attention to the fact that eBusinesses are vulnerable to encroachment from overseas digital business ecosystem competitors, yet new opportunities are offered at the same time to those willing to take on global markets.

To be competitive in today's new business paradigm, clever business models need to be developed to help in turning would-be, one-time purchases into recurring revenue streams, reaching customers who cannot be reached by existing sales forces, and expanding an organization's supplier base by letting more firms bid or tender online by means of online auctions and marketplaces. Effective business models are those that empower organizations to outperform the competitors and accomplish the desired performance target in a given market place (Afuah and Tucci 2003).

Development of an effective eBusiness model requires an understanding of the forces that significantly affect the performance of eBusiness. These are markets, value creation and realization strategy, people, processes and technology. Conversely, market, technology, process and people issues arise from quite different domains, each with a different logic and vocabulary. The functional managers of varied disciplines often fail to comprehend and face difficulties in communicating with each other. Each sees and understands a different piece of the elephant.[1] No one has all the answers, or a complete view. Organizations need a comprehensive framework to synthesize all the divergent aspects of eBusiness into a unique objective-driven business model.

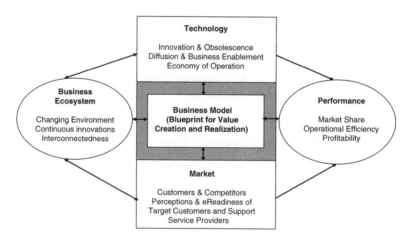

Figure 9.1   Keystones of the eBusiness model

MAP-STEPS is one such normative model that assists organizations to figure out their opportunity window in a given market and digital business ecosystem. It empowers organizations to analyse and synthesize the technical, commercial and social issues of emerging digital business ecosystems.

FRAMEWORK FOR FORMULATION AND GOVERNANCE OF eBUSINESS

Formulation of the eBusiness model is deciding on the frame and fabrics of an eBusiness endeavour, ranging from ideation to governance. It involves a series of analyses that entrepreneurs have to conduct to understand their market opportunities and to develop matching action models for implementation and control. Figure 9.2 exhibits the blocks of analytic requirements of the MAP-STEPS framework. Organizations of DBE need to conduct a series of analyses for identifying organizations' windows of opportunity, developing appropriate eBusiness strategies for the creation, delivery and realization of unique value. The MAP-STEPS framework specifies the key analytic issues that must be checked for the transformation of general market opportunities into the distinctive competitive advantages of a specific organization and development of a competitive edge.

The MAP-STEPS is a normative framework for market opportunity assessment, strategy formulation, project execution strategy and governance of eBusiness operations and processes. Figure 9.3 highlights the four phases of the MAP-STEPS framework. Each phase illustrates the key

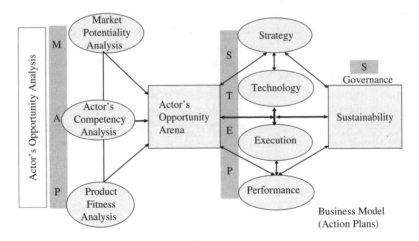

Figure 9.2   A framework for formulation and governance of eBusiness

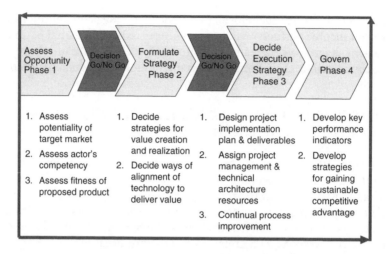

Figure 9.3   Four phases of the MAP-STEPS model

issues that are to be addressed to develop viable strategies and actions required to seize an opportunity and to maintain a competitive edge in the market place.

Market Opportunity Assessment

Market opportunity assessment is a three-step process called 'MAP'. Every eBusiness-initiating firm (actor) has to conduct the MAP: (1) Market potentiality analysis, (2) Actor's competency analysis, and (3) Product fitness analysis. By conducting the MAP analysis, a firm or entrepreneur can make calculated 'go/no go' decisions about pursuing the opportunity.

To launch a business in a market economy, one has to begin with market potentiality analysis. As business is creating and delivering values to the target customers, understanding what customers perceive as valuable is essential. Secondly, eBusiness is an alternative way of doing business and any alternative business approach must analyse the pains and preparedness of the existing markets and customers to find out the scope of improvements.

The analysis of eBusiness-potential of the target market is a two-stage process that the actor has to undertake: (1) broader macro-economic analysis of the marketing environment, and (2) analysis of end users' disposition. The end users' outlook illustrates the potential of the market. The macro-economic factors of the market significantly influence end users' perception and outlooks. Both the macro and micro factors of the target market have to be analysed within the context of the eBusiness readiness of the market to understand the eBusiness potential of the market. The prerequisites of making electronic business transactions (eBusiness) possible are: (1) availability of Internet infrastructure; (2) eBusiness preparedness of the entrepreneurs as well as their suppliers and distributors (web-enabling of the business processes for conducting online transactions); (3) availability of Internet access to a sufficient number of intended or would-be customers; and finally (4) the willingness of significant numbers of customers (that is mental acceptance or readiness) to use the Internet as an alternative or complementary channel of business communication and transactions.

Once the eBusiness potential of a market is known, the actor or entrepreneur has to assess whether or not he or she has the required competency to make use of the general market potential of specific benefits for the enterprise. In other words, is the actor capable of taking advantage of this opportunity? Can the actor transform the eBusiness potential of the market into an eBusiness and reap real benefits for the firm?

Market potential does not make any sense to an actor if the actor does not possess the capabilities and resources required to seize the opportunity. Transformation of the eBusiness potential of a market into profit requires a comprehensive assessment of an actor's key competencies.

In a borderless digital business ecosystem (DBE), firms can only outperform their competitors if they possess not only the required capabilities and resources but also have a distinctive competitive advantage. Without having any distinctive advantage in what you can do the best, it is hard to survive in this hypercompetitive eBusiness market place. Finally no business is free of risks. Every actor entrepreneur must assess the financial and technical attractiveness of the potential market with respect to its strengths and the mission of the business. Hence, whether the market opportunity in question is the right opportunity for the actor or not is to be judged from the viewpoint of the distinctive competencies of the actor.

To transform the general market opportunity into a specific business plan, firms not only need to analyse their competencies, but also the 'fitness analysis of the proposed product'. The eFitness of a product depends on four factors: (1) digitality of the product, (2) service requirements of the product, (3) degree of fragmentation in the value chain, and (4) sensitivity of the product and services.

Digital products can easily be exchanged across the Internet. Similarly, the products that require a higher degree of service can be delivered through the network in DIY (do it yourself) mode. In fact, all digital and remote customer services are ideal for eBusiness. The Internet is a unifying agent. The more fragmented the industry and its value chain partners, the more suitable is the industry for eBusiness. Finally, speed and pervasiveness are the unique feature of eBusiness technology. Thus the products and services that are sensitive to time and convenience are best fitted for eBusiness. Also, eBusiness can improve quality and reduce costs; most importantly it helps to improve convenience, communication and coordination.

Strategy Formulation

The second phase of the MAP-STEPS model is strategy formulation. The heart of the eBusiness model is its strategy. The three paradigms of eBusiness strategy are: (1) value creation strategy, (2) value realization strategy and (3) value delivery strategy. Figure 9.4 demonstrates the relationship and the interconnectedness of these three paradigms.

The four other sub-models of eBusiness strategy are: (1) execution model, (2) resource model, (3) cost model and (4) revenue model. The eBusiness model will not function if any of these sub-models is inappropriate. However, there is no golden rule or magic for value creation.

An organization may be for-profit or not-for-profit, but every organization must create value for its customers and realize value for its initiators. For a profit-making organization, the focus is on realization of money for its investors, and for not-for-profit organizations, the focus is on serving more recipients of the products or services with less money.

The bottom line of any business is its financial results, which depend on the soundness of its pricing and revenue collection strategy. To survive and thrive in hypercompetitive digital business ecosystems, eBusiness firms have to look for multiple sources of revenue.

The virtue of an eBusiness model depends on the cohesive effectiveness of the five business vehicles: people, process, culture, technology and content. The eBusiness is based on the philosophy of 'pull' rather than the

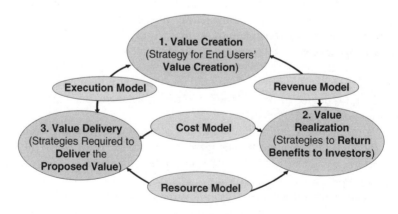

Figure 9.4   Three paradigms of the eBusiness model

'push' of bricks and mortar business. If technology is not geared to address the soft issues of eBusiness, it will hardly be able to pull sufficient numbers of customers to use the eBusiness solutions. Alignment of people, process and technology is a critical factor of success.

The contents should trigger the core desire of the target customers. In 'Technology' are the enablers and the differentiators of eBusiness. Hence, after strategy the next step of eBusiness is articulation of the architecture of eBusiness technology.

Technology Architecture of eBusiness

Technology is a major pillar of eBusiness. Figure 9.5 displays the architecture of eBusiness technologies. This means that to make eBusiness work, one has to manage five different sets of ICT. Moreover, to make the system work, one most critical task is the seamless integration of various layers of technology and convergence of the business processes. If any of the layers of eBusiness technology becomes non-functional, eBusiness will not function. Buying technology is not a problem; but using technology for creating exceptional strategic value for the business is the key issue of eBusiness

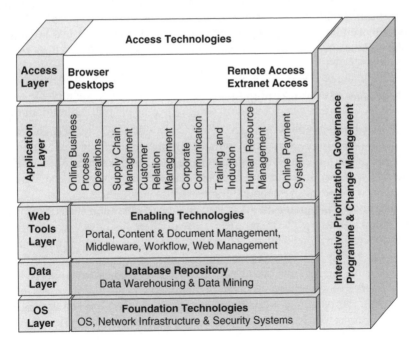

Figure 9.5   Architecture of eBusiness technology

management. Management of technology is choosing which innovation you have to consider for your business and how the technology has diffused to your area or locality; how you leverage the technology to create, deliver and realize value is the key to success.

Execution of eBusiness Project

The strategy or the blueprints of eBusiness will not produce any result if the process of execution is wrong. Conversely, wrong strategy and right execution will glorify the failure. The execution of an eBusiness project is a new ball game – a completely new approach of strategic convergence and coordination. Technologists create eProcess, and business acumen is required to embed the technology in the business process to protect the business values from the competitors. Execution is critical. One does not possess 100 per cent of the knowledge required for execution before actually doing it. It depends on the need for a quick turnaround, rapid learning and redesigning approach rather than doing everything right in the first place. The assumption is that we do not know every detail of eBusiness. The only way to bridge the knowledge gap is learning by doing.

Successful execution of an eBusiness project requires a radically different approach. Building an eBusiness is not a sequential process but a series of interdependent and overlapping work streams. It requires a fast learning and enhancement approach. If you cannot be a 'fast mover' you have to be a 'fast learner'.

Governance of eBusiness Initiatives

The fourth and last phase of the MAP-STEPS model is governance. The governance of eBusiness is radically different from physical business. It requires an integrated framework to define and establish the linkage between strategic analytics, performance measurement analytics and operational analytics. Figure 9.6 presents an integrated framework of governance.

The goal of integrated analytics is to enhance a firm's ability to transform its vision into value. The integrated framework demonstrates that corporate governance is a judicial balancing act between long-term strategic planning and day-to-day operational planning and involves continuous measuring, monitoring, analysis and taking performance improvement actions. The key component of governance is creating 'actionable plans and forecasts' and assessing the outcomes when they come through – analyse the variances, apply options and gap management concepts, develop new marketing scenarios, adjust prices, increase service, or introduce a new product line or venture into a new market to deliver better performance results.

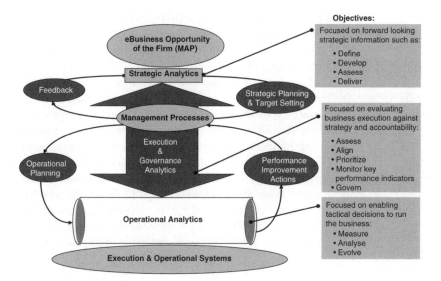

Figure 9.6   Integrated framework of governance

The goal of eBusiness is turning the vision into value through people, processes and technology. The governance of eBusiness requires continuous monitoring of both performance and competitive sustainability. There is nothing called e-forgiveness. Customers of DBE have zero tolerance for defects. Poor performance means a pitiable future for eBusiness. The challenge is how to attain high performance for the current year as well for the coming years.

Performance Management

The management of an eBusiness initiative involves monitoring the performances of eBusiness projects. It is an assessment process of the alignment (or lack thereof) of the organization's eStrategy with the tactics taken by its discrete parts. Performance management involves everything an organization does from formulating strategy, to executing operations, to transacting business. It is the essence of visibility. It requires a common understanding of priorities and performance criteria, effective integration and communication of information across the enterprise, visibility mechanics and technology.

The strategic objectives of eBusiness must be cascaded down into operational activities, to ensure that maximum value is created at all levels and accrues to the shareholder. Nevertheless, the business process and technology of digital business ecosystems are continuously evolving. The heterogeneity and diversity of eBusiness functions are too many. For effective governance of eBusiness, top management needs to focus on the key performance indicators of the strategy execution process.

The bottom line of performance is the financial results. The key financial performance indicators are: (1) market share, (2) revenue generation and (3) profitability. The soundness of an eBusiness strategy execution process is to be measured by these bottom-line performance criteria of the business, that is by (1) increase of market share, (2) improvement of operational efficiency, and (3) increase in profitability. Each criterion arises from a different management discipline; eBusiness operators need a comprehensive framework or system that allows them not only to define the strategic actions but also to monitor the effects of the actions on the bottom-line financial results of the business. The only remaining question is: how to de-risk, and maintain and sustain growth and leadership in this ever changing, hypercompetitive business ecosystem.

Sustainability

In the digital business ecosystem, change is consistent. How long the distinctive competitive advantage of a firm will last depends on what actions the firm takes to enhance and protect it and what actions the competitors take and how long each action takes. ICT is a great equalizer and offers the same advantages and privileges to everyone. It has produced a transparent economy, removed the walls of protection and offered equal opportunity to all. How one creates distinctive competitive advantage with the common ICT depends on how uniquely one blends this technology with its business activities and how long the firm can protect its uniqueness from its competitors. In a connected economy both good news and bad news move fast and send alert signals or inspire and provoke competitors to take counter actions to match, alter or supersede them. This raises many questions. How can a firm uphold its key strategic advantages?

Sustainability of competitive advantage in the digital business ecosystem depends on the protective ability of the advantage. Protecting a business model in the Internet economy is impossible. Everything is highly visible on the Internet, and it is relatively easy to copy an innovation without infringing on patents. Creation of sustainable eBusiness requires a radically different technique and approach. The sustainability of an eBusiness depends on the effectiveness of the business processes and the degree of encapsulation of complex operations within the simple process capsules or devices which many can use for multiple purposes.

The competitive advantage of an eBusiness model depends on the pulling power of the model and calls for reversing the rule of competition to cooperation. The aspirants and entrepreneurs should be encouraged to join together as business collaborators in order to create a larger resource pool for product and process enhancements. The concepts are encapsulated as: pull, co-work and create multiple sources of revenue for a longer period and create a larger base for further innovation.

The framework suggests that one can obtain and sustain a competitive advantage even in the hypercompetitive digital business ecosystem if one can encapsulate processes and transform the cooperation, thereby creating a pool of talents and resources and continuously adding additional resources for creation of multiple renewable sources of revenue.

MAP-STEPS: THE COMPREHENSIVE ANALYTICS OF eBUSINESS MANAGEMENT

Figure 9.7 presents a list of analytical issues that organizations of a digital business ecosystem have to address to formulate and manage eBusiness operations. This is not a one-time longitudinal affair, but is a continuous affair of surveillance.

CONCLUSION

MAP-STEPS is an integrated analytic framework from ideation to implementation and governance. It advocates the necessity of continuous and repetitive analysis of the key issues from different viewpoints. Many of these issues are interrelated and inseparable. For instance, one cannot formulate eBusiness strategy without the eBusiness technology strategy. Similarly, performance is the outcome of the strategy and its execution. No one can formulate an eBusiness strategy to ensure competitive sustainability without collecting feedback and developing ways of preventing reoccurrences of the undesirable.

MAP-STEPS recommends that to remain competitive in a digital business ecosystem, organizations have to create rare and inimitable value for their customers, associates and shareholders by the appropriate alignment of people, processes and technology across the value chain.

In conclusion, to deal with sustainability, eBusiness entrepreneurs have to have a pool of talent and resources to take up new challenges and to discover new sources of revenues over the passage of time, while governance of eBusiness requires high performance mindsets and work culture and

- **M = Market Potentiality Analysis**
  - C = Customers
  - C = Competitors
  - O = Opportunities for Improvements
  - R = eReadiness of the Target Customers and the Market
  - S = Societal, Ethical and Legal Issues
- **A = Actor Competency Analysis**
  - C = Capability
  - R = Resources
  - C = Competitive Advantage
  - A = Attractiveness of the Market Segment (Technical & Financial)
- **P = Product Fitness Analysis**
  - D = Digitality (Degree of Digitization) of the Product
  - U = Use & Utility
  - P = Position in the Value Chain
  - S = Sensitivity to PQST (Price, Quality, Service, Time and so on)
- **S = Strategy Formulation**
  - P = Value Proposition (Place & Process of Value Creation)
  - R = Value Realization (Positioning & Pricing)
  - A = Alignment of Process, Content, People, Culture & Technology for Value Delivery
- **T = Technology Enabling of Processes**
  - S = Selection & Business Enablement
  - U = Upgrading
  - M = Management
- **E = Execution Strategy**
  - A = Assess Intents & Risks; Acquire and Allocate Resource; Accelerate Implementation; Address Technical & Non-Technical Issues; and Adjust Styles of Management with the objectives of the Business
  - C = Control Cost of Implementation
  - T = Time & Task Management
- **P = Performance Measurement and Governance**
  - M = Market Share
  - R = Revenue Generation
  - P = Profitability Ratio
- **S = Sustainability of Competitive Advantages**
  - V = Valuable
  - R = Rare
  - I = Inimitable
  - N = Non-substitutable
  - P = Protectable

Figure 9.7   MAP-STEPS: A methodology for formulation and governance of eBusiness

a passion for continuous learning. The fast mover's advantage does not last long. To remain at the top, entrepreneurs of digital business ecosystems have to be fast learners and proactive managers of change.

NOTE

1. Some blind people found an elephant. One held a leg and thought it was a tree; another held the trunk and thought it was a snake, and so on.

BIBLIOGRAPHY

Afuah, A. and C.L. Tucci (2003), *Internet Business Models and Strategies*, 2nd edition, New York: McGraw-Hill/Irwin.

Amit, R. and C. Zott (2001), 'Value creation in eBusiness', *Strategic Management Journal*, **22**, 493–520.

Kaplan, P.J. (2002), *F's Companies: Spectacular Dot.com Flameouts'*, New York: Simon and Schuster.

Laudon, K.C. and C.G. Traver (2003), *E-Commerce: Business, Technology, Society*, New York: Pearson Addison Wesley.

Majumdar, S.K. (1999), 'Electronic ecosystems: global economy's ambassador', *The Chartered Accountant*, **XLVII** (10), 26–29.

Majumdar, S.K. (2005), *Macro and Micro Variables of eBusiness Model*, Paper presented at the British Academy of Management conference 'Challenges of Organizations in Global Markets', University of Oxford, 13–14 September.

Peltoniemi, M. (2004), *Cluster Value Network and Business Ecosystem: Knowledge and Innovation Approaches*, Paper presented at the conference 'Organizations, Innovation and Complexity: New Perspectives of the Knowledge Economy', University of Manchester, 9–10 September.

Porter, M.E. (2001), 'Strategy and the Internet', *Harvard Business Review*, **79** (2), 63–78.

Rayport, J.F. and B.J. Jaworski (2001), *Introduction to E-commerce*, New York: McGraw-Hill/Irvine.

Tarban, E., D. King, J. Lee and D. Viehland (2004), *Electronic Commerce: A Managerial Prospective*, Upper Saddle River, NJ: Prentice Hall.

10. Tools and frameworks for digital business ecosystems

Erik Brynjolfsson, John Quimby, Glen Urban, Marshall Van Alstyne and David Verrill

INTRODUCTION

Companies using a business ecosystem approach in order to understand their environment and develop their strategies have had tremendous success. John Chambers explains how Cisco became the dominant global networking equipment provider through an active involvement in its ecosystem (Stauffer 2000). Moore (1996) describes the competition between Microsoft and Netscape as the competition for the Internet ecosystem dominance, while Iansiti and Levien (2004) explain the keystone role of IBM and Microsoft in the computing ecosystem.

The ecosystem metaphor was developed by J.F. Moore, who described a business ecosystem as an economic community supported by a foundation of interacting organizations and individuals which co-evolve their capabilities and roles. This economic community produces goods and services of value to customers, who are themselves members of the ecosystem (Moore 1996). Business ecosystems include business and financial service companies, technological providers, regulatory agencies and makers of complementary products, as well as competitors and customers. Each business ecosystem needs an infrastructure supporting interaction and a knowledge-exchange mechanism.

A digital business ecosystem could be defined as the eBusiness infrastructure enabling a business ecosystem, with each of the ecosystem players as participants. The digital business ecosystem is the space in which digital organizations interact, compete, collaborate and co-evolve around innovation, using eBusiness technology.

Since its foundation in 1999, the mission of the MIT Center for eBusiness has been to be a leading academic source of innovation in management theory and practice for eBusiness. As part of the 'practice' of eBusiness, the MIT Center for eBusiness has developed a series of tools and frameworks for eBusiness practitioners.

This chapter describes tools and frameworks related to:

- relationships a firm can develop with its customers and market;
- the productivity of a digital organization in its business ecosystem.

TOOLS AND FRAMEWORKS FOR CUSTOMERS AND THE MARKET

To understand customers and the market better, eBusiness companies can use two tools developed at the MIT Center for eBusiness – trust, and customer experience life-cycle management.

Trust

Key relationships that a firm develops with its customers and market in the digital economy can be enhanced with a trust-based strategy (Urban 2004). Customer power is growing – customers now have the right tools to make them informed about the true state of affairs, to avoid the pushy messages of marketers and to be supported in their decision making.

The following seven trends increase the relative power of customers and decrease the relative effectiveness of a push-based marketing strategy – increased access to information, access to more alternatives, simplified transactions, increased communication between customers, increased skepticism, decreasing media power, and overcapacity and saturation of markets. There is a convergence of forces that amplifies customer power and makes the consideration of trust-based strategies imperative. Consumers now have more tools with which to verify a company's claims or to seek out superior product and service options. At the same time, companies have less power to push messages on to customers.

Companies must decide what to do in the face of this overwhelming convergence of forces. One answer may be to 'push harder' with traditional marketing methods to torment customers. Another choice may be 'trust-based marketing' and partnering with customers to succeed jointly. Trust is more than just a self-congratulatory adjective to be appended to a company's press releases. It means advocating for the customer's long-term interests; it is hard to earn – and easy to lose – but when a company gets it, there are sustained benefits. Trust increases customer loyalty as satisfied customers return to buy repeatedly and widen the range of their product purchases. Trust creates business benefits in MIT areas – reduced customer acquisition costs, higher profit margins, growth and long-term competitive advantage. Increasing customer power will drive a new paradigm for marketing, a paradigm based on advocating for the customer by providing open, honest information and advice.

Customer power is reducing the effectiveness of old-style push-based marketing. Thus, the shift to trust-based marketing may be more of a mandatory imperative than an option. Trust-based marketing is an approach to marketing that shifts and deepens the relationship between a company and its customers. Rather than bombarding passive customers, a trust-based strategy creates a positive relationship with an increasingly loyal customer base. Trust-based marketing contrasts with traditional push-based marketing in the assumptions that it makes about the customer. The old paradigm of push-based marketing assumed that customers did not know what was good for them. Under this old assumption, companies broadcast their hype to push products and services on to an ignorant customer base. The key is in changing the marketing assumptions that companies hold about their customers. Although some might view trust as a pleasantly nice idea that cannot withstand the brutal reality of modern day business, at MIT we argue that it is business that may not withstand the brutal new forces that underpin the trust imperative.

Although this chapter stresses the consumer side of marketing, these recommendations are even more applicable when the customer is another business. In industrial marketing, the 20 per cent of the sales force that sells 80 per cent of the volume owes much of its success to building trust-based relationships with clients. Moreover, customer power is also rising among industrial customers. Enterprise software systems help companies track the performance of suppliers. In some cases, the customer company might even have better data about the supplier than the supplier itself does.

The sales of commodity items may be done on a cost-based, push approach, but sales of the raw materials and component parts that go directly into manufactured goods are a different matter. In fact, trust is far more important in the supply chain where companies establish long-term relationships with strategic suppliers. Collaborative development of products – co-creating the supplier's products to mesh perfectly with the customer's products – is a good example of the types of trusted-based strategic relationships in the supply chain. An example is GE's 'At the Customer, For the Customer' program, a corporation-wide initiative to help customer companies to learn from GE's management experience with Six Sigma[1] and business process improvement. As companies move to lean manufacturing, just-in-time or outsourcing, they become more and more dependent on suppliers. Thus, good suppliers must be trustworthy.

In order to capture the benefits of trust, a company must have a pervasive strategy to establish itself as the trusted partner of the customer. Eight strategy elements provide milestones to achieving the trust imperative.

A co-evolutionary strategy is the best path to establish trust with customers, to earn loyalty, to achieve sales growth and to be rewarded by customers with margins that lead to premium profits and stock prices. The trust imperative involves the following strategic actions:

- Strive for transparency;
- Realign to be on the customer's side;
- Help customers help themselves;
- Put the customers to work;
- Build outstanding products and services;
- Compare your products to those of your competitor;
- Create a trust-based supply chain;
- Make trust transcend all functions of the firm.

One exercise a firm can perform very easily is to rate its marketing approach, as shown in Figure 10.1 and Table 10.1. Figure 10.1 show four of the eight dimension of a specific trust profile. The complete set of dimensions is: Transparency, Product/Service Quality, Incentive, Partnering with Customer, Co-operating Design, Product Comparison, Supply Chain

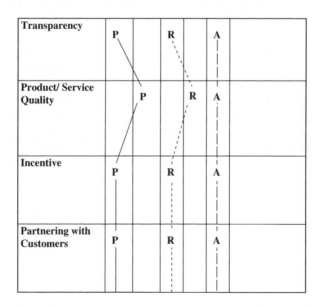

Note: P = Push; R = Relationship; A = Advocate.

Figure 10.1   A simple rating tool

Table 10.1   Overall trust rating for three marketing strategies

Distrust				High Trust
Skeptical				Believe
Not confident	**P**	**R**	**A**	Confident
Disloyal				Loyal

Notes:
P = Push
R = Relationship
A = Advocate

and Comprehensiveness. The simple approach in table 10.1 is a technique to self-analyse your own trust profile selecting for each dimension where you are and where you want to be.

A trust-based strategy is not suitable for everyone. Indeed, many companies face competitive situations, company operating conditions, or customer characteristics that preclude the use of trust. Yet, with each reason to not use trust there are exceptions – reasons why conditions that preclude trust might change or might provide competitive advantage to those companies that do choose a trust-based marketing strategy. Issues that deter the use of trust include commodities, monopolies, uncontrollable quality or quantity, short-term financial focus, short-term customer base, and low impact products.

Somebody might feel that the preceeding exceptions to the application of trust mean that the old 'push' tactics are best. Yet these exceptions are specific and do not apply to every company or market. Managers need to determine if their situation falls into one of these exception categories. But even if an exception does apply, managers can make a strategic decision as to whether they want to continue to fall into an exception category. For example, if a company offers a commodity or a low-relevance product, the company could continue to use a status quo push strategy or attempt to differentiate with an innovative product, quality, involvement and trust. With each possible exception they are the counter-strategies that let a company move away from push and toward trust. For example, companies can implement quality measures, improve forecasting and work to change the locus of competition. The point is that many of the firm's issues that appear to be counter-arguments to trust are at the discretion of the management.

Other, highly successful, companies might argue that they have already got a source of competitive advantage – that explicit efforts to create trust are unneeded by companies with obvious superiority. Yet history suggests that many forms of competitive advantage can be transitory. New entrants, new technologies, new government regulations and new customer needs all create hurdles to long-term competitive advantage. Thus, one can argue that a superior company should use its superiority to gain the trust of its customers while it has the advantage. Trust, with its attendant deep customer relationships, also helps the company to adapt to most of the dynamic forces that might otherwise derail a one-time market leader.

The rise of customer power mutes any argument for push even where exceptional conditions would seem to rule out the use of trust. Independently-verifiable reputation and long-term relationships with customers will be more important than easily debunked hype. Customer ability to learn or track the true performance of companies makes it hard for companies to sustain selfish strategies that emphasize short-term gain at the customer's expense. Likewise, company ability to learn or track the true behavior and profitability of customers makes it less likely that customers will consider only price and sustain disloyal behavior. Thus information technology stabilizes cooperative long-term trust-oriented strategies.

Evidence is building that the paradigm of marketing is changing from the push strategies so well suited to the last 50 years of mass media to trust-based strategies that are essential in a time of information empowerment. Managers need to decide where their firm should be on the spectrum from push to full trust.

There are advantages of being a first mover in this strategy space because once customers develop a trusting relationship with a firm, they are not likely to switch easily to a competitor. Trust creates a barrier to entry by increasing customer loyalty and by forcing would-be competitors to spend more time and resources to develop a trusted reputation. In contrast, not embracing trust presents a risk to the firm's growth and returns if other competitors gain the trust of customers first. The movement to a trust-based strategy does present short-run challenges but it also offers long-run opportunities. Trust will increasingly become the norm of behavior in the next ten years as the new paradigm becomes established and firms meet the trust imperative.

In this view, the Experience Lifecycle Mapping (ELM) knowledge framework allows managers to apply a co-evolutionary trust-based strategy, since it prepares 360 degree views of the entire customer experience. Practitioners can use ELM to view their portfolio of products and services, understand how their internal capabilities are meeting the needs of clients and measure changes in their customer approach. The primary investigator for this work is John Quimby, supported by MasterCard International.

Customer experience life-cycle mapping
Facilitating a deep understanding of how the experience of customers is supported, nurtured or ignored by information systems and organizational

design is a central goal of a new knowledge management system – ELM. Just as modern spreadsheet templates use a grid/cell metaphor for the capture of multi-paged views of complex financial data, ELM templates use a 'rotational phase/step' metaphor for the capture of multi-paged views of complex customer experience and organizational capabilities. The ELM tool uses XML for its data storage. The ELM XML files are used to save and load prepared methodologies, to incorporate domain-specific capability knowledge from experienced personnel and prior engagements and to hold the data and observations of the mapping participants during a customer experience engagement. The XML format lowers the cost of future stand-alone and web-based tool integration as well as enabling editing as a structured document using XML-enabled word processors.

The ELM framework supports an open-ended mix of qualitative and quantitative inquiry about the phases and steps in the customer experience as well as the organizational capabilities that support them. ELM creates a group facilitation view of the customer experience map which presents discussion questions about each attribute. These discussion questions are brought up in turn with a click, framed in the context of the customer experience circle (Figure 10.2).

In the evolving ELM reference methodology, a capability is the capacity to perform a task. With its definition grounded in coordination science research (Malone and Crowston 1994), a capability involves three equally weighted elements:

- The processes in the capability[2];
- The technology infrastructure supporting the capability;
- The people skilled to execute the processes with the infrastructure to deliver the capability.

A given capability will typically support multiple steps within the customer experience. For example a customer may experience the online customer support capability of a firm before, during and long after a product purchase. Sample qualitative questions about a capability in this methodology include:

- What are the critical dependencies for this capability?
- Which exceptions have been observed in the performance of this particular capability?
- Which specific skills are required for personnel to deliver this capability?

These qualitative questions help to inform the quantitative attribute assessments of individual capabilities. Sample quantitative attributes include

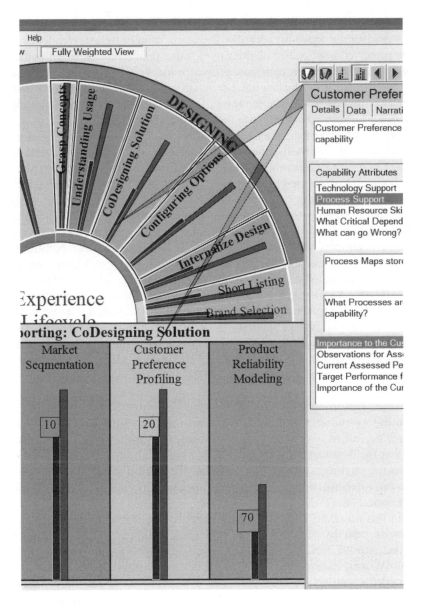

Note: A partial screen shot of ELM mapping one of several uses of the capability –
Customer Preference Profiling – within the context of the customer's experience of co-
designing a product solution. Prepared qualitative and quantitative attribute assessment
dialogs about the capability are ready on the right to be launched by the group facilitator.
During these dialogs, the life-cycle map remains visible in the background providing context.

Figure 10.2   Customer preference profiling

assessment of the current capabilities, their perceived importance, the relative goal for the capability identified in research and by industry leaders and the perceived importance of the gap between the current capabilities and the goals. The system can then provide multiple views of the weighted aggregations within the customer experience metaphor. These 'scores' can then be queried using simple dialogs from the ELM menus, highlighting steps in the customer experience that may be under-supported.

During the execution of a knowledge capture engagement, ELM presents a rich set of dynamically-generated graphic views of the aggregated data to aid the group's collective understanding of the customer's experience. Any of these alternative views can be saved, commented on and organized into an evolving 'slide show' of views within the ELM tool. These saved views provide for a group of professionals to build a suite of views of key questions, opportunities and identified problem areas over time. The evolving narrative support this creates is profoundly different from the traditional frozen PowerPoint presentation as it frees the presenter to respond to sidebar examination of any of the views and save the results as a new view.

Using the ELM search capability and display option (see Figure 10.3), steps in the customer experience that are under-supported may be highlighted or, for emphasis, 'whited out' completely as gaps in understanding the customer. Identification of problem areas within the customer experience map may frame discussions about the need of changing technology investment priorities, organizational structure and skills and/or process design.

To aid easy integration with other tool suites or web-based surveys, ELM can export and import capability assessment tables from Excel as well as generate full MS-Word reports of the collected observations. Live links within the data can point to external documents and web pages of related research, and use cases of live software, threaded discussions or process descriptions in an online process repository such as the Process Handbook (Malone *et al.* 2003).

In this way the ELM Framework supports the development of the customer's trust by a collaborative knowledge mapping of the customer's experience life cycle that allows the evaluation of how information technology, organizational personnel and processes combine in capabilities that support a customer's full experience over the lifetime use of products and/or services. ELM presents a rich set of dynamically-generated graphic views of the aggregated data to aid the group's collective understanding of these issues. Early indications suggest that the perspectives supported with this tool may significantly aid an organization in understanding and tasking itself to address the customer's experience, thus allowing the acceleration of the customer's trust development process.

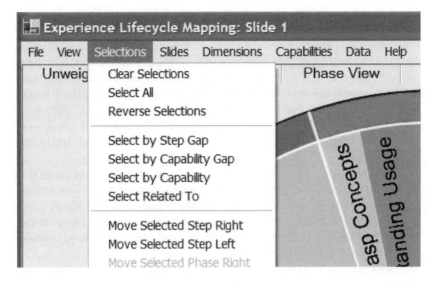

Note: Options for selecting customer experience steps to focus discussion on using various queries. Steps found meeting the selection criteria become highlighted in the life-cycle map while the remaining steps remain visible but grayed down.

Figure 10.3   Selecting customer experience steps

Productivity of Digital Organizations

Research at the MIT Center for eBusiness has focused on better understanding and analysis of the productivity of 'digital organizations'. Below is a summary of two projects – one focusing on measuring productivity at the level of the firm, the other on measuring the productivity of individual information workers.

Productivity at the firm level
Since 1995, the United States has experienced a remarkable resurgence in productivity, with current productivity rates nearly double those of the preceding twenty years. Despite an official recession, productivity growth has maintained its strength, defying the pattern of previous recessions. This recent robustness of productivity levels has been linked to record improvements in the quality-adjusted price of IT equipment and high levels of investment in these technologies. However, investment in IT capital alone does not guarantee productivity in an organization.

Through a series of interviews with executives at over 1000 large US-based firms, data of various types were gathered, including sales, inputs of labor, capital, materials, purchased services, R&D, a number of distinct metrics of computer and communications technology, business practices and corporate culture. The data were analyzed using multi factor productivity (MFP) as the key performance metric. Multi factor productivity measures the amount of output for all inputs including labor and various types of capital used, taking into account prices as well as quantities of inputs and outputs. Unlike labor productivity metrics, which divide output by labor input alone, MFP is more closely related to the economic concepts of how firms can create value and has been linked to profitability and shareholder value.

Analysis of the data indicates that, while investment in IT capital is strongly associated with higher productivity, technology alone is not the most important driver of productivity (see Figure 10.4). This research instead reveals a distinct set of organizational practices and corporate cultures common to the most effective users of IT, defining what Professor Erik Brynjolfsson calls the 'digital organization'.

Statistical analysis shows that the characteristics common to digital organizations include the following:

- Converting traditional analog processes to digital processes. By embedding standard procedures in technology, employees (as well as customers) are able to work with less supervision. Two examples of this are Cisco's policy of minimizing paperwork by routing all

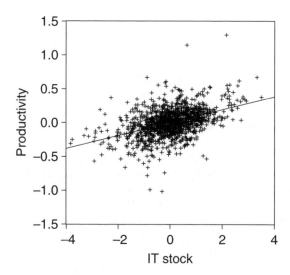

Figure 10.4   IT and productivity

processes through the Internet and UPS's system of providing tracking information to customers online.

- Distributing decision rights and empowering line workers, through increased decentralization and delegation when it comes to choose which tasks to do, the methods of doing them, the pace of work and the allocation of tasks.
- Adopting a policy of free information access and communication which includes encouraging open information access to internal and external documents throughout the organization, using technology to foster both lateral communication (coordination among employees) and vertical communication (between employees and their managers).
- Offering strong performance-linked incentives, including individual performance-based incentive pay and use of stock options for a broader set of employees.
- Maintaining corporate focus and communicating strategic goals. A sharp corporate focus is maintained by weeding out marginal or non-core products and services and then regularly communicating strategic goals throughout the organization with an emphasis on promoting a strong corporate culture.
- Recruiting and hiring top-quality employees and committing the necessary resources to the process. Executives in these firms tend to be more involved in the recruitment process and new employees are more likely to be screened for interpersonal skills and for fit within the corporate culture, as well as across a variety of criteria such as education, analytical skills and computer skills.
- Strong emphasis on the investment of 'human capital', including hiring highly educated employees and then providing ongoing training (much of which is provided online).

These seven characteristics work together to form a coherent system of complementary practices within a digital organization. It is necessary that the practices are adopted together as a whole system; adopting any of the processes in isolation might result in an adverse effect on productivity by introducing barriers to change.

Just as IT investment creates a capital good, so too does 'investment' in these organizational practices. In fact, this research reveals that the stock market value of firms which invest heavily in both organizational capital and IT capital is substantially higher than the value of those who invest in one without the other (see Figure 10.5).

This research provides a framework for better understanding specific organizational characteristics that correlate with productivity gains.

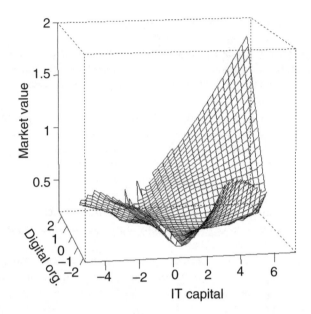

Figure 10.5   Interactions between IT and digital organizations

The vertical axis represents market value (ln(mv)), while the horizontal axes represent the
Digital Organization (org) and the IT Capital (ln(i)).

However, understanding these practices does not translate into automatic
success for firms. There are a couple of important factors that prevent the
system from being applicable to all firms. The first is that not all of these
practices are well known or understood within firms and even when they
are, there may be circumstances particular to an individual firm that make
certain practices inappropriate. The second factor that prevents many
firms from adopting such a system is that knowing what to do is, at best,
only half the battle. Most of the managers interviewed by Brynjolfsson
reported significant barriers in implementing any new set of organizational practices, such as financial constraints, technological infrastructure,
existing work rules and contracts and in some instances even corporate
culture.

From this research at MIT, we created an online questionnaire that
allows companies to input simple data into MIT methodology. The output
measures the firm's capabilities along the seven practices found to be critical for companies who take full organizational advantage of investments
in IT. A 'web' of the digital organizations against its market segment shows
relative strength while prescriptive text suggests ways of improving the
organization's score.

Productivity at the level of individual information worker

If IT is to have a significant effect on the firm, it must almost surely be via its use by information workers and the tasks they perform. However, the real output of most information workers is difficult to measure. Counting the number of meetings attended or the number of memos filed is not closely linked to the value they may or may not create. Does the use of IT lead professionals to complete their tasks more quickly? Does it allow a given worker to do more tasks in a given time? Can information work be explicitly linked to revenues?

In this study researchers focused on executive recruiters, aka head hunters, whose primary work involves filling specific job openings. Because the projects completed by each recruiter, and the corresponding revenue impact, are explicitly measured in the firms' accounting statements, the measuring of output is readily available. The other 'output variables' for this study include individual worker-level revenues, worker compensation, project completion rates and project duration. 'IT variables' focus on the use of technology (not merely its presence) and include direct, message-level observation of communications volume, the size and shape of email contact networks, professed ability to use database technology and relative time spent on various tasks. When combined with interviews and visits, these data enabled us to specify and estimate several equations relating technology, skill, worker characteristics, task completion, revenue and compensation.

Our findings suggest that using IT has a statistically significant correlation with individual information worker productivity as measured via increased revenues, completed projects and individual compensation. Workers who use IT to manage larger social networks perform better on average, as do those who have ability to use IT to manage data.

What mechanism is the performance of IT use affected by? A natural presumption is that computers speed up information work. Certainly, even the simplest computer can calculate millions of times more quickly than humans. Interestingly however, we did not find that heavy IT users completed projects any more quickly than their peers. Instead, we found that heavy IT users worked on more projects simultaneously and thus completed more projects and earned more revenue, per period, even while taking slightly longer on average for individual projects.

These data also enabled us to model and measure the way effort on various tasks, as well as project completion and revenue generation, affected individual worker compensation. Arguably, this is the production function that employees care about most. We found that compensation was tightly linked to observable output and that more observable tasks were more highly correlated with compensation. Specifically, the more highly visible task of interacting and managing people as opposed to data is also associated with a disproportionately high benefit in terms of compensation.

Using these data, we are able to understand better some of the internal workings of a group of firms which rely heavily on information work and information workers. We can measure some of the correlations among key variables and thereby understand not only the ways that IT affects intermediate and final output, but also the compensation and incentive systems.

However, this approach also has its weaknesses. In particular, since at MIT we have data on such a small fraction of the economy, MIT findings may not be completely generalizable. The results should be interpreted as descriptive of the firms, workers, technologies and practices in the researched sample but are not necessarily valid outside of it.

Almost all information workers use IT intensively. However, their productivity is notoriously difficult to measure. As a result, there is virtually no quantitative research to date on information worker productivity. To address the unusual difficulty in measuring this, we focus on a uniquely measurable type of information work: projects in the recruiting or executive search industry. Projects involve a well-defined contract for locating and vetting high-quality executives on behalf of a client. Information flows and access also affect project success rates. Data for this study include three data subsets:

- Exact internal accounting records of the following: revenues generated by individual recruiters (1999–2003); project start and stop dates; projects handled simultaneously; labor costs and compensation; project team composition; cancelled projects; and job level of placed candidates.
- Nine months of complete email history captured from the corporate mail server using specially-developed capture software specific to this project. Spam messages were excluded by focusing on internal communications or external contacts who had received at least one message from anyone inside the firm.[3]
- Collected answers to surveys of information-seeking behaviors, perceptions, experience, education and human factors.

Together, these data provide a desktop-level view of how different professional workers use IT in conjunction with measures of individual performance. The sum of individually secured contracts also provides a complete picture of firm-level revenues. In addition, we have direct observation of a stream of communications behaviors (Figure 10.6).

These data afford the opportunity to construct two distinct models of activity, representing a production sequence within the firm. The first is a

(a)   (b)

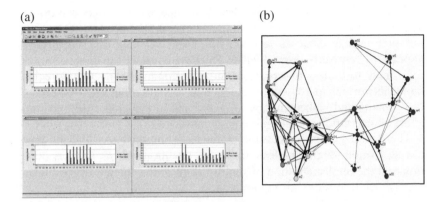

Note: Graphic (a) showing the daily send and reply volumes of four individuals allows fairly precise estimates of communications patterns and labor hours. Figure (b) shows communications volumes for one week among workers in three different industry sectors. A geographic divide also separates two offices. It shows that although all workers are technically connected by email, actual communications cluster by geography and industry sector.

Figure 10.6   Email traffic and communication networks

multi-tasking project model in which agents take on projects, literally a contract, to locate a candidate for a specific client. The number and duration of these jobs then determine total dollar 'billings'. These represent firm revenues and typically equal one-third of a placed candidate's final salary. Taken independently, this fragment represents the white collar production function. Given revenues, the second model (the multi-task incentive model) captures the principal–agent relationship between the recruiter and the firm.

A multi-tasking project model: If we consider white collar workers as managers of queued tasks, each with distinct start and stop points, we may be able to measure the relationship of IT and non-IT factors to intermediate measures of output. Data on project load start times and stop times over the sample period index the rate at which projects are completed.

A multi-task incentive model: For the incentive stage, consider a multi-task mode (Hu 2004). There are two tasks that agents (partners, consultants and research staff) might perform to generate revenue. One IT-related task ('data manipulation') is studying and managing data in the database, modifying stale records and generating search reports. Another IT-related task ('networking') is communicating with potential clients and recruits. The firm can also easily observe total revenues brought in from each client. In particular, the firm can observe and reward the addition of new clients.

Data manipulation increases a firm's revenue, but the effect is indirect. Many activities performed at a computer may not be productive. Indeed, our analysis found that self-reported time spent on public web access pages appears to be weakly unproductive. Thus, we consider the direct effort of data entry to be less observable though not unimportant. On the other hand, networking increases the number and strength of an agent's contacts. New clients and placements by an agent are, in fact, recorded and thus effort on networking can be more easily measured.

The detailed employee-level data we have collected provides an ideal testing ground for the implementation of our proposed production function and the implementation of multi-task incentive theory. In particular, analysis leads to the following findings:

- While it is presumed that IT use will speed up information work, our data suggest that the productivity effects are more complex than that.
- This analysis shows that IT is associated with increased output, but we also gain some insight into the mechanism by which it works. The estimates imply that IT is not used so much to speed up work as it is to increase the number of projects a recruiter handles at a given time. The slight increase in the average project duration for heavy IT users may reflect a willingness to dip further down into marginal projects (assuming faster projects are the first to be selected) or real bottlenecks in recruiter time – even with email and databases, there is still a need for a certain amount of real-time conversation with candidates and clients.
- The data also allowed us to study the compensation systems of the recruiters. This is a setting where the classic principal–agent model might be expected to fit fairly well and the data suggest that it does. A significant fraction of the pay that the executive recruiters earn from their employers is explicitly linked to the revenue they generate. This reflects a job design that leads to a relatively high observable output: recruiters work on specific projects and the successes or failures of those projects and the associated earnings are easy to monitor.
- We also find that approximately one-third of new billings are paid to employees who are responsible for generating those revenues. This provides very high-powered incentives.
- The modest surprise was that both uses of IT – email contacts and database skill – are correlated with greater project completion rates and revenues. However, only email contacts, which by definition involve interactions with other people and are thus more observable, are correlated with greater compensation.

CONCLUSION

The mission of the MIT Center for eBusiness is to be a leading source of innovation in management theory and practice for eBusiness. Several tools and frameworks have been developed for eBusiness practitioners as a result of collaborative research between MIT and its sponsors.

First, trust will become an increasingly important approach for digital organizations as customers have the power of information. Through the Customer Experience Lifecycle Mapping (ELM) framework, companies can view the collaborative knowledge mapping of the customer's experience life cycle and how information technology, organizational personnel and processes combine in capabilities that support a customer's full experience over the lifetime use of products and/or services.

Second, another key goal in MIT research has been to model and measure the productivity of digital organizations and individual information workers. Organizations that invest in IT, as well as business practices to support these new technologies, are clearly more productive than those that do not. We have developed a tool which allows companies to compare their organization with industry peers across seven dimensions that correlate directly with productivity. Further, at the level of the individual information worker, we have been able to develop a number of tools that provide great insight into the root causes of individual productivity. We found that specific measures of IT use were significantly correlated with output at several levels: final revenue, completed projects and intermediate measures like number of projects managed simultaneously. At the same time, by peering into the black box of production at these firms, we found that some of the effects of IT can be counter-intuitive: greater IT use does not seem to speed up task completion. On the contrary, it is correlated with greater duration time for projects, although the increase in multitasking more than offsets this effect in terms of completed projects per year. The ability to multitask projects is highly significant and its effect, however, appears slightly paradoxical. Individuals who multitask more (complete more work over the course of a year) take longer to complete their individual projects. We also found that relatively observable activities like email interactions with colleagues and others were correlated with both revenue generation and compensation.

These tools enable eBusiness practitioners to benefit from a scientific approach to analyzing how their company can benefit within their business ecosystem.

NOTES

1. Sigma is a disciplined, data-driven approach and methodology for eliminating defects (driven towards six standard deviations between the mean and the nearest specification limit) in any process – from manufacturing to transactional and from product to service. See http://www.isixsigma.com/sixsigma/six_sigma.asp
2. In the processes of a capability the acquisition or design phase of the capability and its repeated execution are included as well as its evolution. Note that the skills required of actors of these different phased processes within a capability may vary greatly. For example, the skills required to prepare meals in a typical restaurant are different from those required to design a menu and train staff on a new set of techniques for a new restaurant.
3. A joint F test comparing performance means of those who opted out with those who remained did not show statistically significant differences. F (Sig): Rev02 2.295 (0.136), Comp02 0.837 (0.365), Multi 0.386 (0.538).

REFERENCES

Hu, Y. (2004), *Factors Influencing the Choice of Pricing Models in Online Advertising*, Unpublished Doctoral Thesis, MIT Sloan School.

Iansiti M. and R. Levien (2004), *The Keystone Advantage*, Cambridge, MA: Harvard Business School Press.

Malone, T.W. and K.G. Crowston (1994), 'The interdisciplinary study of coordination', *ACM Computing Surveys*, **26** (1), 87–119.

Malone, T.W., K.G. Crowston and G. Herman (eds) (2003), *Organizing Business Knowledge: The MIT Process Handbook*, Cambridge, MA: MIT Press.

Moore, J.F. (1996), *The Death of Competition: Leadership and Strategy in the Age of Business Ecosystems*, New York: HarperBusiness.

Stauffer, D. (2000), *Nothing but the Net, Business the Cisco way*, Milford, USA: Capstone Publishing.

Urban, G. (2004), *Digital Marketing Strategy: Text and Cases*, Upper Saddle River, NJ: Pearson Education, Inc.

11. Enabling the flexible enterprise – RFID and smart devices

Robert Laubacher

INTRODUCTION

During the 1980s, in the aftermath of the personal computer revolution, businesses substantially increased their investments in information technology (IT). Economists and management researchers expected that these higher levels of investment would lead to increases in economy-wide productivity and firm-level performance. But early studies found that IT investment was not associated with significant productivity gains. In the late 1980s, Nobel laureate Robert Solow characterized this puzzling development with a quip: 'You can see the computer age everywhere but in the productivity statistics' (Solow 1987).

With the rise of the World Wide Web in the 1990s, business investment in IT continued to boom. Yet researchers continued to struggle in their efforts to show a link between IT spending and performance. Starting in the mid-1990s, MIT researchers Eric Brynjolfsson and Lorin Hitt produced a series of papers that examined data on both IT spending and organizational practices from a very large number of firms. Because their sample was substantially larger than the ones examined by prior researchers, Brynjolfsson and Hitt were able to demonstrate that IT had a significant impact on performance. But their work also showed that information technology alone, in the absence of changes in organizational practice, did not have much impact. It was only when firms combined these two factors in tandem that they enjoyed major increases in both profitability and stock market valuation (Brynjolfsson and Hitt 2000).

Labour productivity in the US, which had grown at a 1.3 per cent annual average through the 1970s and 1980s, doubled in the late 1990s. And in the first five years of the 21st century, US labour productivity has been growing at nearly 4 per cent per year. Among academics, there is widespread agreement that information technology has been a major factor driving this jump in productivity.

But even as researchers were coming to agreement on the productivity-enhancing potential of IT, practising managers were becoming sceptical. The flood of spending for Y2K fixes and the subsequent dot.com bubble spurred a tsunami of technology spending. Andrew McAfee has noted that IT spending in the late 1990s was driven by a 'follow-the-pack approach' fuelled not by strategic imperatives but by companies' fear of falling behind their rivals (McAfee 2004). If a firm's competitor put in an ERP system, the firm felt it had to match its rival's move. As a result, a huge outpouring of IT investment was undertaken very quickly, without much deliberation. After the dot.com crash, there was recognition that much of this spending had been wasteful. A Morgan Stanley study estimated that $130 billion dollars of information technology purchased by US companies was simply thrown away – computer equipment and software that was either too difficult to install or already dated by the time buyers got around to installing it.

As a result, today, managers are understandably wary. Their scepticism is reinforced by another line of business writing on IT and performance. Soon after the dot.com bust, Nicholas Carr published an article in the *Harvard Business Review*, contending that information technology is no longer a source of competitive advantage, but rather a mere utility, like electricity – simply a necessary input to run a business (Carr 2003). This article proved highly influential among practising managers. People inside firms who want to make new IT investments today find it much more difficult to get approval from their managers than they did during the late 1990s spending boom.

Managers are thus faced with a challenging conundrum. Economists like Brynjolfsson and Hitt have shown that if implemented in conjunction with complementary organizational changes, information technology can have a major positive impact on profitability and stock price. But, in today's environment, making that case for IT investment inside companies is difficult.

Even as managers face this dilemma, a wave of new wireless technologies is on the verge of having substantial business impact. Two of the major new technologies are radio frequency identification (RFID) and smart devices. RFID provides firms with the capability to locate physical objects in real time and smart devices are mobile phones that allow workers not only to make and receive calls but also to check and send emails, access company calendaring software and search the Web – all with a single handset.

These and a range of other wireless technologies are in the first stages of what computer scientists call an 'internet of things', which involves a proliferation of sensors and processors in the world that are connected at a much greater level than today. This internet of things has great potential to transform the way work gets done and the way companies compete.

The problem for managers is that these are still early stage technologies. It is not clear which ones are going to be the winners and which will end up as forgotten. Managers must make decisions today about what to invest in and when to do it. They must decide whether to be first to market with this technology or to be a fast follower – or to wait for a later generation of technology which will allow them to leapfrog rivals who jumped too quickly. Given these challenges, managers need good tools to help evaluate their IT investment decisions. Activity Based Performance Measurement (ABPM) is such a tool.

OVERVIEW OF ABPM

One of the difficulties associated with measuring the return on IT investments is that IT changes in a significant way how activities are conducted inside organizations and across value chains. Translating these changes in how business activities are done into traditional financial metrics is not an easy task. ABPM seeks to measure costs and benefits at the activity level and to link those fine-grained metrics to the business-unit and firm-level metrics used today by accountants. Assessing the value of IT investments is one important application of ABPM. But ABPM can also be used to measure the costs and benefits of other kinds of management interventions, like quality programmes. It could also be used to assess the effectiveness of incentive and compensation schemes. This chapter gives a high-level picture of the ABPM methodology and presents findings from a field study on RFID.

KEY CONCEPTS BEHIND ABPM

Activity Based Performance Measurement is based on two core insights. The first is that the costs of an activity come from its parts, but benefits come from how an activity affects other activities. The second key concept on which ABPM is based is that it is possible to identify common patterns – what we call family resemblances – in the benefits associated with similar types of processes.

Costs from Parts, Benefits from Impact on Other Activities

If you are measuring the cost of a business process, you can measure the costs of its various sub-processes and aggregate them up. The sum of the costs of the sub-processes is the cost of the whole process. This principle is at the core of the field of accounting, whose conventions have been developed over the centuries, since the days of the Renaissance merchants and the invention of double entry bookkeeping. Over these many years, accountants have developed powerful methods to meet the challenge of measuring costs.

Benefits, by contrast, result from an activity's linkages to other activities. For instance, if a firm puts in place a quality programme in its factory, some of the benefits occur within the factory, such as reduction in the amount of rework that is required. But other benefits of a factory quality programme occur outside the factory. The firm may find that in the marketplace, once word gets out that its product's quality has improved, more customers are inclined to buy and the firm's market share increases. In some cases, the firm might even be able to charge a premium price for the higher quality product. The firm will also have lower costs for customer service, since there are fewer product defects. A key characteristic of benefits is that they cascade outward from the place where the initial intervention occurs, like when a stone is thrown into a pond and ripples go outward from the point of contact. This trait makes it difficult to quantify benefits at a micro level.

Family Resemblances in Benefits Associated with Similar Activities

We now turn to the second key concept that serves as the basis for ABPM. If the same technology is applied to two processes that have similar underlying characteristics, similar kinds of benefits will result. This principle allows us to gain leverage on the measurement problem, since we can make generalizations about the kinds of benefits associated with particular technologies when they are applied to particular classes of technology.

ESTIMATING BENEFITS – HOW ABPM CAN HELP

When firms estimate benefits, there are often some that are relatively easy to measure, since they involve clearly quantifiable changes. One such example is the reduction in the amount of labour required in a factory after the introduction of a quality programme. These are typically referred to as the 'hard cost savings'. But other benefits are more difficult to measure, such as the potential for increased market share that can result from a quality programme. Firms typically refer to these as 'soft benefits'. To estimate soft benefits, companies typically rely on building a business case. The challenge in building a business case for soft benefits is twofold. First, it involves a lot of hard work. And second, once that work is done, senior decision makers often remain sceptical about whether the projected benefits will actually be realized.

Our proposed solution to the problems associated with measurement of benefits is to use the idea that similar benefits are associated with similar activities. This concept can allow us to develop a standardized approach for measuring the benefits generated when a technology is applied to a similar family of activities. Calculating benefits for the first time involves a lot of hard work, but once the first case is completed, the framework generated in that case can be leveraged in subsequent instances.

Today, this is already being done intuitively most of the time in firms. For example, imagine that someone in a company developed a business case that involved a new technology for the firm's customer support group, and that the proposal got approved in 2004 and was successful. If a similar technology were proposed for the customer support group in 2005, it would no doubt refer to the prior year's business case. The finance and management staff responsible for reviewing the new case would be likely to accept quite readily the assumptions that were taken from the prior year's successful proposal. People inside firms have been doing this sort of intuitive comparison of similar business cases for a long time. We are proposing to do the same basic thing, just more rigorously and systematically.

STORING KNOWLEDGE ABOUT BENEFITS – MIT PROCESS HANDBOOK

To compare across different business cases in a systematic and rigorous way, firms will need to be able to keep track of all these benefits associated with relevant sets of activities. To do this, they will need a place to store knowledge about the benefits associated with each key type of business process. One useful tool is a process repository we have been developing for the last ten years at MIT. We call it the *MIT Process Handbook* (Malone *et al.* 1999, 2003). It is a repository of knowledge about business processes, arranged according to underlying theoretical constructs. We see it as a periodic table of processes, since the way they are arranged in the repository is based on an underlying conceptual framework that takes into account the key characteristics of the processes and how they fit together. An on-line version of the *MIT Process Handbook* is available at http://ccs.mit.edu/ph.

FINDINGS FROM THE RFID FIELD STUDY

RFID does all the things bar codes do, but with three key differences: RFID tags have no line-of-sight requirement; can be rewritten from a distance; and hold a number, the Electronic Product Code (EPC), which contains enough information to provide a unique identifier for every atom in the universe. RFID technology is over fifty years old, with many niche applications in use today. Recently a large group of companies, working through the MIT Auto ID Center, have defined a new set of standards that promise inexpensive, battery-less RFID tags. Cheap RFID tags are expected to have a major impact in the retail sector.

The key functionality of RFID in retail is that it enables the counting of tagged items present at key junctures in a supply chain with less work, with greater accuracy, and in less time than can be accomplished by prior methods, such as manual counting or bar code scanning. At short ranges, RFID technology also enables easier and faster finding of tagged items. In a retail supply chain, RFID tags can be applied to individual items that are sold to consumers ('eaches' as they are known in the industry); inner packs containing multiple items; cases of multiple dozens of items aggregated for shipping; pallets comprised of multiple cases; or shipments comprised of multiple pallets.

The firm where our team conducted its field work was a consumer goods manufacturer considering a case-level RFID implementation. Our study employed a three-step approach:

1. Identify processes that would be affected by RFID;
2. Map those processes before and after RFID;
3. Estimate difference in costs and revenues before and after RFID.

High-Level Retail Supply Chain Model

The typical retail supply chain has four key junctures (see Figure 11.1). Goods are made at the manufacturer's factory and sent to the manufacturer's

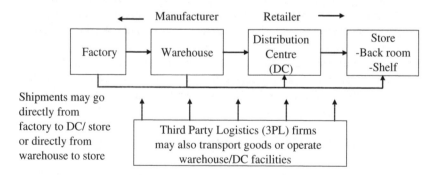

Figure 11.1   Generic retail supply chain

warehouse. The manufacturer then sends goods to a retailer's warehouse, which is also called a distribution centre or DC. From the DC, goods are shipped to the store, where typically they are first stored in a back room, before being placed on the shelves. Sometimes shipments will skip a step in this chain. Third-party logistic providers (3PLs) sometimes provide outsourced warehousing and transportation services. For the sake of simplicity, the following discussion focuses on the simplest case, which involves a manufacturer and retailer only.

RFID in the Manufacturer's Warehouse

In our study, we first examined the manufacturer's warehouse and then extended our analysis to other parts of the supply chain. Inside the warehouse, there are three major processes: goods are received at the receiving dock; they are put into storage; and finally, when an order comes in, it is filled by taking needed items from the warehouse shelves and assembling them into one or more pallets, which are then placed on a truck for shipment to the customer (see Figure 11.2).

After mapping the warehouse processes at this level, we went deeper and decomposed each of the three major processes until we reached the point where RFID would have an impact. By looking at the affected process before and after RFID, we were able to identify the impact that RFID would have. For example, under 'Receive Goods', there are three major parts (see Figure 11.3). In the first of these, 'Accept Shipment', warehouse personnel inspect the shipment to ensure that the number and type of goods present match the accompanying documentation. If the physical goods and documentation match, the shipment is accepted. This is the step in receiving where RFID has an impact. Before RFID, a receiving clerk checked the number and type of goods in a shipment by using a bar code scanner to check each case. With RFID, the readers installed near the warehouse door can do this counting automatically. The 'Accept Shipment' process before RFID required a certain amount of labour and time and also had a characteristic error rate. With RFID, it required less labour and time and had a lower error rate.

We undertook the same kind of mapping for the 'Store goods' and 'Fulfil order' processes. In this way, we were able to identify all the places where RFID would have an impact in the warehouse.

Figure 11.2   Primary activities in manufacturer's warehouse

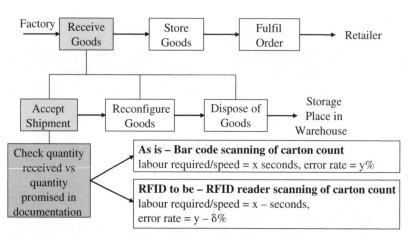

Figure 11.3   Impact of RFID on 'Accept shipment'

Benefits of RFID in Manufacturer's Warehouse

To estimate the benefits of RFID, we relied on several sources. First, we talked to people at the company who had deep knowledge of their firm's processes and could predict what benefits they thought would result from RFID. Second, we reviewed the literature and found a number of studies of RFID implementation undertaken by the MIT Auto ID Center (Auto ID Labs 2003). And third, we brainstormed within our research team about the range of potential benefits of RFID in this warehouse setting. The result was a list of seven types of generic benefits of RFID. The first five benefits are ways the RFID can lower costs and the last two are ways that RFID can increase revenues:

1. Labour savings in counting;
2. Reduction of theft;
3. Reduction of disputes with trading partners;
4. Reduction of excess inventory;
5. Reduction of spoilage/obsolescence;
6. Reduction of out-of-stocks;
7. Greater responsiveness to customer.

The first benefit is automation. Instead of requiring warehouse personnel to scan cases with a bar code scanner, RFID counts the number of cases present automatically, reducing the amount of labour needed in the warehouse.

The second and the third benefits – reduction of theft and reduction of disputes with trading partners – are tied to RFID's ability to provide more precise data about what goods are flowing through the supply chain. These better data allow firms to detect instances of theft more rapidly and also reduce 'claims', the retail industry's term for situations where there is a dispute over the number of cases that were exchanged by trading partners. For example, if the manufacturer says it sent 50 cases, but the retailer says it received only 49, there is an elaborate process that gets triggered on both sides to investigate and resolve the claim. If the shipment proves to have been short, the manufacturer often has to pay a penalty and must send additional cases to make up the difference. Costs associated with negotiating and making good on claims cost large manufacturers and retailers tens of millions of dollars each year.

The next three benefits – reduction of excess inventory, reduction of spoilage/obsolescence, and reduction of out-of-stocks – are tied to the firm's ability to optimize its inventory management practices due to the better data RFID provides. Better information means the firm can have the right goods in inventory at the right time. This can allow the company to reduce inventory buffers and to have fewer instances where there is spoilage or goods that are out of date. It also allows the firm to reduce the number of instances where a customer places an order but the desired items are not present in the warehouse – or, as this is called in the retail sector, 'out of stock'.

The final, and probably most important benefit, is ability to be more responsive to customers. When large retailers mandate that their suppliers put RFID tags on shipments, failing to do so could cause a manufacturer to lose some, and possibly even all of its business with that retailer.

There are several other benefits that apply only in specific instances. For example, luxury goods manufacturers can use RFID tags to help prevent counterfeiting. In some instances, the containers used to hold goods being shipped have an intrinsic value – for example, a brewer's beer kegs. For firms that rely on costly containers of this sort, tagging can prevent container theft and also allow reductions in container buffer stocks.

RFID Benefits in the Retail Distribution Centre and Store

After analysing RFID's benefits in the manufacturer's warehouse, we then turned to the retailer. There are three locations that are relevant for the retailer: the distribution centre (DC) which is the retailer's warehouse; the store back room; and the store shelf.

When we looked at those locations, we found that the processes there were very similar to the ones we had mapped in the manufacturer's warehouse. At each juncture, goods were received and stored, and orders were fulfilled. There were slight differences in some locations; at the store shelf, for example, store personnel do not fulfil orders, but rather, consumers do it on a self-service basis when they take goods from the shelf and place them in a shopping basket.

After observing the parallels between the processes that occur in the manufacturer's warehouse, distribution centre, back room and store shelf, we recognized that these were all specific cases of a larger process, which we called 'hold inventory'. The relationship between general and specific processes is shown in the *MIT Process Handbook* by using the horizontal axis. The more general process is shown on the left, with more specific versions depicted to the right (see Figure 11.4). The important point about identifying these parallels in the underlying structure of the processes is that the types of benefits that RFID can generate will be very similar across all of these specific versions of 'hold inventory'.

We developed a series of equations to calculate the benefits in the manufacturer's warehouse, and we found we could use the same basic structure to create equations to calculate the benefits of RFID in the other settings. Sometimes the empirical data that get entered into the equations are significantly different. For example, there is a great deal less theft in the manufacturer's warehouse than there is in a store. Since the amount of theft is less, the figure for the percentage of inventory stolen is much lower in the equation that describes the 'reduce theft' benefits for the warehouse. But the

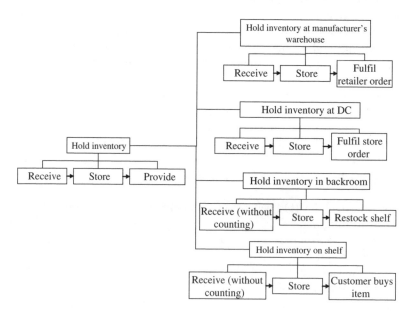

Figure 11.4   Examples of 'Hold inventory' in the retail supply chain

underlying structure of the equation we used to estimate theft remained the same.

In this way, we were able to use the concept of family resemblances between processes to gain leverage on the challenge of estimating RFID benefits. More importantly, if another firm needed to project the benefits it could anticipate from RFID, the framework developed in this case study would allow that firm to get useful estimates much more quickly and easily. A similar approach allowed us to estimate costs throughout the supply chain.

Costs and Benefits of RFID for the Consumer Goods Manufacturer

We then used our framework to estimate the benefits and costs of RFID for the manufacturer. To make the findings comparable across firms, we normalized the data so that the manufacturer had 2005 revenues of $5 billion. The present value of the required investment totalled $17 million. The present value of benefits over which the retailer had control – automation and claims reduction – totalled only $16 million. There were additional benefits of $50 million for the manufacturer, but achieving those required close cooperation with retailer partners (see Figure 11.5).

RFID provides manufacturers with a huge potential return, but one that is dependent on getting cooperation from their trading partners – cooperation which, if the history of bar code adoption is any indicator, cannot be assured (Brown 1997, Haberman 2001). This is one reason that manufacturers have not adopted RFID as rapidly as some industry observers initially anticipated.

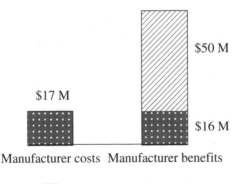

Figure 11.5   Estimated manufacturer RFID costs and benefits

ADVANTAGES OF RFID

Activity Based Performance Measurement helps managers to focus on where and how benefits are derived, which in turn helps during implementation. Firms can focus on the benefits that are most sizeable or the ones over which they have the most control. By leveraging the concept of family resemblance of processes, firms can avoid reinventing the wheel when they estimate the benefits of IT initiatives and other interventions. Over the long term, we envision firms – or cross-firm organizations such as professional societies or industry associations – developing cumulative databases of knowledge of the benefits that are derived when a particular type of technology is used to enhance a particular group of processes.

REFERENCES

Auto ID Labs (2003), *Publications*; www.autoidlabs.org/researcharchive/.
Brown, S.A. (1997), *Revolution at the Checkout Counter*, Cambridge, MA and London: Harvard University Press.
Brynjolfsson, E. and L.M. Hitt (2000), 'Beyond computation: information technology, organizational transformation and business performance', *Journal of Economic Perspectives*, **14** (4), 23–48.
Carr, N.G. (2003), 'IT doesn't matter', *Harvard Business Review*, **81** (5), 41–49.
Haberman, A.L. (ed.) (2001), *Twenty-Five Years Behind Bars: The Proceedings of the Twenty-fifth Anniversary of the U.P.C. at the Smithsonian Institution, September 30, 1999*, Cambridge, MA and London: Harvard University Press.
Malone, T.W., K. Crowston, J. Lee, B. Pentland, C. Dellarocas, G. Wyner, J. Quimby, A. Bernstein, G. Herman, M. Klein, C.S. Osborn and E. O'Donnell (1999), 'Tools for inventing organizations: toward a handbook of organizational processes', *Management Science*, **45** (3), 425–443.
Malone, T.W., K. Crowston and G.A. Herman (2003), *Organizing Business Knowledge: The MIT Process Handbook*, Cambridge, MA: MIT Press.
McAfee, A. (2004), 'Do you have too much IT?' *Sloan Management Review*, **45** (3), 18–22.
Solow, R. (1987), 'We'd better watch out', *New York Times Book Review*, 12 July, 36.

Index

Witzel, M. 138
Wong, S. 142
World Trade Organization 127, 129,
    147, 149, 150
WorldCom 121
Wurster, T. 136

Xin, K.R. 140
XML 204

Y2K 218
Yamaha 95
Yang, M.M.F. 150
Ybarra, J.A. 12
Yin Tongyao 96

Zander, U. 77–8, 88
Zeng, M. 98
Ziedonis, R.H. 163